T0386793

GARIBALDI IN SOUTH AMERICA

RICHARD BOURNE

Garibaldi in South America

An Exploration

HURST & COMPANY, LONDON

First published in the United Kingdom in 2020 by
C. Hurst & Co. (Publishers) Ltd,
41 Great Russell Street, London, WC1B 3PL
© Richard Bourne, 2020
All rights reserved.
Printed in India

The right of Richard Bourne to be identified as the author of
this publication is asserted by him in accordance with the
Copyright, Designs and Patents Act, 1988.

Distributed in the United States, Canada and Latin America by
Oxford University Press, 198 Madison Avenue, New York, NY 10016,
United States of America.

A Cataloguing-in-Publication data record for this book
is available from the British Library.

ISBN: 9781787383135

This book is printed using paper from registered sustainable
and managed sources.

www.hurstpublishers.com

For Juliet

CONTENTS

CONTENTS

LIST OF ILLUSTRATIONS

Southern Brazil, 2018

1. Palácio Piratini, Porto Alegre with flags of Brazil and Rio Grande do Sul
2. State flag of Rio Grande do Sul, incorporating flag of Farroupilha republic
3. Notice honouring *Lanceiros Negros*, black Farroupilha fighters, Porto Alegre
4. Henrique Nunes, driver, with Garibaldi bust outside town museum, Garibaldi
5. Elma Sant'Ana, prolific writer and enthusiast for Anita, with author
6. Garibaldi house and office of *O Povo*, Piratini, with Fladimir Gonsalves, Secretary of Tourism and friend
7. Courtyard of Charqueada São João, Pelotas, one of many 19th century producers of *charque*, dried beef
8. Adílcio Cadorin and Ivete Scopel, outside the Instituto Anita, Laguna
9. Old town with harbour, Laguna
10. Guide in front of one of Anita's homes, Laguna
11. Battlefield memorial near Curitibanos, Santa Catarina, where Anita was captured and escaped, after realising that Garibaldi must have survived
12. Mural of Anita on *Prefeitura*, town of Anita Garibaldi, Santa Catarina

LIST OF ILLUSTRATIONS

Uruguay, 2019

PREFACE

Giuseppe Garibaldi, hero of Italian unification in the nineteenth century, bulked large in the imagination of his contemporaries. Lionised
internationally in an era before television and social media, he was
written up by Alexandre Dumas *père*, French author of *The Count of
Monte Cristo*, and immortalised by a new biscuit in Britain, where lucky
female admirers retained precious locks of his hair.

In his lifetime he was a legendary figure. But the origins of his actual
achievement did not lie in Italy. They were in South America. He spent
over twelve formative years, from the age of twenty-eight until he was
nearly forty-one in the southern part of the continent, roughly a third
fighting for the breakaway republic of Rio Grande do Sul against the
Brazilian emperor, and two-thirds battling for Montevideo and its
Gobierno de la Defensa in a lengthy civil war in Uruguay.

The Canadian-born press baron, Lord Beaverbrook, once said that
anyone who would go on to do anything significant in life would have
shown signs already in their twenties. This was certainly true of
Garibaldi. His time in South America saw how an adventurer with a
commitment to Italian unification through membership of the Young
Italy movement could harden into a skilled and charismatic commander
able to weld unmilitary volunteers into forces capable of overcoming
adverse odds, on land and water.

Along the way in southern Brazil he met the love of his highly-sexed
life, Anita Ribeiro, his fellow warrior. This was one of the great
romances of the time, cut short by her death, still under twenty-eight,
on the retreat from the defeated Roman Republic in 1849. Their chil-

dren, carrying forward their ideals and what became an international brand of liberty and international fraternity, were still soldiering on into the twentieth century.

In South America this aspect of the Garibaldi story is known and this account, designed for a wider readership unfamiliar with it, rests heavily on the scholarship and enthusiasm of a handful of Brazilians and Uruguayans whose assistance I would like to acknowledge with gratitude. I have also been guided by a variety of secondary sources.

My concern is not just with the history of Giuseppe and Anita in Brazil and Uruguay (pronounced *Uruwhy*, without sounding the g), but with their longer-run impact in the region. For this purpose I visited both countries in 2018 and 2019, talking to individuals, visiting museums, seeing monuments and battle sites. Chapters 10 and 11 of this book recount what I found, in tours which were hectic and highly enjoyable.

The way in which the past does or does not influence the present, the way in which historical memory can be captured or reinvented to serve contemporary purposes, and the way in which the twenty-first century with all its marvellous technology can be totally ignorant of exciting and influential persons and events of an earlier age... these are absorbing issues I wished to consider.

My own interest in this region was awakened when I first visited Brazil for six months in 1965, with an award from the Brazilian Foreign Ministry, and I was given leave of absence as a reporter on *The Guardian* newspaper to take it up. I subsequently returned to South America several times, researching a succession of books, and though mostly in Brazil I was in Uruguay in 1971 for elections in that year. In fact, the 1960s, following the success of Fidel Castro's revolution in Cuba in 1959, saw a peak in European and North American study of a region which both before and later was treated in Britain as a backwater.

The US State Department funded scholars at that time; one of the best-known US Brazilianists, Thomas Skidmore, switched then from German history to study modern Brazil. In the United Kingdom the 1965 Parry Report led to the setting up of several Latin American studies centres at British universities. Although briefly attached as a fellow to one of them, a Latin American centre at Glasgow University in the 1970s, my own involvement was freelance and independent.

PREFACE

When a college friend in an Oxford street casually dismissed my serious interest in its politics and development, he snorted that "South America is the last refuge of a romantic."

Garibaldi's period in South America can indeed be construed romantically, as it has been in fiction and film. By chance I discovered that an Italian writer, Mauro Gavillucci, had made a similar tour of Garibaldi sites in Brazil and Uruguay, in 2010–11, less than a decade before I did. His concern, discussed in Chapter 12, was to bring the South American epic of "the hero of two worlds", a description which was already used in the nineteenth century, to a contemporary readership in Italy. He made a point of speaking to members of the modern Italian communities and local officials. While recounting the history, Gavillucci gave due attention to the courage, romance and tourism potentials of the man and his memory.

For me, as will be clear from the pages that follow, the perspective is different. I have a critical admiration for someone who was both a nationalist and an internationalist; a freethinker who fought for the underdog and was prepared to take on the papacy; a man who did not give up on his ideal of a united Italy; an austere man whose poverty affected his family. But like everyone, he had his faults, in his case infidelity, some vanity and gullibility and ideological confusion. And I, as someone whose great-grandmother eloped as a teenager with a young Lincolnshire farmer, have only admiration for the courage and intelligence of Giuseppe's partner Anita, who ran away with him into war and danger.

I hope that my book, lightly footnoted, will be accessible to many readers who only have a vague idea of Garibaldi, and associate him exclusively with Italy. It is structured in four sections: Part 1 covers the history in Brazil and Uruguay; Part 2 describes the aftermath of the South American campaigns; Part 3 is contemporary reportage and a comparison of my own findings in Brazil and Uruguay with those of Gavillucci; and Part 4 contains final reflections. There is occasional overlap, retained to assist the reader.

I would like to start by thanking Juliet, my wife, to whom this book is dedicated, for her patience and support as I worked on this project.

I would also like to thank many persons who have helped me in various ways, some like Elma Sant'Ana, Adílcio Cadorin, Milka Rappa and

PREFACE

Enrique Hernández, and Henrique Nunes, my driver in southern Brazil, also specified in the text, and to apologise for anyone overlooked, and any errors that have crept in. In planning my visit to southern Brazil I was carefully advised by my friends Anthony and Denise Staddon, and it goes without saying that I owe a debt of thanks to my experienced publisher, Michael Dwyer of Hurst Publishers, London, and to Sebastian Ballard, who drew the map.

My warm gratitude therefore goes to: Rosita Angelo, Federico Anschütz, Paulo Armando, Leslie Bethell, Becky Branford, Sue Branford, Eduardo Bueno, Adílcio Cadorin, Luisa Calvete, Maria Laura Canineu, Andrea Carvalho, Sergio da Costa Franco, Nicolás Duffau, Sergio Falchio-Arrigone, Ana Frega Novales, Fabricio Furtado, Gabriella Galeotti, Fladimir de Moura Gonsalves, Cesar Guazzelli, Cary de los Santos Guibert, Enrique Hernández, Raúl Ingold, Nelson Jobim, Silvana Lesca-Barolin, Nicola Locatelli, David McLean, Edward Mortimer, Denise Neddermeyer, Henrique Nunes, Ana Olivera, Moíses Batista Pedone de Souza, Gianni Piccato, Milka Rappa, Márcio Rodrigues, Vitor Ivan Gonçalves Rodrigues, Maria Sagario, Monica Salandrú, Elma Sant'Ana, Silvia Skowronski, Maria Cristina Skowronski Flynn, Alessandra Skowronski Simões Lopes, Anthony and Denise Staddon, Guilherme Stumpf and Claudete Wolffenbuttel Stumpf.

TIMELINE

1807   Giuseppe ("Peppino") Maria Garibaldi born to a seafaring
        family in Nice (Nizza), part of the kingdom of Sardinia and
        Piedmont annexed by the French empire of Napoleon
        I. He is second of five siblings.

1822   Begins a career as seaman, sailing round the Mediterranean
        and the Black Sea, qualifying later as a captain.

1833   Meets Giovanni Battista Cuneo in Taganrog, Sea of Azov, to
        be key friend in South America and early biographer.
        Recruited into Young Italy, movement founded by Giuseppe
        Mazzini to unify Italy and expel Austrians. Meets Mazzini
        in Marseille.

1834   Joins Sardinian/Piedmontese navy under false name and
        condemned to death after failed Mazzinian plot. Resumes
        maritime career.

1835   Arrives in Rio de Janeiro as second in command of
        Nautonnier of Nantes and leaves ship. Uprising in Rio
        Grande do Sul leads to declaration of breakaway republic
        in southern Brazil when Brazilian empire is ruled by
        regency. Joins Young Italy branch in Rio. Influenced by
        Italian revolutionaries sympathetic to new republic.

1837   With letters of marque from Republic of Rio Grande do
        Sul, is authorised to raid empire's shipping and create a
        naval force. Wounded off Maldonado in Uruguay, is cap-
        tured, escapes and then tortured in Gualeguay, in Argentine
        confederation.

TIMELINE

1838 After visiting Piratini, capital of the breakaway republic, he builds boats at Camaquã on strategic Lagoa dos Patos, capturing empire vessels and forcing them into convoys. Manoela, niece of republican President Bento Gonçalves, forbidden to marry him.

1839 Survives attack on shipyard by Moringue, ruthless imperial commander. Loses his ship *Farroupilha* with Italian friends in storm after hauling it overland to Atlantic, but helps capture Laguna, where he meets Anita, Ana Maria Jesus de Ribeiro, who elopes with him. She fights in battle of Imbituba. Julian Republic in Santa Catarina lasts 100 days. He is ashamed to carry out punitive assault on Imaruí. After losing fleet he becomes soldier rather than sailor.

1840 *Farroupilhas*, troops of breakaway republic, caught in surprise attack at Curitibanos and he escapes, Anita is captured. She realises his body is not among corpses, escapes cross country, meets up with him in Vacaria. Big but indecisive battle at Pinheirinho, where he is impressed by *Lanceiros Negros*, black cavalry. Unsuccessful assault on São José do Norte where republicans loot and get drunk. Anita has first child, Menotti, at Mostardas, evading Moringue. Couple involved in bitter retreat.

1841 Permitted to leave by Bento Gonçalves, he takes herd of cattle as pay-off overland to Montevideo, arriving with 300 hides. Helped by Masonic connections, works as teacher. Family short of money. Guerra Grande, Uruguayan civil war 1839–51, moving into more active phase. Capital Montevideo and Fructuoso Rivera fighting against much of rural Uruguay and Manuel Oribe, backed by Argentine dictator, Juan Manuel Rosas.

1842 Garibaldi and Anita marry. Rivera's government puts him in command of fleet and orders him to sail up River Paraná to open up navigation to inland states and Paraguay, vital for trade and Montevideo's customs dues. Survives series of nautical battles upriver with William Brown, Irish admiral serving Rosas and Oribe, and has to fire his vessels after running out of ammunition.

1843	Marches back to Montevideo, now facing extreme danger and siege after Rivera's defeat at Arroyo Grande. Britain and France put marines ashore to rescue nationals if city falls. Europeans form legions. Garibaldi issues proclamation to form Italian Legion and raises funds for four small craft and six guns. Wins a battle at sea against Brown in Isla dos Ratos off Montevideo and, with Anzani, drills legion's volunteers into a fighting unit, recognisable with red shirts, serving in lines of defence. Rosita, second child, born.
1845	Montevideo government rejects his proposal for night landing near Buenos Aires to capture Rosas. British and French blockade Buenos Aires, intervening decisively on behalf of Montevideo. Parallel naval expeditions designed to free navigation in Plate tributaries: British Navy to advance up Paraná, Garibaldi with ships and Italian Legion, to move up the River Uruguay. They combine to take Colonia and British carpenters repair ships for him at Martín García. He takes Gualeguaychú, with looting, and his capture of prize vessels leads to complaints by British. Advances upriver to Salto, in hard-fought battle, where he learns that his daughter Rosita has died following birth of Teresita, third child.
1846	Greatly outnumbered at San Antonio, outside Salto, Italian Legion fights bravely in its most celebrated battle. Montevideo government offers generalship to Garibaldi, who arrests his commander who arrived too late, and sends him back to the capital. Friction with British over his privateering as he sails down river, and his raiding in Plate.
1847	British lift blockade of Buenos Aires. Montevideo loses control of nearly all Uruguay. Garibaldi briefly made commander-in-chief in June but forced out as non-national at time of peace feelers. Disillusioned with politicking, he writes to new apparently liberal pope, Pius IX, offering support to expel Austrians and realises popularity in Italy. Ricciotti, fourth child, born. Sends Anita and three children to Genoa.

TIMELINE

1848	Anita overwhelmed by reception in Genoa. Garibaldi brings only sixty-six from Italian Legion in *Speranza*, arriving off Nice (now again Nizza) on 21 June. Year of revolutions in Europe. Garibaldi fighting Austrians in northern Italy with new Italian Legion. Count Pellegrino Rossi, pope's chief minister, murdered in November.
1849	Roman Republic declared with Mazzini as one of three triumvirs and Garibaldi key defence chief, establishing his heroic reputation in Europe. Joined by Anita. Republic overcome by French troops after a hundred days. He leads remnant force to San Marino. Anita, pregnant and with fever, dies at Mandriole. Escapes, briefly arrested by Piedmont.
1850	In New York, works in a candle factory.
1852–4	Commands a sailing ship and visits New Zealand, Australia, Hong Kong and England.
1856	Acquires home on Caprera, off Sardinia, which becomes his retreat for rest of his life.
1858–9	Leads *Cacciatori delle Alpi*, volunteer force of *Garibaldini* in support of Cavour, Piedmont and French of Napoleon III against Austrians in campaign round lakes Maggiore and Como. Menotti one of guides. Anita's remains reburied in Nizza/Nice.
1860	Leads Thousand Redshirts in successful conquest of Sicily, accompanied by Menotti. Dictator of Sicily in name of King Victor Emmanuel until plebiscite sees it join kingdom. Captures Naples in September and ends Bourbon monarchy with decisive victory at the Volturno, October. Retires to Caprera after Victor Emmanuel tells him he cannot extend dictatorship, but promises to integrate Redshirts in Italian forces.
1861	Peek Frean and Co., biscuit maker of Bermondsey, London, produces the Garibaldi biscuit, filled with raisins, reflecting popularity of English visit in 1854.
1863	Menotti recruits Garibaldi Legion to fight with Poles against Tsarist Russian empire.
1864	Garibaldi visits England at invitation of Lord Palmerston with Menotti but cuts visit short.

TIMELINE

1866	Garibaldi with Menotti, Ricciotti and their brother-in-law win Battle of Bezzecca against Austrians, to bring Venetia into Italian monarchy.
1870	Rome taken by troops of Victor Emmanuel on 20 September, following defeat of Napoleon III at Sedan and end of French support for pope's temporal power. Garibaldi on Caprera. Garibaldi then joins new French republic against Prussians with army of *Garibaldini* volunteers in Vosges, where Ricciotti wins classic Garibaldi victory against odds.
1871	Rome capital of united Italy.
1882	Garibaldi dies at home on Caprera, 2 June, after suffering from arthritis since South America and wounds from Italian campaigns.
1883	Joint houses of parliament in Uruguay authorise funding for statue of Garibaldi overlooking port of Montevideo, styled as admiral. Described as "hero of two worlds" in debate.
1893	Júlio de Castilhos first comes to power in Rio Grande do Sul, beginning state-wide memorialisation of *Farroupilhas* and former republic.
1895	Equestrian statue of Garibaldi in Rome describes him as "hero of two worlds" and quotes his "Rome or death".
1897	Ricciotti leads a force of *Garibaldini* to support Greeks against Ottoman Turks.
1900	Rio Grande do Sul recognises municipality of Garibaldi. Santa Catarina recognises municipality of Anita Garibaldi, changing the name in 1912 and re-establishing it in 1930.
1930	Getúlio Vargas from Rio Grande do Sul leads successful revolution in Brazil with support of state militia, but then crushes state loyalties in name of *Brasilidade* nationalism.
1932	Mussolini unveils statue of Anita on Janiculum, containing her remains.
1938	Lindolfo Collor, former minister of Vargas and grandfather of President Collor de Mello, writes elegant history, *Garibaldi e a Guerra dos Farrapos*.
1940	Group buys Garibaldi house in Montevideo with intention of opening museum.

TIMELINE

1947   Reburial of republican general Davi Canabarro in Porto Alegre becomes major demonstration of *Farroupilha* memory and *gaúcho* folklore after suppression by Vargas.

1957   Casa Garibaldi in Montevideo donated to Uruguayan state, to be managed by Museo Histórico Nacional, but closed to public some sixty years later.

1961   Town in Santa Catarina, founded by German colonists, renamed Anitápolis.

1985   Garibaldi Association founded in Montevideo.

1995   *Farroupilha* anniversary on 20 September in Rio Grande do Sul given support of law.

2004   Uruguay adopts 20 September as Day of Freedom of Expression and Thought after lobbying by Garibaldi Association and as tribute to his convictions.

2016   Separatist movement in Brazilian states of Rio Grande do Sul, Santa Catarina and Paraná, *O Sul é o Meu País*, organises first of two unofficial referenda, demonstrating little support. New inscription on bust of Garibaldi in Salto on 170th anniversary of battle of San Antonio lists ideals of hero of two worlds: "His example continues to guide us."

Map 1: Countries and places mentioned in the text.

INTRODUCTION

Giuseppe Garibaldi (1807–82) was perhaps the greatest liberal, patriotic, heroic soldier of the nineteenth century. Handsome, frugal, totally incorrupt, crazily brave, his life was a romance. In an age when steamships were only beginning to take over from sail and communications were slow, he was an international celebrity. Remembered today for the boldness against all odds which captured Sicily and Naples and helped forge a united Italy, he was offered a command by Abraham Lincoln in the American Civil War and given a triumphal reception when he visited England in 1864. He was a constant thorn in the side of the Italian authorities.

His first wife, Anita, whom he carried off with him in southern Brazil in 1839, was his intrepid partner in war and sorrow. She died of a fever in Italy in August 1849 as he, left with a handful of men, retreated after the failure of the short-lived Roman Republic, for which he had fought gallantly. She too, mother of four children, formed part of his legend. Feisty, not especially attractive, she was a warrior. She escaped from capture after losing touch with Giuseppe as she fought alongside him in southern Brazil. She disobeyed his orders not to join him in Rome.

Lucy Riall has written recently that "Garibaldi's life and experiences in South America are among the least known and most mythological of his entire career".[1] This book seeks to describe what he did in Brazil and Uruguay during these formative years, what he learnt and brought with him back to Europe, what happened after he left, and how he and Anita are remembered in South America today. In a depressing era of

1

identity politics and narrow nationalism in the twenty-first century it is inspiring to recall a man who risked his life for two small republics in peril, who was an internationalist, a fighter against absolutism, and for freedom of thought, of peoples and of individuals.

PART 1

HISTORY

1

A JOURNEY TO SOUTH AMERICA, FROM NICE TO RIO DE JANEIRO

Garibaldi, best known for his part in the creation of a united Italy, first became famous in South America. But why did he travel across the Atlantic, and how did he suppose that fighting as a corsair and guerrilla for faraway causes that seemed to have little to do with Italy, could bring his dream any closer? The immediate explanation lay in a death sentence passed on him in a failed plot against Piedmont, a kingdom in northern Italy which also ruled over Sardinia; he had joined its navy as a conspirator but the plot failed, and he escaped from Genoa on 5 February 1834, heading to Nice. He could not return. For the time being Italy, described by Klemens von Metternich, foreign minister and then Chancellor of Austria, as only "a geographical expression", had rejected him.[1]

He started life in Nice, or Nizza, where Giuseppe, known as Peppino to his childhood friends, was born on 4 July 1807. The town had been part of the Italian kingdom of Piedmont, but it was annexed to France by Napoleon I. After Bonaparte's final defeat at Waterloo, and the restoration of the reactionary House of Savoy which ruled Piedmont, it reverted to being Nizza. Garibaldi's father Domenico was a merchant seaman, and Giuseppe was devoted to Rosa, his mother. He was the second of five children, and there is a suggestion that his mother would have liked him to enter the Church.

At fifteen he ran away to sea, hoping to get to the port of Genoa with friends. His boat was overtaken by those trying to stop them, and his parents gave in to his desire for a nautical career. So began a varied and adventurous life, from the ages of fifteen to twenty-five, in sailing ships. He was captured and released by pirates. The Mediterranean was still dangerous for commerce, and Barbary corsairs based along the North African coastline had only just been restrained by more powerful orthodox navies. He sailed around the Mediterranean and as far as the Black Sea, where he visited Odessa three times. He was engaged, but found that Francesca Roux, his fiancée whom he left in 1827, was married to another when he got back.[2] In 1832 he qualified as a captain.

His own family was conservative, and his education with tutors had been erratic. But in the wider fallout from the French Revolution of 1789, the overthrow of the Bourbon monarchy in France in 1830 and the Great Reform Bill of 1832 in England, the Italian peninsula was not immune. The peninsula was then governed by eight different and auto-cratic states, which included the Papal States where the Pope had unchallenged temporal power in central Italy, and the Austrian empire, which governed Lombardy and Venetia in the north-east. Each had its own currency, court and legal system, and even different weights and measures. Customs barriers restricted trade between and within these states. In the Duchy of Parma, the smallest, it was said that a traveller covering thirty kilometres from Guastalla to the capital would have to stop at seven customs barriers.[3]

By the 1830s what later became Italy was in a ferment of revolt. A minority of young idealists were angry with the absolute monarchies, and were prepared to take up arms against them. Many of these revo-lutionaries were linked in secret societies, the *carbonari* (literally charcoal-burners), who had been operating since the turn of the cen-tury with aims ranging from constitutional reform to the unification of the differing states. Pope Pius VII in 1821 excommunicated them as Freemasons, and many of them were both anticlerical and linked in Masonic Lodges. They had organised risings in 1820, 1821 and 1831, all put down with hangings and bloodshed. Garibaldi was particularly affected by the death of the patriot Ciro Menotti in 1831, hanged after a failed rising in Modena.

Initially he appears to have been influenced by the thinking of the French idealist philosopher, the Comte de Saint-Simon, and a French fellow seaman, Émile Barrault, gave him a copy of Saint-Simon's *Nouveau Christianisme* (1825). This advocated the brotherhood of man and the elevation of the poorest in society on a scientific basis.

Garibaldi was recruited into the underground conspiracies of Young Italy after meeting its devotees when he was ashore in Taganrog, a port on the Sea of Azov, after carrying a shipload of oranges to the Black Sea. Young Italy had spread its networks widely, and he met a group of mariners who had come under its influence. Crucially they included Giovanni Battista Cuneo, who became an important friend in South America. This formative meeting happened in 1833.

The most inspirational figure in the fairly disorganised world of Young Italy was Giuseppe Mazzini (1805–72). Mazzini, who was to use Garibaldi's exploits in South America as propaganda for Young Italy, had been a member of the *carbonari*. Imprisoned in Savona in 1830–1 for six months after a failed plot, Mazzini was forced into exile in Marseille.

There, in July 1831, Mazzini and a group of exiles founded Young Italy (*La Giovane Italia*). Its aim was to create a unified, republican, democratic Italy in the peninsula; its slogan was "For God and the People—Thought and Action". But there were always conflicts between those "moderates" who would be satisfied with constitutional monarchies and Young Italy, influenced by the France of 1789 and the United States of 1776, which wanted a republic.

Mazzini himself was ascetic, magnetic and a skilled and prolific journalist and writer. He was to spend much of his life in exile, living in England from 1837 until he returned to the peninsula in 1849, as did Garibaldi in the same year, when Tuscany and Rome declared themselves republics. He was not a narrow nationalist. He promoted ideas of European unity—a Young Europe movement—and sympathised with Poles and others who wanted to break free from the Russian empire. Garibaldi too shared these broader sympathies. Mazzini preached that Italy could only be free and united by force of arms, and he was watched, and his correspondence followed, by the secret services of the European powers.[4]

Garibaldi joined the Piedmontese and Sardinian navy, with a view to taking part in a revolutionary mutiny, using a fictitious name—

Cléombrato. But the Mazzinian revolt failed and on 3 June 1834 a court condemned him to death as an enemy of the state, a verdict confirmed by King Carlo Alberto. Garibaldi did not sail for South America straightaway. Initially he signed onto a French merchant ship, *Union*, and visited ports in the Levant and Odessa.

For a while he served on a warship built in Marseille, flying the flag of the Bey of Tunis. Twice he rescued men who had fallen overboard, and he helped out as a volunteer during a cholera outbreak in Marseille. But his sense of adventure was unfulfilled. He decided to go to South America. In November 1835 Garibaldi arrived in Rio de Janeiro as second in command of the *Nautonnier* of Nantes, having signed on with a Captain Beauregard. He was twenty-eight, and he left the ship in Rio and came ashore.

Brazil, and South America, were politically unstable. If Garibaldi dreamed of a large, unified Italy to replace its patchwork of autocracies, the issues in the new continent were quite different. How could new states be created out of the ruins of the Spanish and Portuguese empires? The formal outbreak of revolution in the Spanish empire took place in 1810, stimulated by Napoleon's replacement of the Spanish king in Madrid by Joseph, his brother. It took place almost simultaneously in Mexico City in the north, and Buenos Aires in the south. But warfare continued over this huge area until well into the 1820s, with Simón Bolívar's hopes for a Gran Colombia in what are now four countries[5] in the north-west of the South American continent unrealised. Bolívar remarked wearily, shortly before his death: "America is ungovernable. Those who have served the revolution have ploughed the sea."[6]

In Brazil something strange and different took place. Independence in 1822 was won by the twenty-three-year-old Pedro, son of the King of Portugal, who tore the Portuguese colours from his uniform and cried, "independence or death" beside the River Ypiranga in São Paulo. This meant that, for the first time since King George III was removed from the throne of North America, the western hemisphere had acquired a monarchy—indeed the Brazilian empire. But whereas the Spanish empire broke into pieces, an independent Brazil stayed together.

Behind the ending of Spanish and Portuguese rule lay the forceful, if not Machiavellian, role of the British. After Nelson won the Battle of Trafalgar in 1805, and George Canning as Foreign Secretary ordered the capture of the Danish fleet two years later, the British had naval mastery in the Atlantic. They used this in November 1807 to escort the Portuguese court, including the mad Queen Maria and Dom João, the Prince Regent, to Bahia in Brazil; they got away from Lisbon under the eyes of a French army led by Marshal Junot and, resting after a frightful voyage lasting two months, they sailed down the coast to Rio de Janeiro, capital of Portugal's biggest colony.

The arrival of the court gave a boost to the provincial, slave-dependent society of Rio, and João awarded Brazil dominion status in 1815. But developments in Lisbon, where a liberal rebellion was threatening the overthrow of the Bragança monarchy, caused João to head back to the mother country in 1821. Both in the former Spanish and former Portuguese territories the British supported the independence movements, opening ports to their trade and investment, but becoming unpopular in the process.

Admiral Lord Cochrane, a Scot who was one of Nelson's most successful and dashing captains, played an important freelance role as a mercenary. Disgraced in Britain, he took his family to Chile in December 1818 and, as a Chilean citizen, commanded the Chilean fleet, and his victories confirmed the independence of Peru as well. In 1823, at the request of the Brazilian Emperor Pedro I, a fleet under his command defeated the Portuguese in Bahia, and bluffed the defenders of Maranhão and Belém, near the mouth of the Amazon, into surrender.

In 1825 the independence of Colombia, Argentina and Mexico was recognised by commercial treaties with England and, in the same year, under pressure from Canning and with compensation from the Brazilians, Portugal accepted the independence of Brazil. Canning had a far-sighted and neo-imperialist view of these movements; looking back in 1826 at his efforts to prevent Napoleon from extrapolating his victories in the Iberian Peninsula to Latin America, he told the House of Commons: "I resolved that if France should have Spain it should not be Spain with the Indies. I called the New World into existence to redress the balance of the Old."[7]

By the time Garibaldi arrived in Rio de Janeiro the political scene both in Brazil and the River Plate basin was still unsettled. Brazil's first emperor, Pedro I, had become deeply unpopular and was forced to abdicate in 1831 in favour of his five-year-old son, also called Pedro.

The court of Pedro I was venal; he favoured his mistress over his empress, Leopoldina; and he was accused of being too interested in Portugal and the fate of the Portuguese monarchy.[8] There were five rebellions during the abdication crisis, all anti-Portuguese with the exception of one in Recife which supported the outgoing emperor.

The country was ruled by a succession of regents until, in 1840, the teenager agreed to become emperor as Pedro II. The constitution gave the monarch considerable power. He could nominate all members of the senate, veto legislation passed by the elected house of deputies three times, and dissolve it as he saw fit. His *poder moderado* ("moderating power") entitled him to adjust his cabinets in what he decided was the national interest. And four groups of regents, over the period of Pedro's minority, tried to keep Brazil together. There were local revolts in 1831 in Pará, in 1833 in Minas Gerais, and in Mato Grosso and Maranhão in 1834. The causes were various, and reflected both social frictions and continuing conflicts between liberals and authoritarian monarchists, and between "Brazilians" and those who still looked back to Portugal, to which Pedro I had returned after his abdication.

In the southernmost state of Rio Grande do Sul a new and more serious rebellion was germinating just as Garibaldi arrived in Rio de Janeiro. Borders and allegiances in southern Brazil were insecure. Shortly before the end of its rule the Portuguese crown had extended its presence down to the River Plate, occupying most of what became Uruguay from January 1817, when Portuguese troops captured Montevideo. In 1821 Brazil formally annexed what was known as the Banda Oriental and renamed it as the Provincia Cisplatina, its province on the near side of the Plate. Portuguese troops here had been among the last to be defeated by Brazilians.

Yet the Brazilians were not liked in a predominantly Spanish-speaking region and in 1825 Juan Antonio Lavellaja led "the 33 Orientals" in a declaration of independence. A guerrilla war lasted for 500 days, with Uruguayans backed by the United Provinces of Río de la Plata, a proto-Argentina based in Buenos Aires. Brazil was forced to acknowledge Uruguayan independence by combined pressure from Britain and Buenos Aires. Nonetheless Brazilians retained commercial interests in Uruguay, ranchers (*estancieros*) had land on both sides of the new border, and Spanish as well as Portuguese was spoken in Rio Grande do Sul.

The rebellion in Rio Grande do Sul combined political and economic interests. The state, with a population of some 100,000—of whom perhaps 30 per cent were slaves, and the majority of mixed race (*mestizos*)[9]—had come to rely on cattle rearing and the production of *charque*, dried meat. *Charque* was a basic element in the diet of slaves, who formed a larger proportion of the population in Rio de Janeiro and northern Brazil. Liberal supporters in the state were known as *Farroupilhas* or Ragamuffins,[10] and were closely linked to the ranchers in the south who had lost cattle supplies when Brazil ceded control of Uruguay. *Charque* was heavily taxed in southern Brazil, but was being imported cheaply from the Plate region. Imposition of a conservative president onto the state by the Regency helped precipitate an uprising.

Garibaldi had little knowledge of Brazilian politics when he reached Rio de Janeiro. But there were other Italians there already, and he said that the first he met was Luigi Rossetti. In his autobiography he writes: "On entering the port of Rio de Janeiro, it was my good fortune soon to meet with the rarest thing in the world, a friend … after one smile, after one pressure of the hand, Rossetti and I were brothers for life."[11]

It was not until the last quarter of the nineteenth century, after the unification of the peninsula, that Italian migration became a major factor in Brazil.[12] Earlier there were only a handful of adventurers and traders, with a small group of revolutionaries for whom Europe had become too hot. In Montevideo, by contrast, there were already around 4,000 Italians, petty traders or labourers, many of them from Genoa or connected to trade with Genoa. Similarities of language and Catholic culture simplified their adjustment to South America.

Not surprisingly, Garibaldi gravitated to the revolutionaries. He joined a Masonic Lodge and found that Giovanni Battista Cuneo, a fellow patriot who had arrived in Rio a year earlier and then moved on to Montevideo, had set up a Young Italy branch in Rio and started editing a paper with the same name. Garibaldi knew him from his time in the Mediterranean, when he had smuggled Mazzini's letters to friends. Rio was a small town, and Rossetti, with whom Garibaldi shared lodgings, introduced the seaman to other Italian friends, including Luigi Carniglia, with whom he became close, and Domenico Torrisano, a businessman.

After a period of relaxation on his arrival, Garibaldi returned to his trade as a seaman, on ships which carried goods up and down the coast between Rio and Montevideo. In early 1837, for instance, he was using a pseudonym, Borel, on board a twenty-ton boat named the *Mazzini*, running meat and corn the short distances between Rio, Cabo Frio and Campos.[13]

In the state of Rio Grande do Sul the attitudes of the more powerful groups had become polarised between the more liberal constitutionalists, who wanted a federal Brazil at least, if not a breakaway republic, the *Farroupilhas*, and their opponents, the *Caramurús*.[14] The *Caramurús* backed the absolute monarchy. The *Farroupilha* faction was provoked when the imperial president of the state was ordered to set up a Sociedade Militar, a club for advocates of the Regency, exercising enormous powers in the name of the young emperor. In September 1835 General Bento Gonçalves da Silva led a *Farroupilha* rebellion which expelled the regents' nominee from the state capital, Porto Alegre. Approximately a year later the rebels declared a republic in Piratini, a small inland town in the south of the state, with Bento Gonçalves as president.

However, Gonçalves and the *Farroupilhas* were forced out of Porto Alegre after only nine months, and suffered a serious defeat nearby when their force surrendered to the imperialists on 4 October 1836. It had been surrounded on the island of Fanfa, in the river Jacuí, by troops backed by eighteen ships commanded by the English mercenary commodore, John Grenfell. A number of leading *Farroupilhas*, including Bento Gonçalves and an aristocratic Italian intellectual, Count Tito Lívio Zambeccari, were taken away to prison in Rio. After Fanfa the surviving *Farroupilha* leadership took a far-reaching decision: to free the slaves of Rio Grande do Sul so that more men could enlist to rebuild their army.

Zambeccari was a scientist and naturalist, and fervent supporter of Young Italy. More than anyone else it seems that he was the advocate who, even as a prisoner himself, persuaded Garibaldi to join up with the *Farroupillhas*. Zambeccari had been born in Bologna in 1802 and, as a teenager, became one of the *carbonari*. He took part in the failed rebellion in Italy in 1821 and was condemned to death. He fought in Spain for a constitutional monarchy and, when that rising was crushed by French troops, he travelled round Europe as a naturalist.

In 1826 he arrived in Montevideo, in the middle of the war against Brazil for the independence of Uruguay. He then crossed to Buenos

Aires, joining a legion of Italians which was fighting against the despotic Juan Manuel Rosas for control of what was becoming Argentina.
When Rosas won, Zambeccari moved to Rio Grande do Sul in 1831,
offering his services as a scientist to the authorities; he also met up
again with friends he had made in the "Cisplatine" war.

Given his outlook, as an anti-authoritarian liberal and internation-
ist, it was not surprising that he threw in his lot with the *Farroupilhas*.
He became secretary and chief of staff to Bento Gonçalves, credited
with designing the flag of the Piratini republic, with its green, red and
yellow diagonal stripes. He had a mystical explanation for this flag;
more recently, as the basis for the flag of the modern state which now
incorporates its coat of arms, it has been interpreted as green for the
countryside, red for pride and yellow for the soil, or alternatively
green for spring, red for enthusiasm and yellow for the soil.

Transported from Rio Grande do Sul in a prison ship, Zambeccari
was incarcerated for three years in the fort of Santa Cruz da Barra in
Rio de Janeiro, and not released until 1839. But he was allowed visitors. Luigi Rossetti and Garibaldi saw him several times in jail. He was
a man after Garibaldi's heart—brave, adventurous, internationalist,
and a campaigner for Young Italy. He suggested that Garibaldi should
enlist as a corsair, aiming to disrupt the empire's commerce at sea, in
the cause of Rio Grande do Sul. The breakaway republic had lost control of the state's ports since the surrender at Fanfa, and he might be
able to recapture them. Garibaldi, hungry to do something more exciting than tramp shipping, and receiving no calls from Mazzini to return
to Europe, was not in a mood to resist. Bento Gonçalves, held in the
same fort as Zambeccari—at his second attempt he escaped by
swimming—approved.

There was then some delay while Garibaldi and the conspirators
waited for letters of marque, the official authorisation for their privateering on behalf of the Piratini republic. Letters of marque were a
concept only marginally different from licensed piracy. A vessel holding
them was entitled to raid and capture other ships, and sell them and
their contents in a shipping court. The letters were actually signed in
Montevideo and entitled Captain Giuseppe Garibaldi, commanding
any vessel he could get hold of, to capture Brazilian warships and
peaceful traders alike, and to put into the ports of neighbouring states.
Italian friends in Rio raised the equivalent of £8,000 to buy a boat.

Their first ship, of only twenty tons, was loaded with arms buried beneath sacks of corn. It was all prepared in secret, by a small group of Italians, including Luigi Carniglia, Rossetti and Domenico Torrisano, the merchant who did the paperwork to enable the freighter to leave the port of Rio. Garibaldi commanded a crew of a dozen men. For him the prospect of command, and life at sea for a cause he came to believe in, was one of pure joy. He wrote to Cuneo, then in Montevideo: "I am disposed to start a new life, in accordance with our principles."[15]

So, one bright May morning in 1837, the *Mazzini* headed out of Rio, sailed past the Barra fort, and raised the flag of Piratini. It was the start of a new, dangerous and exciting adventure, for a handsome, bearded, charismatic man who was still under thirty.

2

FROM RIO DE JANEIRO TO ROMANCE

The expedition started well. Shortly after leaving the port, sailing to the south, Garibaldi ambushed a schooner laden with coffee for Europe. Better still, it was owned by a rich Austrian, symbol of the empire he hated, which occupied the north of the Italian peninsula. He promptly scuttled his own boat and renamed his capture the *Farroupilha*. He rejected the offer of a casket of diamonds from a Portuguese passenger who asked for immediate freedom, but put him and others ashore further south in the ship's tender. Significantly, he liberated five black slaves, who preferred to stay on board with his crew. He sailed on down to the River Plate.

Here he began to run into trouble. He cast anchor at Maldonado in Uruguay, east of Montevideo, close to the modern resort of Punta del Este, where the Plate estuary widens to join the Atlantic Ocean. Uruguay was then, and for some years to come, a cockpit of struggle between two rival *caudillos*, Manuel Oribe (1792–1857), who was recognised as president between 1835 and 1838, and José Fructuoso Rivera (1784–1854), with whom Garibaldi later was for a while a valuable naval and military ally. These *caudillos* were rough and ready leaders, ranchers who led troops of armed cowboys (*gaúchos*), living by their own customs and dispensing their own instant justice; their intricate feuds and changing fortunes were knit together by kinship, intense historical experiences and patrimonialism. Rivera, in 1831, was responsible for what is described as the Massacre of Salsipuedes: most of the surviving Charrúa males, one of the largest indigenous groups in Uruguay, were defeated and killed.

Both Oribe and Rivera had fought against the Portuguese and Brazilians, and Rivera, president from 1830 to 1834, had wanted Oribe to succeed him. But they then fell out and fought. Rivera overthrew and defeated Oribe in 1838. Oribe fled to Buenos Aires, and struck up a close alliance with its dictator Juan Manuel Rosas (1793–1877), who was governing the most powerful province in the Argentine confederation. Rosas was a *caudillo*'s *caudillo*, an ideal and extremely effective representative of this ruthless type.

When Garibaldi arrived off Maldonado, however, Oribe was still ruling Uruguay. Rossetti in Montevideo was trying to get authorisation for him to land. But the local officials in Maldonado, which was a small port, realised that a Piratini vessel was unrecognised. The Brazilian vice-consul put pressure on Oribe to have the boat impounded, and Garibaldi arrested. A Uruguayan warship was sent to take them. The *Imperial Prado*, a Brazilian warship stationed in the Plate, was coming too. Garibaldi, trying to sell some of his captured coffee, obtained his money from a trader in the town at gunpoint. He and his crew only just got away.[1]

Sailing westward up the Plate from Montevideo, with little knowledge of the river or its reefs, the crew narrowly missed rocks when the ship's compass went awry. Having given away their tender they had to improvise a raft, using a table and four casks, and Garibaldi scrambled ashore in search of provisions. He was attracted by the rolling plains of the pampas, with its semi-wild horses and cattle, its rhea, a cousin to the ostrich, and its dangerous jaguars. Arriving on foot, unusual in that landscape, he met a young woman in an *estancia* who wrote poetry and could speak Italian. His sense of romance awoke, and her husband sold him a bullock which he and a comrade killed, skinned and cut up on the beach, returning on the makeshift raft and giving his hungry crew a square meal.

But although the poet and her husband had been friendly, that was not the official position of Oribe's Uruguay. Two small vessels, coming from Montevideo with armed men on board, called on the *Farroupilha* to surrender. They opened fire, and sent a boarding party, which was repulsed. Fiorentino, his Italian helmsman, was shot dead, and Garibaldi was hit between an ear and his carotid artery. He was floored on deck. His South American adventure could have ended there.

Garibaldi suffered a fever from his wound. But the situation was rescued by another Italian, Luigi Carniglia, who took command, got the *Farroupilha* away from the ambush, and steered upriver to Gualeguay on a tributary of the River Paraná. He promised Garibaldi that, should he die, his body would not be thrown overboard as had happened to Fiorentino's. Gualeguay was in Entre Rios, the Argentine province which lies between the Paraná river to the west and Uruguay to the east, and initially Garibaldi was lucky. An Argentinian captain, Luiz Tartabull, helped the corsairs and gave a letter of recommendation to Don Pascual Echague, governor of the Argentine province of Entre Rios. Echague was friendly, and got his personal doctor to care for Garibaldi. A bullet was extracted after an hour long operation, naturally without anaesthetic.

Then the luck ran out. The Brazilian Embassy in Buenos Aires had been putting pressure on Rosas to imprison the *Farroupilha*'s crew. Rosas had a loose overlordship of Entre Rios and he gave instructions to its provincial governor to act. Caught between his orders and his sympathies, Echague found a suave middle way. Garibaldi was put under a form of house arrest, which still permitted him to ride round the surrounding neighbourhood.

After six months, in which Garibaldi recovered but became bored, Echague had to go to Buenos Aires, leaving a Leonardo Millan in charge of the captive. Garibaldi decided to try and escape, walking some distance, then picking up a horse to ride to an *estancia* owned by an Englishman by the Paraná. But he was betrayed: his guide let him down, he was captured and brought back to Millan, who interrogated him. When he refused to say who had helped his escape, Millan whipped him and ordered that he be strung up from a joist. Suspended in agony for a couple of hours, five feet off the ground, with his wrists bleeding and his shoulders dislocated, he was cut down and then shackled with fetters to a murderer in the jail.

This torture was one of the worst passages in his South American odyssey. In his memoirs he recalls the kindness of Echague, and his fear that, when much later Millan and others fell into his hands, he did not want to see him in case he misbehaved.[2] He was transferred to Bajada de Santa Fé, the provincial capital (now the city of Paraná), where he was held for two months, before suddenly being released by the governor.

He boarded a Genoese merchantman for Montevideo where he met up again with Italian friends—Rossetti, Cuneo and Napoleone Castellini—but had to keep a low profile. He lived in hiding with another Italian. He was still under threat, as a result of the deaths he had caused in his first battle with Montevideo's sailors. The threat was only lifted in June 1838 when Manuel Oribe was overthrown by Fructuoso Rivera, and all political prisoners were released.

Rossetti had just returned from seeing the *Farroupilha* leaders in Piratini. After Garibaldi had spent a month in Montevideo, they decided to ride overland there together, taking a team of horses which they rode in turns. The country was hilly, forested and temperate as they came into Rio Grande do Sul. Where it was cultivated it was possible to grow European fruits—peaches, oranges, pears and plums— and Garibaldi was reminded of the area round his home town of Nice. Some of the early settlers had come from the Azores.

When the two Italians arrived in Piratini, a small place with low, tiled buildings, now overrun by visitors and with the aspirations of a capital city, they went to be greeted by Domingos José de Almeida. Almeida was interior and finance minister of the new republic. He was atypical, in that he had been born in Minas Gerais, owned a well-run *charque* factory, and was a *Farroupilha* ultra. Most of the *charque* producers had sided with the empire. He used his own resources to create an arsenal and a ship repair yard to help the rebels. He had been imprisoned for a while, and had opposed Bento Gonçalves in the early stages of the agitation when Gonçalves still preferred peace to civil war, to a battle between brothers.

Throughout the life of the Piratini republic there was friction between those who wanted a totally independent state, and those who were looking to replace the empire with a federation of self-governing provinces, not dissimilar to the Argentine confederation of fourteen states led by Buenos Aires. Bento Gonçalves at times also played with the idea of a federation which would include the Piratini republic, Uruguay and some or all of the proto-Argentina based on Buenos Aires and the River Plate.

Almeida had a daunting task in trying to raise the funds to keep the new republic going; there was little cash money, and cows and bullocks became units of exchange. The strategic outlook was not good. While the *Farroupilhas* were strong in the interior the ports along the coast, including Porto Alegre, the provincial capital, were in the hands of the empire. This was where much of the wealth lay. The coastline was dominated by two long lakes, paralleling the Atlantic. The bigger and longer, the Lagoa dos Patos (the lake of ducks) ran southwards from Porto Alegre to the towns of Pelotas and Rio Grande, where there was a wide link to the ocean. South of these, and divided by a stretch of watery, boggy land was the Lagoa Mirim (the little lake), less important commercially, which ran down to the Uruguayan border where the River Chuí joined the sea. For the Regency in Rio, continuing control of these lakes was crucial.

Although it was clear that Garibaldi's real contribution would be in creating a small force of ships, and leading light craft to harry the imperial navy on the lakes, he took the opportunity to join a column that was riding to join Gonçalves. He was bowled over by the charisma of the *Farroupilha* president—handsome on horseback, looking like a twenty-five-year-old rather than the sixty-year-old he actually was. He wrote back to Rossetti: "He is truly a beloved child of nature, which has endowed him with everything which makes a man a true hero. I saw the grace with which he mounted a horse. No one would have given him more than 25 years. I am not surprised that with such gifts Bento Gonçalves is an idol to his compatriots."[3]

Garibaldi and Rossetti were attached to Gonçalves' staff, and after his column failed to capture Pelotas, at the southern end of the Lagoa dos Patos, he gave the order to withdraw towards Piratini. His entry into the capital coincided with news of a *Farroupilha* victory at the Rio Pardo, where insurgents led by Antônio de Sousa Neto and Bento Manoel had overwhelmingly defeated a larger imperial force, led by Marshal Sebastião Barreto Pereira Pinto. In this more optimistic scenario the Italians were put to work. Domingos de Almeida decided that Garibaldi should help build some small boats, and then captain them. His orders were to construct a shipyard, and then attack the empire's shipping on the Lagoa dos Patos. Rosetti stayed in Piratini, editing *O Povo* (The People), a new paper to speak out for the republic. A third

Italian, Castellini, acted as contact man in Montevideo, charged with buying war material for the rebels.

The *Farroupilhas* had set up a simple shipyard near Camaquã, on an *estancia* belonging to a relative of Gonçalves. An American called John Griggs, a soldier of fortune from a good family, had started to build two sail-driven sloops, one of about eighteen tons, another of just under twelve. Garibaldi spent a couple of months enjoying *estanciero* hospitality from two of the president's sisters with considerable pleasure, while the work was completed. Each vessel was armed with two small brass guns and he recruited two motley crews totalling around seventy men, of whom the majority were black or mestizo.

Initially the modest flotilla was dismissed as a laughing-stock by the imperial navy, which was commanded in Rio Grande do Sul by an English adventurer, John Pascoe Grenfell, a mercenary who had originally fought alongside Cochrane. Because of their shallow draught, however, the small boats of the rebels were perfect for hit-and-run guerrilla warfare in shallow water. They could slip between sandbanks on the lakeshore where the empire's bigger vessels could not follow. They were light, and could be manhandled over land if necessary. The imperial navy was reduced to providing convoys between the lake ports, with shipping restricted to certain days only.

Garibaldi's nuisance value was demonstrated when he opened fire on a steamer, the *Aguia*, which was carrying the emperor's minister of war, Sebastião do Rego Barros, through the lake to Porto Alegre. Porto Alegre was being threatened by two columns of *Farroupilhas*, one from the north under Bento Gonçalves, another of cavalry from the east under two other commanders, Antônio de Sousa Neto and Davi Canabarro. The minister had been sent down to sort out the quarrelling pro-government leaders in the state capital, and he was embarrassingly slipped in to Porto Alegre without fanfare after the attack.

The rebels did not recapture Porto Alegre, however, and Garibaldi's boats were damaged in the exchange of fire. He went back to his base near Camaquã for repairs, and to build two more. In August 1838 he and John Griggs, with their two light craft, captured an imperial vessel, the *Mineira*, richly laden with wheat, rice and even French brandy. This was in the lake, close to Camaquã. Another boat escaped.

Yet, as this prize was taken under the letters of marque, the republic's finance minister, Domingos José de Almeida, ordained that the value should be divided into eight parts and split so that his treasury had half, an eighth went to Garibaldi, another eighth went to the other officers, and a quarter could be shared between the crew.

This was a valuable victory, and it had a further, more romantic aspect. Garibaldi, good-looking, bearded and with strong blue eyes, was an exotic gallant to impressionable, well-brought-up young ladies. He had survived many adventures already, in Europe and South America, and had stories to tell. Although his own education had been ragged he was a voracious reader, loving poetry in particular. When he met the wife of an *estanciero* west of Montevideo, seeking provisions, he had swapped stanzas of Petrarch with her. He had a fine singing voice and could improvise rhymes and verses.

It was not surprising if women fell for him. One of them was Manoela, daughter of one of Bento Gonçalves' three sisters, Dona Maria Manoela. The Gonçalves clan had adjoining *estancias* near Camaquã, and after the victory Dona Antônia, another sister of the president, gave a celebratory ball. These parties were quite something, with music, dancing and feasting, and with girls at their most attractive. Garibaldi had been in and out of the various Gonçalves properties, landing to obtain food and equipment, and was well known to the extended family.

Manoela decided she was in love with the dashing Italian, and thought she was going to marry him. Garibaldi certainly gave her some encouragement and recalled Dona Antonia's ball for one reason in particular: that, after worries that he had died, "a beautiful young girl, on hearing of my danger, had turned pale and anxiously inquired after my life and health; a victory more sweet to my heart than the sanguinary triumph we had obtained". Bento Gonçalves recognised that the piratical Italian was a military asset, but may also have doubted his calibre as husband material for a young member of his family. Tactfully he indicated to both parties that Manoela was already committed to his own son, Joaquim. This was not good news for her. She died without ever marrying.

The war was not going too well for the young republic, which was forced to move its capital from Piratini to the town of Caçapava, further north, in January 1839. Its administration was chaotic. It was short of money. Although it had had some victories its attempts to capture the state capital of Porto Alegre had been frustrated. In these circumstances Bento Gonçalves conceived a plan to break out of this stalemate by launching an expedition northwards, into the adjoining province of Santa Catarina. The republicans thought that there was sympathy there for their plan to reconstitute the empire as a federation of self-governing republics, and knew that a number of *Farroupilhas* had fled into Santa Catarina.

Garibaldi had averted an attempt by the empire's troops to destroy his shipyard, in highly dangerous circumstances. Realising that it could not defeat him on the water, but that it had to clear these irritants out of the Lagoa dos Patos, the government decided to send in its wiliest and most ruthless guerrilla leader, Francisco Pedro de Abreu, to attack him on land. Nicknamed Moringue, the Polecat, Abreu was a *gaúcho*, as tough and locally rooted as the *Farroupilhas*. He led a party of seventy cavalry and eighty foot soldiers, many of them the German and Austrian mercenaries whom Garibaldi hated. They were put ashore a few kilometres from where Garibaldi was working with around sixty of his men, in an old *estancia* and *charque* factory.

It was a foggy morning. Scouts sent out to spot Moringue's advance failed to do so, and cattle spread out as guards, to warn the defenders, never bellowed. The rebels had put their rifles in a shed, outside of which Garibaldi and a cook were having a lazy breakfast, when Moringue, whose troops had been hiding in woods nearby, attacked. Surprised, the two leapt into the shed, and a lance was thrust through Garibaldi's poncho. But he opened fire and luckily killed three assailants with successive shots. The cook passed him loaded rifles in turn, and his speed in shooting made the enemy think they were up against a detachment.

His men heard what was happening and eleven more joined the two in the shed. But Moringue's troops surrounded them, firing from other farm buildings. Some even climbed onto the shed roof, shooting down at them. The battle lasted five hours according to Garibaldi's memoirs,[4] and it was only broken off when one of his black companions, Procópio, identified Moringue as the commander and pierced his arm with a bullet. Moringue called off his men and was taken to Porto Alegre to recover, leaving fifteen dead. Garibaldi lost five of his men, and three more died from their wounds. Moringue was consumed by a desire for vengeance, which had a sequel later when he tried to kill Garibaldi's partner Anita and baby son Menotti.

In a lifetime of close shaves this was one of the closest. But its outcome gave Garibaldi confidence, redoubling the importance he attached to knowledge of and two-way loyalty between himself and his fighters. It also encouraged those living along the lake, suffering from Moringue's raiding and depredations, who realised he could be beaten.

Garibaldi, who had been building two new vessels in Camaquã and had captured others, was put in charge of a seaborne attack on Laguna. Davi Canabarro led the republican troops on land. The problem was how to get the ships from the Lagoa dos Patos to the Atlantic, so that they could sail up the coast to Santa Catarina. Nothing daunted, the captain found a hundred oxen and put two of his vessels on strongly built carts which they pulled for some 54 miles across the land before reaching the small Lake Tramandaí, which abutted through a shallow channel into the Atlantic. This bold move took place over six days, in secrecy, relying on the complicity of local people. Waiting until the tide was high, they navigated the Atlantic breakers.

Less than a day later, catastrophe struck. Garibaldi's boat, the *Farroupilha*, was too heavily laden with a cannon, chests and much equipment for an expedition which might take several weeks. It was carrying too much freight. A storm blew up. The boat was caught in an enormous wave, and turned turtle. The crew were tossed overboard. Garibaldi himself was a strong swimmer and did what he could to rescue two of his best Italian friends, Luigi Carniglia and Eduardo Mutru; but the waves were violent, and both of them drowned. Carniglia had been a good friend in Rio de Janeiro, Montevideo and now in Rio Grande do Sul. Mutru he had known as a boy; they had joined the Sardinian Navy together, and he had been a fellow conspirator in the failed plot in Genoa which had led to his death sentence.

In all, sixteen out of a crew of thirty, six of them Italians, perished in the disaster. Bodies were swept away. Garibaldi and the survivors were frozen, and he made them exercise to recover the use of their limbs. Griggs, the American, was captaining the second ship, the *Seival*. Though not as big as Garibaldi's vessel it was built differently, and rode out the storm.

Garibaldi was understandably depressed at the loss of so many friends and comrades. But after heading along the shore he met someone who sympathised with the revolutionaries and gave him some horses, so that he and other survivors were able to ride to meet Canabarro's advance guard, under Teixeira Nunes. This was rapidly closing in on the town of Laguna, in Santa Catarina.

Much of the southern part of that province was in a state of ferment. Seditious posters and pamphlets were circulating. Young men were refusing to join the imperial militias and were slipping out of Laguna and other small towns to join the rebels. Unknown to the authorities, the *Seival* floated through a narrow canal from the ocean to take up a hidden position near the town of Laguna, where Garibaldi took over the command. In the first centuries of the carve-up of South America between Portugal and Spain, Laguna had marked the southern boundary of the Portuguese possessions.

The battle for Laguna took place by land and water. In his memoirs Garibaldi wrote that "we had not much trouble in gaining possession of the little city", but this was not entirely true. The government had stationed several ships to defend the town, and they were amazed to see that the *Seival*, flying the republican colours, had stolen a march and opened fire. The *Seival* nearly ran aground and was lifted off by the mariners, under fire. Although the government forces were poorly led, and had lost support in the town, they put up resistance and Garibaldi left his ship to fight on land with Teixeira. The defenders surrendered. The rebels captured three small ships and war material. In an order of the day Teixeira Nunes paid tribute to "Lieutenant-captain José Garibaldi, commander of the naval forces of the Republic" for his part in executing the plan of attack.

To begin with, all was sweetness and light in Laguna. There had only been one death from the province among the rebels, as against sixteen who had died for the monarchy. The conquest looked like magic. Teixeira Nunes proclaimed Liberty, Equality, Humanity (*Liberdade, Igualdade, Humanidade*),[5] which was the slogan on the masthead of *O Povo*. There were feasts to greet the liberators. On 24 July 1839 the Julian Republic was declared, as the empire had been overthrown there in July. The town council elected Lieutenant-Colonel Joaquim Xavier das Neves as its first president.

Initially there was no attempt by the *Farroupilhas* to take over the running of this adjoining province and Canabarro promised a provisional government. Rather, Santa Catarina was seen by its *gaúcho* neighbour as another republican administration, building up to a federation of Brazilian republics to replace the monarchy. Garibaldi's *carbonari* comrade, Rossetti, had fought in Canabarro's ranks and became secretary to the new Julian Republic.

As a result of captures and enemy surrenders in the victory of Laguna, Garibaldi was now the admiral of a fleet of six ships. He spent much of his time on board. He confesses in his memoirs that he was unhappy. The deaths of his friends and his remoteness from the hopeless situation of Italy, which he dreamed of seeing united, made him lonely. It was in this downhearted mood that he saw, through his binoculars, a lively young woman in a house on the hill overlooking the water. It was the start of one of the great warrior romances of the nineteenth century.

Ana Maria de Jesus Ribeiro was born on 30 August 1821 to a poor family of Azorean origin. She was one of three children, whose father died when she was young, and whose parents had lost two sons in infancy. She was therefore very different from the more privileged Manoela. Her mother, who recognised that Ana was something of a handful, was not sorry when a shoemaker called Manoel Duarte de Aguiar asked to marry her. She may have coerced Ana, who was only fourteen, who seems soon to have regretted her marriage. There were no children, and there is a question as to whether the marriage was ever consummated sexually.

When the republicans threatened Laguna, Duarte joined up in the National Guard, a kind of nationwide militia. As the imperial army withdrew from the town, he went with them, leaving Ana in the care of a neighbour. Garibaldi, who always had an eye for a woman, was attracted to someone who was not conventionally beautiful. She had powerful black eyes, long dark hair and a vigorous way of walking, and he liked the look of her oval face despite her smallpox scars. She had seen him at a distance at a service of thanksgiving for the liberation of Laguna. When he went ashore, hoping to meet her, she walked in as he was taking coffee with a neighbour of hers on the hill.

Speaking to her briefly in Italian rather than Portuguese, in a sentence that has gone down in history, he said: "Tu devi esser mia"—"You

25

have to be mine." It was love at first sight. Garibaldi realised that she was married, a point overlooked by some of his later admirers such as the great British historian of the Risorgimento, G.M. Trevelyan, who claimed that she was merely engaged to Duarte and that Ana "had a perfect right to go with him".[6] In fact, Ana had married Duarte on 30 August 1835 in the church of Santo Antonio dos Anjos in Laguna, and there was an element of arranged marriage as her mother wanted her off her hands. Garibaldi, passionate and highly sexed, swallowed any sense of guilt.

Why did Ana, shortly to be known to her partner as Anita, elope with Garibaldi? Only a couple of months after meeting him for the first time she had joined him on board his ship, the *Rio Pardo*. She was only eighteen. But she had an adventurous spirit, was bored with her life with Duarte, who appeared to have deserted her, and was swept off her feet by the handsome, single-minded Italian whose derring-do was well-known in Laguna. Issues of language were no barrier, for Garibaldi had learnt to communicate in both Spanish and Portuguese. Although there were misgivings in Laguna that an unsuitable Italian was involved with a married daughter of the town, she did not instantly accept his suit. Her own family was strongly opposed.[7]

Anita was already sympathetic to the revolutionaries. Both her father and her grandfather, Antônio da Silva Ribeiro, were *tropeiros*, herding cattle as traders and for landowners. They shared the anger of the southern elites at the commercial policies of the empire, reinforced by martial law. Antônio in particular was propagandising for southern autonomy as he travelled in his work. His house in Lages was burnt down by the authorities, to make an example, and the whole family moved to Laguna. So Anita had taken on board ideas of social equality and republicanism before she ever saw Garibaldi and, though still illiterate, dictated a letter to her sister Irmã to say that she was helping Antônio plan a revolt.[8]

When she went to sea with Garibaldi, she found herself at once in the middle of the war. Using a decoy to avoid a Brazilian vessel, he took her with his three ships across the bar outside Laguna, out into the Atlantic.

3

FIGHTING SIDE BY SIDE

Overall, the war was not going too well for the *Farroupilhas*. In Rio de Janeiro a more conservative regent had been elected, Pedro Araújo Lima, the future Marques de Olinda, and he led a reaction against a more liberal policy which had given power to provincial assemblies. He sought to crack down on secessionist movements in the empire. As these were snuffed out, the rebels in Rio Grande do Sul realised that the chances of a coordinated move to a federal state were disappearing. At the same time their behaviour towards their neighbours in Santa Catarina hardly made for friendship. Canabarro, an arrogant general, lacking diplomatic skills, favoured the *gaúchos* from his own province. The rickety Julian Republic, lacking effective leaders and public support, lasted only until 15 November, when imperial forces recaptured Laguna.

The empire had reinforced its naval forces in southern Brazil. Garibaldi had captured some vessels laden with rice but lost touch with one of his own three ships, commanded by Griggs; he was then caught in a surprise attack at Imbituba, just north of Laguna. While the cannon from one of his two remaining ships was stationed on a promontory, Garibaldi in the *Rio Pardo*, the only seaworthy vessel he had left, was attacked at close quarters by three Brazilian warships.

With furious cannon fire and musketry, the battle lasted for five hours. It only finished when the captain of one of the Brazilian ships was killed, and they sailed away. This battle was a revelation to Garibaldi, for he realised that Anita was not just his lover but a formidable ally and fighter. She refused to go ashore when he suggested she should, she shot with a carbine and carried a sabre in case the enemy boarded the *Rio Pardo*, and survived a hit from a cannon ball when it killed two men beside her. Garibaldi beseeched her to go below deck. She said she would only do so to drive up the cowards who were hiding there, and duly returned, pushing three fellows ahead of her.

The war in Santa Catarina had turned decisively against the *Farroupilhas*. They had never advanced far northwards towards the state capital of Desterro (now Florianópolis)[1] and in the south they were losing popularity. This was partly due to factious infighting in the Julian government led by a Padre Cordeiro, frictions between the civilians and Canabarro, exactions by the rebel army, and a loyalty to the empire which had an economic rationale. The *charque* producers needed the markets of Rio de Janeiro and the slave regions of northern Brazil. There was also a whispering campaign against Garibaldi for having "abducted" Anita, and Duarte, her absent husband, was presented as one of the victims of the invasion. Canabarro never received the reinforcements he expected from Lages, a town to the west of Laguna, across the mountains. Defeat and retreat were only a matter of time.

It was against this negative backdrop that Canabarro ordered Garibaldi to launch a punitive expedition against the small town of Imaruí, on a lagoon halfway between Imbituba and Laguna. Imaruí had risen against the *Farroupilhas* and it had a small imperial garrison. Garibaldi wrote that he had been ordered to chastise the town by fire and sword, that it was an order he could not disobey, and that he hoped no other human being would be asked to do the like.[2]

While the garrison expected an attack from the sea, Garibaldi landed his troops on 9 November 1839, and assaulted Imaruí from hills to the rear. The imperial troops were routed. Garibaldi lost control of his men, whom he did not know well. Fired up with alcohol, they seem to have behaved without restraint, sacking the town and ravaging its shops, men and women in a way that gave Garibaldi, who did not touch alcohol, lasting shame. He commented that if fifty sober troops from the empire had counter-attacked at that point, his own force would have been wiped out. With great difficulty he got his men back onto their ships.

Shortly after this punitive expedition, the republicans lost control of Laguna; this followed a major battle, which demonstrated once again the heroism of Anita. The regency in Rio de Janeiro sent an armada of twenty-two warships to support its army on land, which Garibaldi with his three small ships tried to stop from sailing from the Atlantic into the lagoon after which the town was named. Anita took charge of a cannon, and refused her partner's request to go on shore to liaise with General Canabarro. The battle was bloody, and five of the six republican officers on board were killed, including John Griggs the American, with Garibaldi the only survivor. The republican boats were burnt to prevent them from falling into enemy hands, and Anita with two oarsmen rowed munitions and men to shore in a series of journeys under fire. Canabarro was forced to retreat towards the boundary of Rio Grande do Sul.

The loss of Laguna meant that Garibaldi was no longer in charge of a fleet, however miniscule. From now on he was commanding troops, fighting on land. His views of the *Farroupilha* troops were mixed. He admired their courage and their skill on horseback, where they fought with lances and lassos. But their indiscipline vexed him, for they would melt away after a victory or when there seemed little to do. On these occasions they could be caught unawares by the more professional army and national militia which served the empire. One aspect which pleased him, however, was the loyalty and fighting quality of freed slaves. As a hater of absolutism and arbitrary authority he totally supported the decision of the republic to liberate and enlist the black slaves, who fought both on foot and horseback.

While Canabarro retreated to the south, Garibaldi and Anita joined an expedition westwards across the Serra to the town of Lages, a transport hub and trading crossroads where Anita had lived for a while when she was younger. The Serra make up a range of hills, inland from the coast, running down through Santa Catarina and southwards through Rio Grande do Sul; the ascent can be steep, and at this period the forested slopes made difficult obstacles. This expedition was led by Teixeira Nunes who won a victory over 500 imperial troops, killing their commander, and entered Lages on 18 December.

However, shortly after, on 12 January 1840 at Curitibanos north of Lages, the *Farroupilhas* were caught in a surprise attack at dawn.

Outnumbered and with their forces divided, they were defeated. Some of their troops, who had formerly fought for the empire, defected and returned to the imperialists. Anita, who had been guarding munitions, became separated from Garibaldi. A shot went through her hat, her horse was killed and she was captured.[3]

This was a bad moment for the couple. Anita thought Giuseppe might be dead. Interrogated with sarcasm by a former boyfriend, now a sergeant, Gonçalves Padilha, she was brought before the commander of the imperial force, Colonel Melo Albuquerque. He knew something of her, and was impressed by her courageous bearing in a man's uniform. He gave her permission to look over the battlefield to see whether she could find Garibaldi's body. But she could not see it. It was not there.

Encouraged that he must be alive, Anita resolved to escape. It is possible that the enemy did not try too hard to prevent her. Getting away at night and already just pregnant, a *Farroupilha* sympathiser living in the forest gave her a horse. She rode some sixty miles across difficult terrain, up and down hills, through bush and woodland, with her horse swimming two wide rivers. Staying one night in Lages, and looking like a man with short hair in a soldier's uniform, two women who offered her refuge in their house wanted proof that she was actually female. She showed them her breasts. After riding for a week, with only a cup of coffee to sustain her, she caught up with the retreating republicans where she was reunited with her lover.[4]

Although the rebellion had been running for five years the situation of the republicans was not improving. They had failed to capture the provincial capital of Porto Alegre in spite of bombarding it in a lengthy siege. They were dependent on support from Montevideo, and Brazil had more resources and was increasingly willing to deploy them. In fact, one of the imperial columns had come up from the Uruguay border and had briefly occupied their latest capital, Caçapava. The regency also undercut republican support among the ranchers, and the Montevideo alliance, by introducing a 25 per cent tax on *charque* imported from Uruguay. The republican leadership was factious, and often timid; Colonel Bento Manoel, one of the *Farroupilha* commanders, changed sides three times in the war. There were desultory peace talks, involving Garibaldi's friend Rossetti. Garibaldi's loyalty and fighting spirit, backed up by Anita, stood out in this gloomy picture.

What might have been a decisive engagement near the River Taquarí, west of Porto Alegre, saw armies forming up on either side, but not initially engaging. Garibaldi and other leaders were critical of Bento Gonçalves for not taking advantage of a superior position, even though the rebels were inferior in numbers. The empire's forces had substantial artillery. Two columns of *Farroupilhas* had come together, including the *Lanceiros Negros* (Black Lancers), freed slaves fighting for their liberty, first recruited from the municipality of Piratini, who had a reputation for fearless courage. But Gonçalves failed to attack, and the Brazilians staged a strategic retreat. Time was not on the side of the republicans, whose troops were hungry and tired from constant marching. When the two armies did clash at arms, on 3 May 1840, at Pinheirinho, *O Povo* claimed a victory for the rebels. On the other side, the imperial commander, Manuel Jorge Rodrigues, was awarded a barony, as Barão de Taquarí, as if he had won. It was more of a draw than a victory for either side. Although numbers are disputed, one estimate is that the empire fielded 4,500 troops against 3,400 for the republic, with fifty-three deaths and 125 wounded among the former, and thirty-five killed and 114 wounded among the latter.[5] Other estimates were much higher, and it is doubtful that anyone was counting accurately.

The battle was not the definitive fight that had been anticipated, and which could have brought the war to an end. Garibaldi, never fazed when the odds were against him, had a position in the centre of the republican army. He was particularly impressed by the discipline and effectiveness of the *Lanceiros Negros*, who were turning into the best troops in the republic. "A true forest of lances was that incomparable corps, almost totally composed of slaves liberated by the republic, and chosen from among the best horse-tamers of the province; all were black, except the superior officers," he recalled later, and they were a terror to the enemy.[6] But Pinheirinho was not an all-out victory, and the republican commanders ended up blaming each other.

A more clear-cut disaster took place in the south of Rio Grande do Sul later the same year, when Garibaldi took part in a surprise attack on São José do Norte. The idea was to capture a port in the south of the province and block the Lagoa dos Patos to imperial shipping. It started well, and the defenders were cooped up in their barracks. But Bento Gonçalves ruled out a scheme to set the barracks on fire, as risking too many innocent lives. The capture of the town had already been bloody, with streets lined with corpses. The republicans, as so often in moments of victory, started looting and drinking. The empire sent reinforcements by water. An explosion killed troops and civilians and Gonçalves released prisoners in an exchange for medicines. Then he ordered a retreat.

There were continuing rumours that republican leaders were in talks with the enemy. The failures disheartened Garibaldi, and his friend Rossetti concluded that it was better to seek a federation than to pursue an independent republic. After the retreat from São José do Norte they reviewed together a situation in which a number of Italians had died, while others had moved on to Montevideo. It was a moment in which Garibaldi seems to have thought seriously, for the first time, that he might follow them. The war could not be won and, poorly armed and hungry from trying unsuccessfully to live off the land, *Farroupilha* troops were deserting. Rossetti himself had explored the prospects for peace with the empire, and his imperial correspondent in Porto Alegre had pointed out shrewdly that it was illogical for Italians who wanted a united Italy to fight to break up Brazil.[7]

Giuseppe and Anita were overjoyed, in the midst of this frustrating war, when Anita gave birth to a little boy, on 16 September 1840. They named him Domenico Menotti, but he was always known as Menotti. This was a tribute to Ciro Menotti, the patriot hanged in Modena in 1831, whom Garibaldi greatly admired. Anita had her baby in the home of a family near Mostardas, on a strip of land that divides the Atlantic from the Lagoa dos Patos.

The baby emerged with a dent in his head, the result of his mother's fall from the horse in Curitibanos or in the course of her flight and, in the midst of a war, there was no escape. Garibaldi had gone to buy some necessities for his family. While he was away, Moringue launched an attack on republican troops in the neighbourhood, undoubtedly hoping to catch Garibaldi. Anita had to ride off, at night and in the rain, escaping with her baby of some twelve days clutched to her breast.

The winter of 1840 was wet and cold. The republicans had been defeated at São José do Norte, at the southern end of the Lagoa dos Patos, and an attempt to get Garibaldi boat-building again—for the Brazilians controlled the lake—left him disheartened. The *Farroupilhas* were defeated again at Settembrina, where Rossetti, Garibaldi's best friend since he first arrived in Rio, was killed. "After performing prodigies of valour, falling from his horse desperately wounded, and summoned to surrender, he had preferred being killed to giving up his sword. Another sharp pang for my heart," Garibaldi wrote later.[8]

Garibaldi and Anita took part in a terrible retreat across mountains and through pine forests and flooded rivers, short of food and with the camp-followers, women and children, dying like flies. It did not help that their guides lost their way. The cavalry were having to kill their horses, to provide food. The only consolation was that the indigenous Amerindians supported them, and ambushed the imperial troops.

"Anita shuddered at the idea of losing our Menotti, whom we saved only by a miracle. At the most dangerous passages of our route and in crossing rivers, I carried the poor child, three months old, suspended from my neck by a handkerchief, and by that means I could warm him with my breath," Garibaldi wrote.[9] In March 1841 the family reached São Gabriel, the latest capital of the republic, where he built a hut to shelter them, and reviewed the situation. He had signed up with the republic as a seaman and captain, but it no longer had ships. He was influenced by Rossetti's conclusion that continuing the war was futile. He was receiving news about his family in Europe and the progress of Young Italy from Montevideo, currently enjoying a pause in the Uruguayan civil war.

At the end of April 1841 Garibaldi decided it was time to take a break. Bento Gonçalves, president of the tottering republic of Rio Grande do Sul, which actually lasted much longer, until February 1845, gave him permission to withdraw from the struggle. It is possible that he told Gonçalves that his departure was only temporary.[10] Gonçalves may also have used Garibaldi to take messages to his allies in Montevideo. The *Farroupilhas* were in no position to give him compensation or a pension. Instead he was authorised to collect 900 head of cattle, to provide him with capital. *Gaúcho* cattle were semi-wild, and it took him twenty days to round up his convoy. He resolved to ride overland to Montevideo, where he could sell his herd.

There seems to have been a mixture of reasons for his final decision, which meant saying good-bye to the country of Anita's birth. He had heard that his father had died,[11] and in Montevideo he would have more news from the Italian states via shipping and the large Ligurian community. He was conscious that Anita and Menotti deserved a rest from the dangers of campaigning, and he thought wrongly that a more peaceful Montevideo would not pose such a challenge to family life. Anita herself had shown she was an adept linguist. Having learnt Italian with Giuseppe, she was starting to pick up Spanish too. And, most likely, he was just tired of a war that was plainly being lost.

Going to Montevideo with cattle was not straightforward. Garibaldi had no experience as a herdsman. Wild cattle made their escape. He was robbed by the four *gaúchos* he employed to help him. The couple took a roundabout route to avoid Brazilian patrols and, riding hard, covered some 360 miles in fifty days. By the time he crossed the dangerous Rio Negro his herd was down to 500 beasts, and he had them killed. In the end he only had 300 hides to sell in Montevideo. After six years in Brazil, a new chapter in his South American adventures was about to open.

What had he learnt from his adventures so far? He admired the hardiness of the *gaúcho* horsemen, who could live and fight for days with minimal supplies of boiled, grilled or dried beef. He admired the wilderness and forests of an untamed geography, so different from Europe. He admired the courage and ingenuity of the freed slaves who fought alongside him, making nonsense of racism and slavery. He learnt the huge importance of high morale, and not to be intimidated by adverse odds. He loved above all Anita, as a fellow warrior and soulmate.

But he had also seen the downsides. He watched internal squabbles and timidity in the *Farroupilha* leadership, and political and military arrogance as those leaders sought to extend the revolution to Santa Catarina. He saw occasional cowardice and the lack of commitment of irregular soldiers who might go home after a battle or defeat. In this scenario the loyalty of fellow Italians, fighting like him for a distant cause, shone out as an inspiration.

4

MONTEVIDEO, AND ANOTHER WAR

Initially Garibaldi and Anita seem to have hoped that Montevideo would be a haven, where they could be a normal family and recover from the hardships and danger of Rio Grande do Sul. It was also a city with a vibrant Italian population, estimated to have numbered some 6,000 out of a total of 42,000, with friends and contacts including Giovanni Battista Cuneo; there was abundant news from home and of the continuing struggles of Young Italy. But at the same time the new family was poor, for their hides were not worth much.

Giuseppe, Anita and Menotti stayed with a *carbonaro* friend, Napoleone Castellini, and Giuseppe tried several ways to make a living. He taught maths, history and calligraphy at an institute run by another friend, Paolo Semidei, and at the same time checked cargoes on the docks and worked as a salesman. "I carried samples of all kinds about me," he wrote.[1] He was helped by his Masonic connections, since the *carbonari* were linked in Masonic brotherhoods which the partisans of Young Italy saw as progressive. He may have been assisted financially by the French "Amis de la Patrie" Lodge, and in Rio Grande do Sul he and Rossetti had belonged to the "Asylo de Virtude" Lodge, which had both Italian and *Farroupilha* connections.

For less than a year Garibaldi lived this "civilian" existence, a life for which he was not well suited. He decided to regularise his situation with Brazil, and in September 1841 he approached José Dias da Cruz

35

Lima, the Brazilian chargé d'affaires in Montevideo, requesting an amnesty so that he could resume a nautical career without fear of reprisals from the imperial navy. He did so in the light of a decree from Emperor Pedro II that forgave any rebel who laid down his arms, and he promised in writing not to fight any Brazilian naval vessel. Yet by February 1842 he had been put in charge of a small Uruguayan warship and early in the following year, when Montevideo was facing crisis, he ran into trouble with the Brazilians after capturing a small Brazilian vessel in Uruguayan waters. Cruz Lima's successor described him as a robber and demanded his expulsion, there was talk of a duel, and the Montevideo government had to smooth things over.[2]

On 26 March 1842 he and Anita were married at the church of San Bernardino, Montevideo, with Paulo Semidei as one of two witnesses. Although he was anticlerical Garibaldi wanted to marry in church, and have his children baptised. Anita's mother came from Brazil and said that Anita was now a widow as Manuel Duarte de Aguiar, her first husband, had died. Anita was free to marry again. This did not stop rumours among those hostile to the couple that it was a bigamous union, since solid proof of Manuel's death was lacking.

But although to start with the Garibaldi family was living quietly, in relative poverty, Giuseppe's reputation as a courageous commander was well-known, particularly in the Italian community. Young Italy and the *carbonari* had been boosting his reputation in Europe. War came knocking at his door again, and it was as a dashing naval commander that the Montevideo government initially turned to him.

The Guerra Grande in Uruguay, 1839–51, was the product of the complicated politics of the River Plate region, involving both the Argentine confederation of fourteen states, now directed by Rosas from Buenos Aires, and a divided Uruguay. Rosas would have liked to bring Uruguay, and its capital the port of Montevideo, under his control. In this he was allied to Manuel Oribe, who had been overthrown as president of Uruguay by another *caudillo*, Fructuoso Rivera, in 1838. Both had played a patriotic role earlier, and they had worked together until they fell out.

Oribe had been one of the legendary thirty-three patriots, who, led by Juan Antonio Lavalleja, had launched an uprising against Brazilian control in 1825, and Fructuoso Rivera had joined Lavalleja soon after.

Rivera was president from 1830 to 1835 and supported Oribe to succeed him. But there was a breakdown between the two and Rivera led
a successful revolt, defeating Oribe in October 1838 and precipitating
the Guerra Grande. Rivera's supporters wore red armbands, so that
their political party became known as the *Colorado* (red) Party; Oribe's
wore white, so that their Partido Nacional was popularly called the
Blancos (whites). The long war impoverished what was still a new state,
and Uruguay saw a sharp fall in population.

Oribe proved to be one of Rosas' most effective generals. He won a
series of battles in 1840 and 1841 which saw off a threat to Buenos Aires,
and enabled Rosas to win domination of all the Argentine states. He
moved back into Uruguay, supported by Rosas with some of the best
Argentine troops, and a full-scale civil war developed. This became
extremely bloodthirsty. His faction, the *Blancos*, were more pro-Argen-
tine and less internationalist than Rivera's *Colorados*, whose base lay in the
city of Montevideo. Victors took no prisoners. Captured soldiers were
decapitated, a practice that was also common in the fighting in Argentina.

In June 1842 Garibaldi was asked by Rivera and the Montevideo
government, the Gobierno de la Defensa, to take command of a small
fleet of three vessels, captaining the largest. This was the *Constitución* of
256 tons, with eighteen cannon. He was ordered to go up the River
Paraná, and free it from Argentine threats to commercial shipping from
Paraguay and inland ports like Corrientes. This trade was crucial to the
port of Montevideo, which Rosas and Oribe were trying to blockade,
while Oribe was building his own custom house just outside the capital. Customs dues were essential to the revenues of both Montevideo
and Buenos Aires at this time, in an era before income or sales taxes. In
his memoirs Garibaldi wrote that his enemies wanted him out of the
capital, and thought he might never survive to return.

There was also a political purpose. The state of Corrientes was at the
extreme north of the influence of Rosas and Oribe, and Montevideo
was hoping to swing it behind the Gobierno de la Defensa. This would
have the benefit, too, of closer communications with its ally, the breakaway republic of Rio Grande do Sul.

In heading upstream on the Paraná, Garibaldi was confronting a
larger fleet of seven ships commanded by Rosas' celebrated Irish admiral, William Brown. The experienced Brown, now credited as father of

the Argentine Navy, had been winning naval battles in the Plate for nearly forty years. Garibaldi managed to get past the Argentine fortress on the island of Martín García, guarding the entrance to the Paraná, but then the *Constitución* became stuck on a sandbank, and he had to transfer its cannons to his smallest vessel, the *Procida* of only seventy-one tons. He re-floated his flagship while Admiral Brown then ran his own ship, the *Belgrano*,[3] aground, giving him precious time to get away.

Using all his skill and various tricks to deceive the enemy, Garibaldi won a victory in mid-July; the Paraná has many islands, useful for marine guerrillas. By the beginning of August he had travelled as far upstream as La Paz, where he was joined by some vessels sent downriver from Corrientes. But he was still being pursued by Brown. He decided to confront him at a place called Costa Brava, in a three-day battle, where Garibaldi ran out of munitions. He decided at length that the best thing he could do was to put his sailors ashore, and set fire to his ships.

He had not exactly been defeated, and thought he had taught Brown a lesson. He then marched north, past Goya to the riverside town of Santa Lucía, where he waited two months for instructions. It was not until early 1843, after a difficult overland march, that Garibaldi and his force returned to Montevideo—a capital facing the worst moment of danger from Oribe. For Rivera had just been beaten at the battle of Arroyo Grande in December 1842.

This was also the end of an alliance between Fructuoso Rivera, and his *Colorado* faction in Uruguay, and Bento Gonçalves and the *Farroupilhas*. They had worked closely together in 1837–8, when Rivera had overthrown President Oribe, and they had signed a treaty of mutual support in December 1841. Bento Gonçalves had offered 400 infantry and 200 cavalry to support an invasion of the adjoining Argentine state of Entre Rios. This regional approach, which had been in the minds of some in Rio Grande since the start of the uprising in southern Brazil, had its epitome in October 1842 when Rivera, Gonçalves, the governors of the Argentine provinces of Santa Fé and Corrientes, and the ex-governor of Córdoba, signed a secret anti-Rosas protocol in Paysandú. This could have led to a confederation, and a different political geography for the south of South America.

But the dream lasted less than two months. Rivera's troops were comprehensively defeated in December 1842 at Arroyo Grande inside

Entre Rios state, beyond the Uruguayan border, where he had half the numbers of his opponents, Oribe and Urquiza, ruler of Entre Rios.[4] Rivera managed to get back across the River Uruguay, eluding Oribe, and reached Montevideo on 1 February 1843. Oribe, however, was free to advance on Montevideo. At first Oribe thought he would be welcomed without resistance.

In February 1843 he started to besiege the city—the great siege began. He was occupying all the land surrounding Montevideo, and had set up headquarters at Los Cerritos, a few miles to the west.[5] His position was strong, as Rosas saw him as a legitimate ruler who had been wrongly overthrown in Rivera's coup, and was supplying Argentine troops to help him regain the presidency. Oribe was running a parallel government, which was ruling nearly all of Uruguay.

Rivera and the various expatriate and exile communities anticipated an assault at any moment, and thought there was little to stop it. Some panicked. Rivera guarded a convoy of 9,000 people, including children, fleeing the city. Many Argentinians, in the liberal, Unitarian faction opposed to Rosas, had also taken refuge there. Between 1839 and 1842 Rosas' hoodlums had been killing his opponents in the streets of Buenos Aires, and his opponents feared vengeance. Montevideo's small navy was virtually wiped out.

In March, just after the siege had begun, the strategic balance seemed to turn against the city. The Brazilian empire signed an offensive and defensive alliance with Rosas, aimed both at the *Farroupilhas* and the defenders of Montevideo.

5

ITALIAN LEGION, AND NAVAL COMMANDER

At this point two European powers, as well as slaves who were freed in the crisis and expatriates living in Montevideo, came to the rescue. France and Britain had much stronger navies than that of Rosas. Both nations were active in trade in the Plate basin, with Buenos Aires, Montevideo and the upstream river ports. Freedom of navigation in the Plate, and in the big Paraná and Uruguay rivers which ran into the Plate, was a vital commercial interest. French warships had blockaded Buenos Aires from March 1838 to October 1840, just prior to Garibaldi's arrival in Montevideo, in a row over the status of French nationals. Should Rosas have controlled both shores of the Plate the European states would have had to do his bidding.

In late 1841 the British legation in Buenos Aires had twice unavailingly offered its good offices to Rosas to resolve his dispute with Rivera, and in August 1842 the two European states had proposed a joint mediation.[1] In December Britain signed a treaty of friendship with Uruguay, guaranteeing freedom of navigation, which the Montevideo government hoped would turn into a guarantee of military support also. By early 1843, with Oribe and his Argentine troops threatening Montevideo and British residents and merchants becoming jumpy, there was increasing pressure on Britain to take action, and an Anglo-French naval squadron sailed from Europe to the Plate.

It was the British Navy which broke the Argentine naval blockade of Montevideo, permitting food, materials and people to reach the besieged city. The five Argentine warships off the coast under Admiral Brown were put under surveillance and kept at anchor. Britain wanted not only to maintain free navigation in the Plate, but to protect the independence of Uruguay as a buffer state between the Argentinians and the Brazilian empire. It was British diplomacy in 1828 that had intervened to guarantee the new state of Uruguay, sandwiched between two more powerful neighbours.

In spite of frictions between admirals and diplomats, and between those on the spot in South America and their chiefs who were some weeks away by sail in the capitals of London and Paris, there was coordinated Anglo-French naval intervention in the mid-1840s. It was designed to baulk Rosas, protect British and French traders and citizens, and safeguard an independent Uruguay.

The crisis for Montevideo was at its height after the battle of Arroyo Grande. Ramparts were thrown up around the city and batteries placed at intervals. It is possible that less than a third of the capital's population may have been Uruguayan, and the European and Argentinian majority, threatened by the cruelty of Rosas and with their livelihoods at risk, began to raise legions in its defence. In Buenos Aires foreign nationals, including Italians, had unsuccessfully tried to stop Rosas from capturing the city. In February 1843 the British and French admirals each put 120 marines ashore in Montevideo, to protect an evacuation of their nationals in the event of the city's fall.

Rivera handed over the presidency of the besieged city in March 1843 at the completion of his term to a civilian, Joaquín Suárez, retaining his role as general. Then, on 1 April, their enemy Oribe committed a strategic error. He issued a circular to the foreign consuls in Montevideo that any foreigner found to have fought for or supported the government would be regarded as a Unitarian and dealt with accordingly by his Argentine allies. Unitarians were the more liberal party in Argentina, long opposed to Rosas and defeated by him in Buenos Aires. Many survivors had taken refuge in Montevideo. Knowing what had happened to Unitarians at the hands of Rosas' thugs on the streets of Buenos Aires, this was a death sentence. It was also counterproductive.

Commodore John Purvis, the Royal Navy commander who did not hide his sympathy for Montevideo, called on Oribe to withdraw his threat. He told Admiral Brown, by now blockading the city with his

Argentine ships, that if Oribe did not withdraw his circular and guarantee the lives and property of British citizens, his ships would not be allowed to move. "When Brown ordered two of his ships to strike sail, Purvis opened fire from the *Alfred* and caused the Argentine ships to drop anchor."[2] Although Purvis' action caused a diplomatic rumpus in Buenos Aires and with John Mandeville, the British plenipotentiary there, the blockade had been broken.

But the threat to Montevideo from Oribe's army, and to its large expatriate population, had already caused the foreigners to take up arms. French, Spanish and Italian legions were ready to take to the field. Oribe's circular to the foreign consuls confirmed them in their determination. As in the Piratini republic, all the slaves were freed by a law of emancipation of December 1842, and some 5,000 were willing to put their lives on the line in the struggle.

Garibaldi had first helped Montevideo in his capacity as a naval captain, leading the Paraná expedition. He could not now return to a civilian life as a teacher or trader when the city was in imminent peril. His commitment to liberty, his opposition to despotism, were defining aspects of his character. He issued a proclamation to Italian residents, calling them to arms.[3]

He simultaneously set up the legion and, by public subscription, raised funds to pay for four small craft with six guns and sixty crew; these light vessels were not enough to break the Argentine blockade but, as in Rio Grande do Sul, had the capacity to harry larger warships. As before, he became an admiral for a threatened republic. His experience in southern Brazil had taught him not to distinguish between land-based and water-based forces, and he was ready to command a force of troops, sailors or marines as required. He once told Alexandre Dumas that he was "born an amphibian". He was an original, not an orthodox military thinker.

The Italian Legion, initially with 500 men, grew to number some 800, but was not as large as the French Legion of 3,500, led by Colonel Jean Thiébaut. When the French government seemed hesitant about helping the embattled city, now surrounded by 14,000 troops, and threatened its citizens in arms, the French volunteers renounced their nationality and became Uruguayan. Some of the Spanish, by contrast, with monarchist and Carlist sympathies, went over to the enemy; the Basques stayed loyal to Montevideo.

Garibaldi was disappointed when his legion retreated in panic on its first sortie outside the city defences. He suspected treachery as well as cowardice, and indeed twenty officers and fifty soldiers did go over to the enemy. The Italian recruits were commercial people and labourers seeking a better life in South America, as well as escaped revolutionaries with a price on their heads, who might have fought earlier in Italy or Spain. Some had been born in Uruguay. The troops were not paid, and their provisions were likely to be misappropriated.

In the course of 1843 this unpromising material was drilled into a useful military force, and shortly after the panicky retreat, Garibaldi and Melchor Pacheco y Obes, the minister of war, led a successful attack on Oribe's troops in March at Cerro, west of Oribe's camp at El Cerrito, where some Montevideo troops were holding out. This involved them in an amphibious landing: "The legion, consisting of 400 men, charged a battalion of 600. Pacheco fought on horseback but I on foot or horseback, as circumstances required. We killed 150 of the enemy, and made 200 prisoners. We had five or six killed, and about half a score wounded…"[4] Garibaldi, who had already fought off Admiral Brown in a three-day battle at the Isla dos Ratos just off Montevideo, showed his personal courage in leading legionaries to rescue Italians cut off in a house, and mounting a successful counter-attack.[5]

News of the Italian Legion was reaching Europe by more objective routes than the pen of Mazzini. *The Times* of 20 July 1844 recorded a sortie from the city when Oribe's troops "were gallantly charged by Garibaldi at the head of the Italian Legion, and were cut up, suffering severe loss". The correspondent estimated that Montevideo had lost nearly 230 in killed and wounded, and Oribe nearly 600.

Garibaldi paid tribute to his friend Francisco Anzani, who had been quietly working in a trading house, for coming in and organising the legion into three battalions, imposing discipline, dealing with traitors and cleaning up its administration. Anzani was a revolutionary and proscribed by the rulers of Italy as a veteran of liberal struggles in Europe. He became Garibaldi's second in command. He focused on building up the legion's "Italian" morale, and its role as an exemplar for the coming struggle for unification of the Italian peninsula. It had its own flag, designed by Cuneo. This was black, to symbolise an Italy in mourning, with a fiery Vesuvius volcano in the centre, to represent an unquenchable revolutionary spirit. The flag was presented to the legion in a ceremony on 9 July 1843 by the wife of Rivera, who became a good friend of Anita's, and Santiago Vázquez, Montevideo's foreign minister. Garibaldi recorded that the flag was handed to Gaetano Sacchi, then aged twenty, who had fought well at Cerro and later went with him to Italy.

The Italian Legion was democratic, and highly dependent on its loyalty to Giuseppe. There was a commission to oversee it, to which he reported. Like the other legions in the city it was not entirely popular with the civilian and Uruguayan citizens, who saw it as swaggering and taking too much of the besieged city's precious food supplies, causing prices to rise. In the Italian case this was because its commander was a close friend of Stefano Antonini, a *carbonaro* and leading merchant.

The legion was recognisable everywhere by its redshirt uniform—later a symbol of Garibaldi's forces in Italy. The shirts became available by chance. A shirt maker in Montevideo had a contract to supply a slaughterhouse in Buenos Aires with shirts already the colour of blood, but went bankrupt as a result of the Argentine blockade.[6] It was an inspirational move to use this stock to clothe the legionaries. For some these shirts echoed the ponchos worn by the *Lanceiros Negros* of Rio Grande do Sul. The more cynical saw that they would make cowards and traitors more obvious on the battlefield.

Garibaldi's willingness to pursue unorthodox strategies was illustrated by a proposal he made in 1845, after a successful guerrilla ambush by the legion near Montevideo, charging with the bayonet and capturing cattle. He suggested to the government that he could make a night landing near Buenos Aires, advance on Rosas' house, take him prisoner and bring him across to Montevideo. "This expedition succeeding, the war would be terminated at a single blow."[7] Perhaps unsurprisingly the government turned down his offer. In 1845 the course of the war—*La Guerra Grande*, as it became known—changed decisively as the Anglo-French diplomacy switched from attempts at mediation to a clear-cut intervention on the side of Montevideo. Buenos Aires was blockaded by sea, to teach Rosas a lesson. The Anglo-French naval force also found itself collaborating with Montevideo in its efforts to defeat Oribe. In particular, this meant fighting alongside the sometimes insubordinate and hardly controllable Garibaldi, admiral of its puny navy.

The two diplomats in charge of operations were William Gore Ouseley for the Britain of Queen Victoria and her successive foreign secretaries, Lord Aberdeen, from 1841 to 1846, and the uncompromising Lord Palmerston, from 1846 to 1851, and Baron Anton Deffaudis for the France of Louis Philippe I, the last Bourbon king, who was following a policy of friendship with Britain while losing popularity at home.[8] Each, of course, had their own interests, and the British seemed keener on access up the River Uruguay, and up the Paraná which served inland Paraguay, for import-export commerce. Together they did not rate Montevideo's tiny navy as of high military value, and relations between the three allies were not close. Nonetheless the British agreed to subsidise Montevideo's navy for wear and tear, and took steps to strengthen it.[9]

In the second half of 1845 two parallel naval operations developed, both encountering stiff resistance from Rosas, Oribe and local *caudillos*. The Royal Navy launched an expedition up the Paraná, where a significant number of merchant ships were stranded because of the war; some of these were British and, from the viewpoint of Montevideo, their customs revenue was vital for the impecunious city state. Meanwhile Garibaldi, with his small flotilla and the Italian Legion, advanced up the Rio Uruguay.

To begin with there was tactical cooperation. Garibaldi's boats joined the Royal Navy in blockading Buceo, a supply point for Oribe close to Montevideo, and in capturing the strategic island of Martín García, at the estuary of the Rio Uruguay. Admiral Samuel Inglefield, in charge of the Royal Navy squadron, handed Garibaldi a couple of captured Argentine vessels. Garibaldi and the legion, working with both the British and the French and other Uruguayans, then landed at Colonia on 31 August 1845.

Colonia, opposite Buenos Aires on the north bank of the Plate, was potentially a crucial base for the Anglo-French blockade of Rosas' capital. Its layout was still that of a Portuguese town, for it had been founded by Manuel Lobo, a Portuguese, in 1680 and for much of the period until the Treaty of San Ildefonso in 1777 had been the southernmost point of Portuguese territory. It had then briefly returned from Spanish to Portuguese rule in the Cisplatine province from 1809 until 1825, at the dawn of Uruguay's independence.

A letter from Garibaldi to his friend Cuneo, who was editing *Legionario Italiano*, stated that two companies of the legion, and some Uruguayans, went ashore ahead of the British and French. The legion tackled both infantry and cavalry with success and with only five wounded, but Garibaldi was critical of his British and French allies. Reports in *Presse*, a French journal in Paris, maligned him in turn, and a French officer who subsequently went over to Rosas turned "friendly fire" onto the Italians who were also criticised for pillage. But the town and port were safely in the hands of Montevideo.

Garibaldi was now in a position to sail up the Uruguay, assisted by cavalry on shore who were able to bring supplies. His navy consisted of ten ships, and the French and British also helped as escorts and suppliers. The aim was to get upriver as far as Salto, where the river became narrower. This would help to clear eastern Uruguay of Oribe's troops, release stranded merchantmen and open links with Brazil, where pro-Montevideo refugees could be recruited to join up in the capital's struggle. Between 1845 and 1852 it is estimated that over 10,000 Uruguayans, soldiers and civilians had taken refuge in Rio Grande do Sul and Santa Catarina, causing diplomatic stress between Montevideo and Rio de Janeiro.[10]

Royal Navy carpenters at the British base on the strategic island of Martín García helped fit out Garibaldi's vessels for the expedition; they were paid from Britain's secret service funds. But it soon became obvious that he was not good at obeying orders, and the British belief that it was buying the support of the Uruguayan Navy was not translated into the close and unquestioning cooperation they had hoped for.

Montevideo wanted to issue its admiral with letters of marque, which had constituted his authority to take prizes for the *Farroupilhas*, and could bring in a handy income for the government. But the British were committed to ending piracy of all kinds, and restoring safe navigation for merchantmen in the Plate and its tributaries. Ouseley and Deffaudis rejected the proposal. Nonetheless Garibaldi went ahead, capturing small boats and treating their freight as prizes when he could see some value. Within a fortnight of the victory at Colonia, for instance, he was sending a consignment of hides to Montevideo for auction and he ran into serious trouble with the Royal Navy when one of his captures had a British owner.[11]

His freebooting style led opponents like Rosas to conclude that he was at heart a corsair, adventurer and pirate. Nationalists in Latin America had dismissed many British heroes, such as Sir Francis Drake, in the same terms. Garibaldi never threw off this hostile reputation. But there is much evidence that he was austere, and the poverty in which he, Anita and his family lived in Montevideo led to comment among their friends, and housekeeping problems for Anita. Given that his government was in no position to pay either his sailors or his legion, and that it needed all the funds it could find, his attitude that he was taking spoils of war for good ends was at least understandable.

The British also had a more vital military objective, from their commercial angle. This was to reopen the Paraná and its traffic. The Paraná serves a huge watershed, running up between the Argentine provinces of Entre Rios and Santa Fé towards Paraguay, with significant inland ports including Rosario, Corrientes and the Paraguayan capital, Asunción. By the end of October 1845 an Anglo-French naval force, comprising five British and four French warships, was ready and on 20 November they won an important victory at Obligado, en route to Rosario. They destroyed Argentine shore batteries, defeated enemy troops on land and broke through hulks that had been chained across the river. By March 1846 Lord Aberdeen, current foreign secretary, was calling for an end to this intervention, but the delay in communications meant that it was not until June that a convoy, including rescued cargoes worth £500,000, returned to Montevideo.[12]

All this meant that Garibaldi did not have to look over his shoulder too hard as he sailed up the Uruguay in 1845. His was a fighting expedition, far from unopposed, frequently contending with shore batteries. The governor of Entre Rios, in alliance with Rosas in the Argentine confederation, was Justo José Urquiza y García, who had a formidable army of his own.

Garibaldi's men won battles at Gualeguaychú, which fell into his hands by surprise on 20 September, and Paysandú. Gualeguaychú, or more probably Gualeguay, some seventy miles to the south-west and away from the river, was the scene of one of the most memorable moments in Giuseppe's sojourn in South America. He found he had captured Leonardo Millan, responsible for torturing him at the start of his service with the *Farroupilhas*. "I think I need not say I gave him his liberty without doing him any injury, leaving him as his only punishment the fright he experienced on recognising me."[13] It was testimony to his generosity of spirit.

His 1861 autobiography edited by Alexander Dumas suggested that this event took place in Gualeguaychú, but it appears that a similarity of names may have led to an unusual slip in Garibaldi's memory. There is no evidence that Millan was in Gualeguaychú in 1845, where Garibaldi's actions have been subject to much critical analysis. But it is possible that he was still living in or near Gualeguay,[14] which Garibaldi's cavalry may well have raided in search of provisions as they fought their way up the river, or that they captured him somewhere else during this campaign. The episode remains mysterious, but there is no reason to suppose that Garibaldi invented it.

However, Gualeguaychú also saw another side to him. The town was undefended, neglected by Urquiza's forces, and was attacked at dawn when many were asleep. Garibaldi captured and then released the mayor, Eduardo Villagra the commander, and other authorities. But he also authorised his men to sack thirty-one shops and warehouses, as well as family houses, to obtain clothes, food and fodder for the horses. Panic ensued among the townspeople, and the foreign merchants who had suffered some of the biggest losses estimated that he cost them, in pounds sterling, the equivalent of £30,000. Garibaldi also took away 5,000 pesos in cash on board one of his ships, *Joven Emilia*. He sailed off a day later, as enemy troops were nearing.

By November he had reached as far up the Uruguay as Salto. Here he ran up against stronger forces of José Urquiza, the powerful governor of Entre Rios, the province lying between the Paraná and Uruguay. He was a *caudillo*, an unreliable ally of Rosas, bridling at the despot of Buenos Aires who sought to control all the states in the Argentine confederation. In the end he was to orchestrate Rosas' downfall in 1851–2, defeating Oribe in 1851, raising the siege of Montevideo, and defeating Rosas at the battle of Caseros in February 1852. By then he was allied to Brazil, the Uruguayan liberals and all the Argentinians who were discontented with Rosas' tyranny.

But in 1845 he was still an ally of Oribe and Rosas, and after Garibaldi captured Salto he attempted to recapture the town in a battle which involved house-to-house fighting, over a period of twenty-three days. The Italians, who numbered 600, were supported by 300 Uruguayan cavalry and two small ships of the British and French navies. Urquiza, by contrast, had 3,500 cavalry and 800 infantry and artillery. Garibaldi spread his outnumbered force round the streets. They fought well. Urquiza was forced to retreat. Garibaldi criticised his small British complement for running away at one point, permitting Urquiza to take valuable cattle which were essential food for his troops and the townspeople, and forcing his troops to eat their own horses. But his hold on Salto enabled refugees from the town to return, and Uruguayans who had fled to Brazil came back to join up in the Montevideo army.

This lengthy battle in the town of Salto began on 6 December 1845. It coincided with a major tragedy for Garibaldi and Anita. On 23 December their much-loved daughter Rosita, only two years of age, died of a throat infection, probably diphtheria, making it impossible for her to breathe.[15] She had been named Rosa, after his mother, but was known by the diminutive. The news reached Garibaldi in a brutally brief message from Minister Pacheco y Obes, who had been a friend: "Your daughter Rosita has died... I prefer not to give details. Please accept my sympathy."

He at once realised what this would mean for his wife. She decided to join him. It is not certain whether she came on her own, leaving her two other children with friends in Montevideo, or whether she brought them with her; it seems more probable that she left them in the care of friends. Menotti was then six and Teresita was only one, when she managed to reach Salto and the legion.[16] Here she was able to continue as a nurse, the role she had played throughout the siege of Montevideo, and to be nearby for the most celebrated battle of the Italian Legion.

On 8 February 1846 Servando Gómez, one of Urquiza's commanders, launched an attack at Ipavey, just outside Salto. The battle, considered the most famous victory for the legion, was known as San Antonio and was fought in suffocating heat. It began with enemy cavalry carrying foot soldiers up to close range of the heights on which the Italians were dug in. The soldiers then leaped down, and began to attack.

The affair started badly for Garibaldi, whose mount was killed. Realising that if his men saw him fall they might think he too was dead, he fired his pistol in the air. Willing hands rescued him. Abandoned by some Brazilian cavalry, the legion consisted then of only 190 men, attacked by 1,200 horse and 300 foot. But, nothing daunted, Garibaldi shouted: "The enemy are numerous, we are few; so much the better! The fewer we are, the more glorious will be the fight. Be calm! Do not fire till they are close upon us, and then charge with the bayonet."[17] He led a charge into the thickest of the enemy ranks and, although most of the Italian officers were wounded in the action, he himself was unscratched.

His men were exhausted and thirsty, but it was only when the enemy fire slackened that he ordered a fighting retreat. Able-bodied troops protected the many wounded as they marched, and only two men were abandoned on the field. But there was an enemy camp between San Antonio and Salto. After an hour's relaxation he led a bayonet charge, cutting through the enemy and reaching the river where they could find water to drink. On arriving in Salto there was an emotional reunion with Anzani, who had been left in the town with a number of sick and wounded. He also had had to fight off an attack, and had rejected a call to surrender, saying: "Italians do not surrender."

The Italians had lost thirty killed, and fifty-three were wounded at San Antonio.[18] Their general had been inspirational. At one point he had carried a wounded lieutenant on his shoulders, Gaetano Sacchi, who was bearing the banner presented to the legion. Writing to the commission which oversaw the affairs of the Italian Legion in Montevideo, he described it "as the most terrible and the most glorious of our battles". He ordered that a large cross be erected, to honour the dead and the legionaries who had fought there.

His own account, written in Salto on 10 February 1846, two days after the battle, stated:

> The four companies of our legion, and about a score of cavalry who had taken refuge under our protection, have not only maintained against twelve hundred of the men of Servando Gómez an engagement which lasted more than twelve hours, but still further, have entirely destroyed the enemy's infantry, three hundred men strong. The firing commenced at mid-day, and ended at midnight. Nothing succeeded with the enemy, neither the numerous charges of their cavalry nor the reiterated attacks of their infantry.

> Without any other rampart but a bad shed in ruins, only supported by some posts, the legionaries sustained the assaults of the enemy, assaults

incessantly repeated. I and all the officers fought like common soldiers. Anzani, who remained at Salto, and from whom the enemy endeavoured to force the surrender of the place, replied with a match in his hand and his foot upon a cask of powder, although the enemy assured him that we were all either killed or made prisoners. We have had thirty killed and fifty four wounded. All the officers are wounded, except Scarone, Saccarello, the Major and Traversi, but all slightly.

I would not this day give my title of an Italian legionary for a world of gold.

At midnight, we set off on our retreat for Salto. We were about a hundred Italian legionaries, with sixty wounded, perhaps even more. Those who were but slightly wounded, with such as were safe and sound, marched in advance, keeping in check an army 1200 strong, and repulsing them without fear.[19]

In retrospect some historians have questioned how absolute was this result. Was it really a victory, or more like a draw? But at the time San Antonio was acknowledged by the government as something special. President Suárez issued a decree which, among other things, ordained that the legion's flag should have gold lettering—"Victory of 8 February of 1846, obtained by the Italian Legion under the orders of Garibaldi"—and doubled the pensions of families of the soldiers who were killed. Garibaldi himself was promoted to the status of general, an honour he was reluctant to accept.

Another who respected Garibaldi for the battle of San Antonio was Admiral Émile Lainé, who was commanding the French fleet. He had been allied with him in the capture of Colonia, when the drunken Italians had misbehaved. Now he wrote to congratulate him, and called round in person later to his small unlit home in Montevideo to show his appreciation.

And the triumph was not wasted in Europe. There the revolutionaries of Young Italy could point to the valour of young men fighting heroically in what was widely perceived as a liberal cause, of relevance to all those struggling against despotic governments.

The last significant battle for the legion took place on 20 May 1846 on the River Dayman, south of Salto, where it was up against a larger, well prepared force, and won. In fact, Garibaldi and his troops were based in Salto from December 1845 until 20 August 1846, and for most of this time he had Anita with him. This was a long enough period for some of his soldiers and mariners to marry local girls in Salto cathedral.[20] As a generalisation, the Italians, in spite of some lapses in their campaign up the Uruguay river, seem to have had a better reputation with the locals than other detachments in the conflict.

However, the government in Montevideo decided that Salto was no longer a viable stronghold, so far from the capital, and this was the view of General Anacleto Medina, Garibaldi's commander, with whom he clashed. In one of his most celebrated acts of insubordination he arrested the general, who had arrived too late to be of use in the battle of San Antonio, and ordered him back to Montevideo.

There were other factors, too. The strategic purpose of the expedition up the Uruguay, along with the parallel British push up the Paraná, was to persuade Oribe to abandon the siege. This had not happened. Further, the British and French were anxious to end their intervention, and there were rumours that they were going to do a deal with Oribe. In the complex politics of the Plate region, moreover, the *caudillo* in Entre Rios, Urquiza, was veering towards neutrality in the Uruguayan civil war, and was increasingly hostile to the control that Rosas in Buenos Aires was exercising over the Argentine confederation.

The retreat of Garibaldi's force downstream was marred by continued friction with the British. They stopped him from making another attack on Paysandú as he went downstream. HMS *Lizard* fired on his ships at the mouth of the Rio Negro, opposite Gualeguaychú and close to the modern town of Fray Bentos—of tinned corned beef fame. He also faced compensation claims from both Brazil and the British, after capturing a merchantman in the upper Uruguay owned by David Law, a British trader who was based in Brazil. He towed it away and made off with contents valued at 3,500 dollars. Traders in Montevideo, whose loans had helped to keep the embattled city almost solvent, were aggrieved that Garibaldi's buccaneering approach to captured prizes was costing them some 60,000 dollars. They complained to Martin Hood, British assistant consul in the capital.[21]

The Italian Legion now went back into the lines defending Montevideo while Garibaldi, in his capacity as admiral of the fleet, sailed around the Plate. He was supposed to be assisting the Anglo-French blockade of Buenos Aires, but in fact was taking prizes off Colonia and from up and down the estuary. Hood wrote to Lord

Palmerston, once again foreign secretary in London,[22] to protest on behalf of the British businesses. Hood, who had been intimate with Oribe before, had his own agenda and was trying to negotiate a settlement with Oribe and Rosas. He was frustrated by the sympathy Ouseley showed for the Montevideo government and by his concern to maintain the Buenos Aires blockade. It was not irrelevant that Ouseley's wife was an ardent admirer of Garibaldi. Grumbling grew that Garibaldi was profiteering, and possibly splitting the proceeds with Rivera until they fell out.

By the middle of 1847 the strategic situation had turned against the Montevideo regime. Oribe's control over most of Uruguay was becoming more solid and he had recaptured the port of Maldonado, east of the capital. Another attempt at mediation, by an Anglo-French team of Lord Howden and Comte Colonna Walewski, failed because Buenos Aires would not accept freedom of navigation in the River Uruguay, and Rosas was ideologically opposed to the idea of two European states guaranteeing the sovereignty of an independent Uruguayan state. In July Lord Howden ordered Captain Sir Thomas Herbert, who had replaced Admiral Samuel Inglefield as commander of the Brazil station, to lift the Royal Navy's blockade of Buenos Aires. This was in advance of any action by France, but was a serious blow for the Montevideo government.

6

LIFE IN MONTEVIDEO, AND THOUGHTS OF EUROPE

When Giuseppe, Anita and Menotti arrived in Montevideo in 1841, they were poor. Although they were known to *carbonari* and others in the Italian community, and had active Masonic contacts, Giuseppe was not yet a celebrity. It was only from June 1842 onwards, when he was given command of Montevideo's small fleet and led vessels up the Paraná in an effort to free navigation upriver, that his importance became recognised. For a while the encirclement of the besieged capital required defence by soldiers on land, while any serious attempt to recapture the rest of Uruguay, or to break the blockade and rebuild the maritime trade and revenues on which Montevideo depended, needed success on water. Although the city was not hermetically sealed, much of its food had to be brought in by blockade runners.

But it was on that first foray up the Paraná, when he spent two months in Santa Lucía after burning his boats, that he had an affair with the daughter of a rich rancher. It wounded and angered Anita when she heard of it. Handsome and dashing, a lover of poetry and with stories to tell, Giuseppe could be irresistible to women. He was libidinous and had been away from home for several months. Lucía Esteche, the lady in question, was the daughter of Don Esteche, with whom he was staying. News reached Anita later that Lucía was pregnant. Her baby girl was named Margarita Garibaldi.

The reality of Anita's life was that she was on her own for much of the time and, according to Adílcio Cadorin, her biographer, she suffered from depression and jealousy. On one occasion, Garibaldi appeared with his flowing hair drastically cut—Anita thought this would make him less attractive to admirers. On another, she was asked why she had two pistols, and said that one was to shoot Giuseppe and another to kill his mistress. Her situation was not eased by poverty. Garibaldi recorded that his friend the minister of war, Pacheco y Oribe, seeing that there were no candles in their small house, sent them money so that they could buy some. But he insisted on giving half the money away to the widow of one of his Italian legionaries.

A rather happier view of Anita was recorded by H.F. Winnington-Ingram, one of the young British naval officers who passed through Montevideo in 1846. He recalled:

> Whilst engaged in this strife Garibaldi wooed and won the beautiful Anita, a Creole born, but with all the habits of the senoritas of old Spain [Winnington-Ingram may not have realised that she was Brazilian, and that they had met in Laguna]. She had become, from the habits of her country, a splendid horse-woman, and it was a sight to be remembered as she rode a curveting animal by the side of her husband, when the Italian band played his legion home from their day's duty at the outer lines of Monte Video [sic] to the plaza in the city, where they were dismissed to their respective billets.[1]

The Garibaldis had three children in Montevideo: Rosita, who was born on 30 November 1843; Teresita, born on 22 March 1845; and Ricciotti, a boy who like Menotti was to become a fighter in Italy alongside their father, on 24 February 1847. Like Menotti, too, he was named after a martyred patriot in the still-disunited peninsula—Nicola Ricciotti had recently been shot along with the Bandiera brothers after a failed revolt in the Kingdom of Naples.

Giuseppe was an erratic husband, often away from home. It seems as if he was particularly fond of his eldest daughter, Rosita, who died when she was only just over two. Attractive and precocious, her death before Christmas was a serious blow to both of them.

Garibaldi's image and reputation in Uruguay were also complicated by the perception that he was a soldier of fortune, a mercenary or condottiere. There were many such people in South America in the period, following the breakdown of the Spanish and Portuguese empires and the ruthless competition for trade and near-genocidal assault on Amerindians and their land in which both Rosas and Rivera had been at the forefront. Admiral Cochrane, a Scot, had fought for Brazil and Chile. Admiral Brown, who was Irish, was serving Rosas. It was not surprising that Garibaldi, an Italian-speaker from Nice who had already enlisted for the republic of Rio Grande do Sul, should be seen as a kind of pirate. Taking prizes in the Plate, though aggravating the British and the merchants who had suffered losses, was only to be expected from the type.

One incident showed that there was much more to Garibaldi. In 1844 General Rivera and his wife had offered a large grant of land from their estates to Thiébaut and his French Legion. Although no part of the country was securely in the hands of his government it was an important gesture, when all the foreign legions were poorly clothed and fed. The grant to the French amounted to at least ninety square miles, and included cattle and buildings. Thiébaut and his men accepted.

Early next year, on 30 January 1845, Rivera made a similar offer to Garibaldi and the Italian Legion. He had been impressed by the bravery of the Italians in recent battles, at Cerro and Bayarda, and said they deserved recompense. The letter included a deed to land beyond the Rio Negro owned by Rivera and, due to delays and the need for consultation with his officers, Garibaldi did not reply until 23 May, turning the offer down. He wrote:

> The Italian officers, after being made acquainted with your letter and its contents, have unanimously declared, in the name of the legion, that they did not contemplate, when asking for arms and offering their services to the republic, receiving any other reward but the honour of sharing the perils of the children of the country which had afforded them hospitality. They obeyed, while acting thus, the voice of their consciences...[2]

Mazzini, in a letter of 29 January 1846 to *The Times* from his exile in High Holborn, London, made much of this. Garibaldi had returned the deed of donation. "I shall not add one word to the above document," which Mazzini had quoted in full, "observing only that the French Legion did accept a donation of the same nature as the one declined by my countrymen; and when the deed of General Rivera, and the answer of their staff were officially read by the soldiers of the Italian Legion, there arose from the ranks one unanimous cry, 'We are no hirelings, we are no Swiss.'"

This was not the attitude of an ordinary mercenary. There were also rumours, reported by Ouseley, that Rosas had unsuccessfully tried to persuade Oribe to buy Garibaldi's support, offering him command of the Buenos Aires fleet after Brown, and a large sum in gold dollars; a possibility that Oribe had dismissed as unrealistic, because, he said, Garibaldi was so pig-headed. In the meantime Anita was living in a small, poorly lit house, while her husband was often away, and focused on the war and his links with Masons, Young Italy and *carbonari* in Montevideo, and Mazzini and the Italian nationalists in Europe.

The pull of Europe was growing for Garibaldi. This combined with his disillusion with growing political divisions among the besieged defenders of Montevideo. The cause was a breakdown in relations between Suárez and his periodically unsuccessful commander, General Rivera. On 27 March 1845 Rivera had been badly defeated for a second time at India Muerta, when he had been trying to raise the siege. Oribist forces commanded by Ignacio, Manuel's brother, combined with the troops of Urquiza and Servando Gómez to impose a crushing and cruel defeat. Garibaldi thought that Rivera had been foolhardy. The beaten general lost 400 men, and over a hundred prisoners were decapitated on Urquiza's orders. This led to a significant exodus of Rivera's supporters, seeking safety in Rio Grande do Sul.

Rivera himself went into exile in Brazil and, for the rest of Garibaldi's stay in Montevideo, he became a destabilising factor in its politics. In March 1846 the government wanted to send him to Europe, to get him out of the way, but on 1 April there was an uprising of his followers in the city. The minister of war, Pacheco y Obes, resigned, Rivera was made commander-in-chief, and he then had a run of minor military successes. He survived an attempt on his life in September.

However, at the turn of the year Rivera, who was advancing up the River Uruguay, suffered first a propaganda setback and then another military disaster. His troops, supported by a bombardment from two French warships, attacked the town of Paysandú, looting and murdering prisoners. This was reported internationally, damaging the credibility of the gallant "second Troy". Shortly after, he was defeated at el Cerro de las Animas.

As the British historian David McLean has commented: "Now in all Uruguay, only Colonia and Maldonado, with their British and French

1. Palácio Piratini, Porto Alegre with flags of Brazil, left, Rio Grande do Sul, right

2. State flag of Rio Grande do Sul, incorporating flag of Farroupilha republic

PASSAGEM DE PEDESTRES

LANCEIROS NEGROS

Nossa comunidade reverencia a cultura e a história da população negra de Porto Alegre, dos remanescentes de quilombolas do bairro Mont'Serrat e moradores da Auxiliadora, em especial, e dos negros do Rio Grande do Sul, em geral, com homenagem à valorosa, corajosa e honrada participação do Corpo de Lanceiros Negros, livres ou libertos pela República Rio-Grandense, em 1836.

EXCELENTES COMBATENTES DE CAVALARIA

Os Lanceiros Negros (oito companhias e total de 426 combatentes) se entregavam ao combate com grande denodo, por saberem em jogo a cada combate, como verdadeiros filhos, a mãe liberdade.

Manejavam como grande habilidade suas armas prediletas (as lanças) usadas mais longas do que o comum. Combinada esta característica com instrução ao combate e disposição para a luta, foram usados como tropas de choque da Revolução Farroupilha.

Como lanceiros não utilizavam escudos de proteção, mas sim seus grosseiros ponchos de lã (bicharás), que serviram-lhes de cama, cobertor e proteção do frio e da chuva. Quando em combate a cavalo, enrolado no braço esquerdo, o poncho servia-lhes para amortecer ou desviar um golpe de lança ou espada.

No corpo a corpo desmontado, servia para aparar ou desviar golpes de adaga ou espada, em cuja esgrima eram habilíssimos, em decorrência da prática continuada do jogo do talho; nome dado pelo gaúcho à esgrima simulada com faca, adaga ou facão. Por tudo isto infundiram grande terror aos adversários.

A SURPRESA DOS PORONGOS

Em 14 de novembro de 1844, os Lanceiros Negros de Teixeira Nunes salvaram o desfecho da Revolução Farroupilha de um desastre total.

Capichando e grande parte das tropas, tornaram possível a negociação

3. Notice honouring *Lanceiros* Negros, black Farroupilha fighters, Porto Alegre

4. Henrique Nunes, driver, with Garibaldi bust outside town museum, Garibaldi

5. Elma Sant'Ana, prolific writer and enthusiast for Anita, with author

6. Garibaldi house and office of *O Povo*, Piratini, with Fladimir Gonsalves, Secretary of Tourism and friend

7. Courtyard of Charqueada São João, Pelotas, one of many 19th century producers of *charque*, dried beef

8. Adílcio Cadorin and Ivete Scopel, outside the Instituto Anita, Laguna

9. Old town with harbour, Laguna

10. Guide in front of one of Anita's homes, Laguna

11. Battlefield memorial near Curitibanos, Santa Catarina, where Anita was captured and escaped, after realising that Garibaldi must have survived

12. Mural of Anita on *Prefeitura*, town of Anita Garibaldi, Santa Catarina

garrisons, were still under the control of the beleaguered government in Montevideo."[3] This had wide repercussions. It looked as though Oribe and the Argentinians had won the war. Urquiza, who had been talking of mediation between Montevideo and Oribe, was tempted to support Oribe and Rosas once more. The British and French, under pressure from their merchants for a peace, were keen to disengage, with the high-powered delegation of Lord Howden and Comte Colonna Walewski talking to Rosas and the rival Uruguayan governments.

But in June and July 1847 this Anglo-French diplomacy, which had promised an armistice and a recognition of Oribe, broke down. Ouseley, the diplomat who had spent government money and stretched his orders to the advantage of Montevideo, was recalled. Hence, as mentioned earlier, the British stopped their blockade of Buenos Aires, which some thought was just a racket to ensure that customs duties were paid in Montevideo. Lord Howden sailed for Rio de Janeiro and home. French influence in Montevideo rose, and there were further political convulsions in the surrounded capital.

In the middle of this time of danger Garibaldi, already an admiral, received a fleeting promotion. He was made commander-in-chief. This may have been an attempt to bolster morale and was the peak of his recognition in the war. His authority lasted only from 25 June to 7 July, when he was forced to resign. He met a wave of hostility, and Anita, writing to his mother in Europe, told her that Montevideo did not appreciate all he had done out of idealism for its cause. In August an attempt on his life was discovered, and thwarted.

It was thought wrong to have a non-national in charge of all the armed forces, although in reality Lord Howden estimated that by then there were only 300 Uruguayans and 300 freed slaves among the defenders, compared with 2,400 in the French, Basque and Italian legions. External navies had been propping up this government, and Garibaldi's corsair raids were not appreciated by the British and French traders. Uruguayans inside the city were not always keen on the foreign legions either.

Montevideo decided to fight on, against the odds. Its final victory came in 1851 with Oribe's surrender after Urquiza, in alliance with Brazil and Rosas' opponents, raised the long nine years' siege of the city. But in 1847 Garibaldi was associated with the war party which wanted to continue the struggle, now deserted by Rivera who was interested in making peace with Oribe. Garibaldi's last campaign was in November of that year, on water. He led a flotilla in the Plate and was instructed to capture merchant shipping trying to evade the Montevideo customs. Among his prizes were Brazilian and Sardinian vessels. But the British called on him to desist.

Throughout his nearly thirteen years in South America Garibaldi's real concern was with what was happening in the Italian peninsula. He scrounged information as ships crossed the Atlantic. He was aware that Mazzini, and others, were spreading accounts of his valour and of the Italian Legion, a symbol of unity, though probably most of its troops hailed from northern Italy. This propaganda was effective, as fifty years after his death the Milan correspondent of The Times was able to report: "The defence of Montevideo made him a popular hero."[4]

In 1847, just as his disillusion grew with the politicking in Uruguay, it looked as though the chances of change were rising in the peninsula. Unrest there was growing. Two factors persuaded him that it was time to return to Europe. The first was the arrival of Pope Pius IX, elected in June 1846. He seemed markedly liberal for the first two years of his pontificate. He had been Bishop of Imola in northern Italy, was elected by the more liberal cardinals, and raised the hopes of Young Italy by releasing political prisoners in the Papal States, attending to poverty and making concessions to the press.

In October 1847 Garibaldi and Anzani wrote to Pius IX, via the papal nuncio in Montevideo, in a thinly veiled offer of military help if the pope was to authorise a campaign to fight the Austrians and liberate the peninsula. Mazzini had also written to the pope, telling him that the unification of Italy was a work of God, and would happen with him or without him. Garibaldi had had to swallow his anticlericalism to write to the pope, and he did not receive a reply.

But the second signal, which made him realise that times were indeed changing in Italy, and that his own heroism had had a real impact, came in a present sent to him. Mazzini wrote to tell him it was on its way. It was a sword of gold, the idea of two Florentine merchants who raised a subscription among his admirers. The fundraising was so successful that there was enough money to give each of the legionaries a silver medal as well. These gifts—the sword was hung on the wall of his small and simple house—were accompanied by a request that he come back to Europe. The port of Genoa, he was told, awaited him to launch the "sacred crusade for Liberty".

Of particular significance was the fact that Carlo Alberto, the king of Sardinia and Piedmont, was one of the signatories to the subscription. This was a king who had condemned Garibaldi to death thirteen years earlier. Carlo Alberto was now moving towards the idea of a federal Italy, which would lead him to fight the Austrians in what has been described as the first war of Italian independence, in 1848–9. His royal House of Savoy would subsequently help to unify Italy. More immediately, his signature told Garibaldi that it could be safe to go home.

But how best to return? Garibaldi had two considerations: his family and the force of volunteers he wanted to bring with him. He had some difficulty in recruiting and financing the return of the legionaries. So Anita, who was up to date with the tribulations of Italian revolutionaries, and corresponding with her husband's mother in Nice, would go first. On 27 December 1847 she set sail from Montevideo in the *Carolina* with her three children, bound for Genoa. She was accompanied by the wives and widows of some of the other Italian troops.

She reached Genoa on 2 March 1848 and was overwhelmed by an excited reception. Around 3,000 people greeted her at the port, shouting *vivas* for the Garibaldi family, for Garibaldi and for Italy. Anita, speaking in Italian, acknowledged their welcome and said that she put herself at the disposition of the patriotic cause. The publicity for the Garibaldis by Giovanni Batista Cuneo and Luigi Rossetti, writing from South America, as well as Mazzini's *Il Popolo*, meant that the courage of Anita, as well as Giuseppe, was known. She came not just as the wife of a hero, but as a heroine in her own right.

The *Corriere Mercantil* of Genoa, in its edition of 4 March 1848, stated that a multitude of citizens had called on her where she was staying, presenting her with a national flag. She was reported as telling them:

> People of Genoa, your generous and intense acclamations, at my arrival in your city, show that I have found myself in a land inhabited by Italians, born with the virtue of your ancestors. Together with Captain

Tommaso Risso of the Italian Legion of Montevideo, who has come with me, I offer you as a tribute from the obligation of my heart. Up to now I have had the bliss to belong to a man who, for the cause of liberty, has spent courage on foreign soil that he could not use in his own country. I will have reached the peak of hope when he is able to fight for this land, and I too can show that I am an Italian.

This was flowery stuff, shrewdly attuned to her audience, and showed that Anita was wholly committed to the struggle for a united Italy. In Genoa she was hosted by the families of Stefano Antonini and Napoleone Castellini, whom she knew in Montevideo. She wrote to her husband to say that the negative accounts of Genoa she had received from an Argentine friend, Carlos Alberdi, were untrue. She returned the city's affection. But in less than a week she moved on to Nice, Nizza, to stay with Garibaldi's widowed, seventy-two-year-old mother.

Garibaldi was worried as to how the two would get on—Anita was only twenty-seven, came from a different culture, and had had a turbulent life, surviving two wars. Rosa, his mother, was conservative and religious, a strong character and likely to be sceptical of a high-spirited girl who had run away as a teenager from her marriage to be with her son. In fact, Anita and the children did not stay with her for long. Instead, she used her time in Nice wisely, to read classics of Italian literature, to see the sights, and to deal prudently with an offer by King Carlo Alberto. He wrote to say that he could give Menotti, now a boy of around eight, a school place at the prestigious Royal College of Racconigi. She replied that such a decision should await her husband's return. There was still a question-mark over the relations of her husband with a king who had sentenced him to death much earlier.

Getting an expedition together in Montevideo, which Garibaldi could bring to Italy, proved harder than he had expected. Propagandist talk about bringing a thousand battle-hardened men to set the peninsula alight was far from reality. Many of the Italians who had fought in the legion had acquired partners and families, or were even born in Uruguay. They did not want to return to a land of now distant memories. Furthermore the expedition needed finance, and a boat.

It was not until 15 April 1848 that Garibaldi was able to sail from Montevideo for Europe. He was still a controversial figure, attacked and defended in the press, and although he was elected from Salto to an Assembly of Notables and swore an oath to the Uruguayan republic on 15 February 1848, he had had to survive threats to his life. He wrote to Anita to say that various disagreeable incidents were holding him back. Anzani had suffered a violent infection. Sacchi's knee had been injured, and he was lucky to save his leg.[5] Recruiting suffered when Garibaldi's enemies warned the legionaries that they would be executed on arrival in Italy, like the Bandiera brothers, murdered after a failed insurrection. As he had done before, he tried to raise money by public subscription to pay for a ship, but most of the funds were provided by Stefano Antonini, his Genoese friend.

Although the Montevideo government offered to help, he knew it was poor, and he accepted only two cannon and 800 muskets. He felt that he was swindled by the Sardinian from whom they acquired the boat: "His extortion was such that we were obliged to sell our very shirts to satisfy him, so that during our passage several were obliged to remain in bed for want of clothes to dress themselves in."[6] In turn Garibaldi himself was accused of plundering local people to get the supplies he needed.

In the end, Garibaldi only had sixty-six men with him on a ship which was renamed *Speranza* (Hope) and which ran up an improvised flag of a united Italy as it neared Nice.[7] There were fifty-six from the Italian Legion, while two of his best friends, Francisco Anzani and Gaetano Sacchi, were still gravely ill. Anzani died of tuberculosis shortly after they reached Italy; Sacchi took time to recover, having been badly wounded in the knee. Among the Uruguayans one of the most visible was Andrés Aguiar, a freed black slave who was a big man, nicknamed "the Moor". He had helped Anita in household duties in Montevideo and was a loyal batman to Giuseppe. Along with these men, Garibaldi brought with him a precious urn containing the ashes of Rosita. He was carrying out a promise to Anita.[8]

He arrived off the port of Nice on 21 June 1848. Anita could not wait for him to land, but took the children out to see him in a small boat. This was the moment of reunion, the start of the Italian adventure.

What had he learnt in his long sojourn across the South Atlantic? His own courage. Tactical skills. A democratic way with troops. The importance of idealism and charisma in maintaining morale and discipline. An inability to give up when faced with setbacks. That overwhelming odds could be defeated. That Anita was a very special companion. That his commitment to a united Italy was the dominant motive in his life. The reality was that he had successively left both the Republic of Rio Grande, and then the *Colorados* besieged in Montevideo, when their causes were at a low ebb. Only Italy would retain his undying allegiance.

PART 2

AFTER THE SOUTH AMERICAN CAMPAIGNS

7

SOUTH AMERICAN LEGACIES IN ITALY

It is not the purpose of this account to trace the adventurous and historic contribution of Garibaldi after he returned to Europe in 1848. His charisma, courage and generalship have assured him recognition as, along with Cavour, Mazzini and King Victor Emmanuel, an unquestioned maker of united Italy. His major contribution, with his Thousand Redshirts, was the liberation of Sicily and Naples from the Bourbons in 1860. Rome was captured on 20 September 1870, without his participation. It became the capital of a new Italian state, effectively the expanded Piedmont and Sardinia of Victor Emmanuel, in August 1871. Garibaldi himself lived on until June 1882 when he died aged seventy-four, suffering from arthritis which had begun in South America and wounds from successive Italian campaigns. He married twice more, following Anita's death, and had eight children in all.

But what had really crossed the Atlantic with Garibaldi as Europe experienced its year of revolutions?[1] There were people and ideas as well as Giuseppe himself. It is worth starting with the people—his wife Anita and his children, and three of his commanders, Giacomo Medici, Gaetano Sacchi and Inácio Bueno, actually born in Rio Grande do Sul, who were among those who carried the torch across from Montevideo, to help set "Italy" on fire.

Anita, the "heroine of two worlds", was in many ways a tragic figure. She reached Genoa on 2 March 1848 with her three children after two months at sea. She was rapturously received as her husband's representative. After less than a week she took a steamer to Nice, where she was faced with a diplomatic challenge of two kinds. First, King Carlo Alberto, who had signed Giuseppe's death warrant before he sailed to South America, now wanted to offer the eight-year-old Menotti a scholarship to attend the Royal College of Racconigi. The offer was made via a senior official, and Anita turned it down tactfully and respectfully, saying that she could not make such a critical decision without her husband.

After dealing with King Carlo Alberto her other challenge was to get on with her husband's beloved mother, Rosa Raimondi. Rosita, the child who had died, was named after her, and Garibaldi was anxious that the two women should get on, although their life experience had been so different. "I could not bear the idea of a misunderstanding between the two people who represent my future happiness," he wrote to Anita.[2] Although the two women started off well it would appear that there was friction, probably related to her son's runaway romance with Anita and concern that their marriage in Uruguay lacked the full blessings of the Church. Anita and her three young children went to live with friends. Nonetheless, it was Rosa who brought them up after Anita's premature death the following year.

Garibaldi had left Anita alone for much of her time in Uruguay and, after arriving in Nice and offering his services to Carlo Alberto, which annoyed the republican Mazzini, it looked as though the same would happen. The king turned down his offer of military support at a time of democratic upsurge and hostility to the Austrian empire, but Garibaldi was determined to raise another Italian Legion of volunteers to fight wherever he could. There were risings in Milan, Venice and elsewhere, and although the pope had backtracked on his apparent enthusiasm for reform, Garibaldi led outnumbered guerrilla forces of volunteers to fight the Austrians in northern Italy after they had defeated Carlo Alberto's army at Custoza. Some accounts suggest that Anita was with her husband when his volunteers were defeated at the battle of Luino, that her horse was shot and she fell; together on his, they cut their way with sword thrusts through the Austrian lines.[3] Garibaldi returned to Nice via Switzerland, suffering badly from arthritis and recurrent malaria. There, with Anita and the children, he recuperated for barely three weeks in the house of an old friend, Giuseppe Deidery.

Then he was off to Genoa, accompanied by Anita, initially wanting to take his freelance force to Palermo in Sicily, but when they got to Livorno they changed direction and went to Florence, where radicals had taken control. Garibaldi, foreseeing a cold campaign in the Apennines as winter approached, sent Anita back to Nice. His force was stopped from crossing the Papal States by the pope's Swiss troops.

But then, on 15 November 1848, everything changed. The pope's chief minister, Count Pellegrino Rossi, was murdered. Rome was in uproar. The pope fled south. On 5 February 1849, following a passionate speech by Garibaldi in the city, the Roman Republic was declared. Mazzini was one of the three Triumvirs who took command of its destiny, and much the most powerful.

The siege of Rome lasted until the French troops of General Charles Oudinot, representing President Louis Napoleon, marched in on 3 July. Louis Napoleon, who declared himself Emperor Napoleon III four years later, was keen to restore the pope and prevent the Austrians from dominating the peninsula. The defence of Rome, in which Garibaldi and his volunteers played a heroic but ineffective part, became a key point in his mythic reputation in Europe. It was matched only by his role with The Thousand, in the liberation of Sicily in 1860.

By June 1849, when it was already clear that the Roman Republic would have difficulty surviving the systematic assaults of French regular troops, Anita decided that she wanted to join Giuseppe inside the city. She was five months pregnant, unwell and was disobeying his instructions. She had left the children with her mother-in-law. She found a horse in Livorno and, riding across Tuscany, Umbria and Lazio disguised as a man, she slipped through the French lines to enter Rome via the Porta Pia. Garibaldi, surprised but delighted, was with his staff when she arrived. He told them: "Gentlemen, this is my wife. We've got another soldier!"

The siege saw the deaths of several South Americans, among them the colourful Andrés Aguiar, nicknamed "Garibaldi's Moor". Aguiar was a huge man, dressed in vivid colours which contrasted with his commander's appearance, described sometimes as that of an orderly, sometimes a lieutenant. Anita, who fought in the lines, saw him die and Garibaldi paid tribute to his valour in an order of the day for the legion, describing him as a symbol of the love of free peoples for "our unhappy Italy".

Disobeying the terms of the armistice that ended the siege, Garibaldi led 4,700 armed troops out of the city, initially aiming for Venice. They had to dodge French, Austrian, Spanish and Neapolitan troops. His hopes that people would rally to his standard were not borne out, and troops deserted. Among them was Inácio Bueno, the Brazilian who led his cavalry and went over to the Austrians; he ended up going to the United States. The *Garibaldini*, making exactions of food and money, were unpopular.

Reaching the safety of the little republic of San Marino, he allowed his remaining followers to disperse, keeping only a handful and Anita with him. These loyalists included Ugo Bassi, the priest who accompanied Garibaldi and was subsequently executed, and Giovanni Batista Culiolo, a seaman who had deserted his ship in Montevideo and joined the Italian Legion there, following his leader back to Rome.

Anita was seriously ill. Giuseppe had offered to leave her, to speed her recovery. She would not hear of this, saying: "You *want* to leave me." Anxiety about and jealousy of her husband's popularity with women had been a driving concern since Montevideo. Chased by the Austrians as they reached the Adriatic coast, Anita and Giuseppe were lucky to meet a supporter, Gioacchino Bonnet. But by the time he could get a doctor to see Anita, feverish, delirious and mortally ill, there was nothing the doctor could do. She died in Giuseppe's arms on 4 August 1849 at Mandriole, near the estuary of the River Po.

After several narrow escapes Garibaldi managed to reach Piedmont, where he was an embarrassment and the government arrested him, but he was allowed to leave via Nice, where he could see his mother and children. He only spent twenty-four hours in Nice, but wrote that one of his worst moments was when the children asked after their mother, and he had to break the news that she was dead. Menotti was nine, and would remember their mother more clearly;[4] Teresa was four and Ricciotti was only two. Garibaldi was then away from Italy for five years, one of a series of breaks from his mission in the peninsula.

Anita was dead, but war, and the unification of Italy, became a family business. Menotti, their eldest son, was still only seventeen in 1859 when he joined his father's guides in Giuseppe's new army of volunteers, called the *Cacciatori delle Alpi*. The *Cacciatori* were *Garibaldini* authorised to support Piedmont, now allied with France, in a campaign to liberate northern Italy from the unpopular Austrian empire. Their second brigade was commanded by Giacomo Medici, one of Garibaldi's officers from Montevideo. Menotti had had a mixed upbringing since his mother's death—partly educated at a military college in Genoa, and alternating between his grandmother, who died in 1852, and Augusto Garibaldi, a cousin of his father, in Nice, and his father's island home on Caprera, off Sardinia, acquired in 1856.

The *Cacciatori* were grudgingly backed by Cavour and poorly equipped. Much to Garibaldi's fury, Cavour had surrendered Nice and Savoy to France as part of a deal to take on the Austrians. But Menotti witnessed his father's gifts as a general as he fought a short and spectacular campaign around lakes Maggiore and Como, the enthusiastic way in which he was received by the people who rose up with patriotic committees, and the attraction which led 12,000 volunteers to join up. Cavour sought to push this growing army aside and the war came to an end when Louis Napoleon made peace with the Austrians over the heads of Piedmont, after the bloody Battle of Solferino in July 1859.

Only two months later, Menotti accompanied his father in September 1859 when they took Anita's remains from Mandriole for burial in Nice. Menotti took part in the Sicily campaign in May and June 1860, when The Thousand, with a mixture of courage, guile and good fortune, captured the island. This, and the subsequent capture of Naples in the autumn after he had won major battles at Milazzo and the Volturno saw the peak of Giuseppe's military reputation. His skill and management of largely untrained volunteers against regular troops, along with his dramatic appearance and austere way of life, created a powerful image that his political and diplomatic weaknesses did not negate.

Menotti, injured with his arm in a sling in Sicily, was sent to watch the surrender of General Lanza's troops in Palermo. In 1863, reflecting the internationalism that was intrinsic to the family's cause, he recruited a small Garibaldi Legion of Italians, who went to support Polish nationalists in a rising against Russia. He then joined his father in a trip to London in 1864, which did not go well. His father cut it short and he was put up in cheap hotels. Two years later, at Bezzecca, in the campaign to win Venetia from the Austrians, Menotti, his brother and brother-in-law joined their father in winning a victory for the

Garibaldini. His own military prowess was recognised in 1867 when his father asked him to lead volunteers in an abortive invasion of the Papal States, where it was clear that the population was hostile to the *Garibaldini,* and his father was badly beaten by French troops at the Battle of Mentana.

Yet France's defeat by the Prussians at the Battle of Sedan in 1870 made it possible for Rome to be forced to join in a now united Italy. The Emperor Napoleon III had been protecting the pope and his temporal rule in the Papal States. While the pope lost his temporal authority, however, he had just bolstered his spiritual claims, as a Vatican Council proclaimed his infallibility. A loyal *Garibaldino,* Nino Bixio, was now a commander of Victor Emmanuel's troops when they entered the city on 20 September. Garibaldi himself was marginalised, in Caprera, when his dream was realised. But there was a final military sequel, for himself and his two soldier sons, Menotti and Ricciotti.

This was in the Franco-Prussian war of 1870–1. Initially, when it appeared that the war was provoked by Emperor Napoleon III, *Garibaldini* had offered their services to the Prussians. Bismarck, ruling Prussia on behalf of the Kaiser, declined them. But after the emperor surrendered, and the empire was overthrown, the new French republic carried on the struggle. At this point Giuseppe, now feeling his age and far from well with arthritis, joined the French. He was buoyed up by devotion to the revolutionary spirit of 1789, and sympathy for the underdog. He was carried on a stretcher and supported by Menotti and Ricciotti, commanding two of his four brigades, and by Stefano Canzio, the *Garibaldino* officer who had fought in Sicily and was married to Giuseppe's daughter Teresita. Léon Gambetta, trying to shore up the republic's defences against the Prussians, was sceptical about the *Garibaldini,* but Italians, French and many other nationalities volunteered to join the celebrated, now elderly, hero. This was a last hurrah, and his biographer, Christopher Hibbert, wrote: "He himself considered the part he took in the Franco-Prussian War as the crowning military achievement of his career."[5]

The campaign in the Vosges in 1870–1 was at best marginal and not sufficient to change the course of the war against a dominant Prussia. Regular French troops, some of whom had defeated Garibaldi at Mentana, were not keen to fight alongside him. But there was one grace note for him, in that the twenty-three-year-old Ricciotti, put in charge of a vanguard at Châtillon-sur-Seine, scored a classic Garibaldi victory on 14 November 1870. Ricciotti's 400 men routed a thousand Prussians, capturing troops, officers and munitions. Unfortunately for the *Garibaldini* this victory was followed by defeat at Dijon. But Ricciotti was the only person to capture a Prussian flag in the whole campaign. His father was offered a position as deputy in the French republic's parliament, but turned it down.

Garibaldi now retired as a warrior. Menotti, a Freemason like his father, became a deputy in the Italian parliament. His younger brother, Ricciotti, was also a deputy from 1887 to 1890 and in 1897 led a force of *Garibaldini*—for this had now become a volunteer brand—to fight for the Greeks against the Ottomans. Ricciotti, who had broken a shoulder when young and spent four years in a military school in Liverpool up to the age of fourteen, had married an English woman, Harriet Constance Hopcraft, in London in 1874. He was welcomed back from the Greek campaign as an authentic Garibaldi hero.

Ricciotti returned to South America in 1900, when he made a brief visit to Montevideo, his city of birth. He was more interested in setting up a colonisation scheme in Patagonia, meeting the military president of Argentina, General Julio Argentino Roca. Roca was in his second term as president, having become a national hero over twenty years earlier. He had consolidated the Argentine state after finally defeating the Amerindians in "the conquest of the desert", opening much of the pampas and northern Patagonia to settlement. It was a reminder, per-haps, that Ricciotti had not seen the Amerindians in the same light that his father had regarded the *Farroupilhas* and the Gobierno de la Defensa, as peoples struggling to be free.

Both Menotti and Teresa died in 1903, and there had been some frictions between Giuseppe's children. However, all three of Menotti, Ricciotti and their brother-in-law, Stefano Canzio, became generals in the army of united Italy. It was Ricciotti and his children who most typified the Garibaldi legacy. In 1900 a regiment of 360 *Garibaldini*, including Ricciotti's son Peppino, had fought for the Boers against the British in South Africa; arrested by the Austrians when they returned to Trieste, they were again arrested by the Italians at the request of the British government. Peppino, who had been fighting since he was twenty, had also taken up arms for the Greeks and with Pancho Villa in Mexico, who fell out with him.

Between 1903 and 1911 Ricciotti was trying to organise expeditions to help the Albanians to independence and as late as 1912–13, when he was sixty-five, he led an Italian-Greek division in Greece. At the start of the First World War Giuseppe's grandchildren joined the French Foreign Legion in which two of them were killed. After Italy joined Britain and France in the war in May 1915, all surviving grandchildren signed up with the *Cacciatori delle Alpi* as regulars. Ricciotti himself lived until 1924.

Death, and defection in the case of Bueno, who had captained a squad for Giuseppe in Uruguay, reduced the number of Montevideo veterans who fought for any length of time in the Italian campaigns. But Giacomo Medici was someone on whom Garibaldi relied as a recruiter of volunteers and commander. Born in Milan and influenced by Mazzini, he was one of the revolutionary nationalists who turned up in Uruguay and joined the Italian Legion. In Italy he played a distinguished role, trusted by Garibaldi, though sometimes quarrelling with him.[6] He shared his chief's frustration when he was put down by Carlo Alberto's minister of war when they first returned to Europe, and commanded some of the Italian Legion troops in an exposed position, the Vascello Villa, during the bloody battles for the Roman Republic. He went on to command the second brigade of Garibaldi's *Cacciatori delle Alpi*, technically part of the royal army of Piedmont, in 1858.

Medici was one of an inner group, along with Nino Bixio and Dr Agostino Bertani, that persuaded Garibaldi to abandon a foolhardy plan to disrupt the plebiscite in Nice that would approve the annexation by France. Medici was outvoted by the others, who wanted to support the insurrection in Sicily instead. In fact, Garibaldi himself had been initially cautious about the Sicilian venture. But Medici then brought badly needed reinforcements—the "second expedition" of 2,500 men—to join The Thousand in Sicily in June 1860. He played an important role in the Battle of Milazzo in Sicily in July, and commanded a division at the hard-won victory of the Volturno in October; the Volturno was the battle which confirmed the conquest of Naples for Piedmont. Then, as a royal general, he was on a commission which had the difficult task of selecting which of the numerous *Garibaldini* officers should be selected as officers in Victor Emmanuel's army.

Subsequently, like Menotti and Ricciotti, he was elected a deputy, and was later a senator.

Gaetano Sacchi was another Montevideo veteran who brought the spirit of South America to Europe. He had been with Garibaldi since 1842, was the flag-bearer, was wounded and then carried on the shoulders of his commander at the iconic battle of San Antonio. He was listed as captain of the first company of the Italian Legion in a report of the legion's organising commission in April 1847.[7] Back in Europe he fought in the siege of Rome and commanded one of the two divisions in the retreat. By 1860 he was an officer in the royal Piedmontese army and was placed in a difficult position when Garibaldi was planning the expedition of The Thousand.

After the 1859 campaign in the Alps with the *Cacciatori*, Sacchi was one of the *Garibaldini* who chose to join the royal army. As colonel he was put in charge of the 46th regiment, which contained other former volunteers. When they heard of Garibaldi's plan to take troops to Sicily to liberate the island from the brutal Bourbon monarchy, they all wanted to be there. Garibaldi asked Victor Emmanuel for permission to bring officers from the 46th with him. The king and Cavour forbade this, however: they did not want their kingdom left defenceless, and were worried about Austria and possibly even their new ally, France. Hence, at a time when the king and Cavour were highly ambiguous about the expedition, very few from the royal army were part of it. This changed after the spectacular success of The Thousand in Sicily. By October 1860 Sacchi was serving with Garibaldi at the battle of the Volturno, though he did not play a major role.

Garibaldi learnt much after returning to Europe. The Volturno victory, where he showed brilliance in commanding a large force as well as his usual courage in leading several charges, was a good example of his maturity. From managing guerrilla groups, where nimbleness, surprise and evasion are essential, he was now in charge of thousands in a set-piece battle, ordering defence as well as attack. His sobriquet in southern Italy, "the General", was not for nothing—a title different from "the Admiral" which would be inscribed on his statue overlooking the port of Montevideo.

What were some of the ideas that drove the volunteers of the *Speranza*? Among the most crucial were the sense of an Italian identity, *Italianitá*;

along with that was the importance of propaganda, show and performance. Then, significantly, was the role of untrained, enthusiastic and relatively young men who were ready to put their lives on the line to promote an ideal. This ideal, of an Italian nation, was sometimes bound up with a commitment to revolutionary international solidarity and republicanism. For Garibaldi himself, and the cause of a major schism with Mazzini, Italy was more important than a republic. He compromised his republican beliefs to support the monarchy of Victor Emmanuel, and swallowed his anger at the cession of Nice and Savoy to France.

The idea of a united Italy may seem obvious in retrospect, but it had to be sold to parochial Italians who had lived for hundreds of years in separate states, with their own laws and dialects so varied that they were almost separate languages. Peasants, lacking education and with narrow and immediate horizons, were especially slow to buy it. They were often influenced by conservative Catholicism. This meant that Garibaldi's campaigns for unification were very different from Mao Zedong's communist guerrilla strategy in China in the mid-twentieth century, which emphasised the role of the peasantry as leaders and supporters of revolutionary change. The *Garibaldini* tended to be more educated, and enlightened; many were students.

The Italian Legion in Montevideo made the idea of *Italianitá* manifest, justifying sacrifice in a far-off land. The Italian Legion fought alongside the French, Spanish and Swiss, legions of men from recognised states, as well as the Basques, who also had no state of their own. Its soldiers were treated as if they belonged to a single nationality, although Uruguayans also joined the Italian Legion.

This proven identity was what Garibaldi and a handful of volunteers brought to Europe, and it fired him up throughout his struggles with Austria, France, the Bourbons of southern Italy and the increasingly reactionary pope, Pius IX. It also led to misunderstandings and conflicts with Victor Emmanuel, Cavour and Mazzini. Mazzini and Young Italy, a small minority, had promoted an ideal. The Italian Legion in Uruguay had made it seem real. Garibaldi ceaselessly inspired his young volunteers with a continuing refrain—that they were involved in the epic and historic creation of a united Italy. At moments of his supreme achievement, in the liberation of Sicily and Naples when he had dictatorial powers, he was clear that these were only stepping-stones to a greater goal. "I came here to fight for the cause of Italy, not of Sicily alone. If we do not free and unite the whole of Italy, we shall never achieve liberty in any single part of her," he declared after the Redshirts had taken the island.[8] Addressing a multitude in Naples in the carnival which followed its capture, he applauded a glorious day and the beginning of a new epoch for Naples and for Italy. "I thank you for this welcome, not only for myself, but in the name of all Italy, which your aid will render free and united," he said.[9]

Linked to the unification of Italy in the minds of Italians were some necessary building-blocks. The most striking of these were propaganda and what today would be called public relations, image and marketing. Garibaldi had already shown his gifts here by adopting the redshirt uniform in Montevideo and bringing it with him to Europe. It has been suggested that as he grew older he may have modelled himself on Gonçalves, the *Farroupilha* leader he admired, who was a fine horseman, picturesquely dressed.[10] The adoption of camouflage came later in military history, and the mid-nineteenth century was still an era of Redcoats and splendid uniforms. For a ragtag army of volunteers, this cheap, visible outfit was a godsend. Garibaldi and Aguiar in the siege of Rome covered their shirts with a white and blue poncho respectively, and a small woollen mill in Aysgarth, in England's peaceful Wensleydale valley in Yorkshire, manufactured the red shirts.[11]

Even before it was adopted by communists and socialists, the colour red had symbolic connotations—of republicanism, bloody martyred sacrifice and revolution. The *Colorados*, with whom Garibaldi had fought in Uruguay, had red flags. So, too, did the revolutionaries in France in 1848, the year he returned to Europe.

Whereas in South America much of his publicity had been at a distance and second-hand, in Europe he was able to talk to journalists and writers such as Alexandre Dumas who edited his autobiography, and win them over by his charm, simplicity and idealism. In fact, the first biography of Garibaldi, appearing in 1850, the year of the siege of Rome, was by Giovanni Battista Cuneo, who had known him since he was recruited into Young Italy in Taganrog. Cuneo had worked with him throughout his time in South America. But Dumas was a much better known author. His novel, *Montevideo ou une nouvelle Troie*, was a romance set in the siege of Montevideo, also published in 1850. It made full use of the history of Uruguay, which was little-known in Europe, and was fiercely opposed to Rosas. It was part of the liberal propaganda in Europe which saw the gallant defenders of the capital as heroes opposed to the barbarism of Oribe and his Argentinian forces, civilisation confronting tyranny, thuggery and decapitation. Dumas had never visited Uruguay, but the Garibaldi in the novel was a reasonably accurate depiction.

Garibaldi had several French fans, including Victor Hugo and George Sand, pseudonym of the French woman novelist, Amantine Lucile Dupin. But Dumas was the most significant. In this novel he described Garibaldi as one of those who led the defence of the capital, his expedition up the Paraná in 1842, his command of the Italian Legion at San Antonio, his compassion for captured opponents, and his poverty and simplicity. He wrote:

> Garibaldi was then a man of 38, of medium height, well-proportioned, with fair hair, blue eyes, a Greek nose and a Greek chin and forehead—features which in general are classical in their beauty. His beard is long. Normally he wears a close-fitting coat which has nothing of a military uniform about it. His voice has a splendid and melodious softness. For the most part he seems absent-minded and a person of more imagination than calculation; but, once mention the word independence, or that of Italy, and he becomes a volcano in eruption.[12]

It was a herogram, a love letter.

Dumas was already a prolific author, a bestselling writer of adventure stories such as *The Count of Monte Cristo* and *The Three Musketeers*, widely travelled in Europe when he wrote his novel set in Montevideo. His *The Black Tulip* came out the same year. He was of mixed race, with a tart line directed at racists. He was a progressive and also a Freemason. Garibaldi for him was better than any fictional hero, and he attached himself to the Sicily expedition in 1860 to take part in a real-life adventure. He arrived on a yacht with an entourage which included a much younger girlfriend dressed as a midshipman. Garibaldi took to him and trusted him in turn, and Dumas accompanied The Thousand through Sicily and across to Naples.

Here Garibaldi, as Dictator of the Two Sicilies after his victories, made a bad and unpopular decision. He appointed Dumas as director

of the National Museum, responsible for Pompeii and other archaeo-
logical treasures. But Dumas, accused of living the high life in one of
the captured royal palaces and with no knowledge of archaeology, then
found a better cause in launching a Garibaldian paper, *L'Indipendente*.

Garibaldi's success with journalists went to extremes in the case of
Nandor Eber, a Hungarian who was *The Times*' correspondent when The
Thousand invaded Sicily. He not only told Garibaldi what the defenders' dispositions were in Palermo as the Redshirts' attack was prepared, but took over command of the Redshirt column which went on
to liberate Catania.

Garibaldi also travelled widely outside the peninsula, where people
tried to lionise him, and his reputation spread without particular effort
on his own part. In 1850, after the retreat from Rome when he had
become an embarrassment in Piedmont, he went to New York where
he briefly worked in a candle factory owned by an Italian.

His role in the Roman Republic had electrified a worldwide public
and the *New York Times* reported that a ship called *Waterloo* had docked in
the city from Liverpool, carrying on board Garibaldi, a person of
global renown, hero of Montevideo and defender of Rome. All those
who know his cavalier character and his services to liberty will give
him a merited welcome, the report added. He turned down the offer
of a reception at the Astor Hotel, however, as well as demonstrations
by socialists, republicans and the Italian community. He spent over two
years in charge of a sailing ship, getting as far as New Zealand, Australia
and Hong Kong, and then ended up in Newcastle, England, in early
1854 before spending a month in London. It was soon afterwards that
Peek Frean & Co., an enterprising biscuit manufacturer, launched the
"Garibaldi" in his honour. Dockers in Newcastle presented him with a
sword inscribed: "Every penny spent for the purchase of this sword
represents a heart beating for European liberty." In Britain he had supporters among both the aristocracy and working people. In 1864 he
visited the country again, at the invitation of Lord Palmerston, and
could not avoid demonstrations of welcome. Greeted by the Lord
Mayor of London when he received the Freedom of the City, he said:
"I have in common with you English the love of the sea. That is why we
understand each other so well."

He tended to be shy of public receptions. His periods out of the
public eye in Caprera, rather like the year he had spent in Montevideo

before joining the struggle against Oribe in 1842, did no harm to his celebrity; it was paralleled a century later by the time that Charles de Gaulle spent in withdrawal at Colombey-les-Deux-Eglises between the Second World War and his return to power in France in 1958.

His own retreat was on the rocky island of Caprera, off Sardinia, where he moved in 1856 and built first a wooden house and then a stone home which looked rather like a South American farmhouse. Although poor himself, he had been left 35,000 lire by his brother Felice when he died the year before.[13] Initially he camped out with Menotti and Giovanni Basso, a friend from Nice and fellow seaman who had sailed round the world with him for a couple of years in the *Carmen*.

His efforts as a farmer were frustrated by the poor quality of the soil and an unfriendly English neighbour who did nothing to discourage his goats from eating Garibaldi's crops. But he built a wooden playhouse for Teresa, kept cows and goats, and grew figs, sugarcane and vegetables. He was looked after there by Battistina Ravello. Battistina was also from Nice, a housekeeper who became his mistress.

Battistina was jealous of his female visitors and admirers. She also bore him an unruly daughter, significantly named Anita, who died when she was only sixteen. Many who knew him were aware that however many liaisons and marriages he had, Anita Ribeiro was the love of his life. He spent much time between his campaigns on Caprera, where he was eventually able to buy the half of the island he did not own, and where he could keep in touch with developments in the peninsula. He had been elected to seven out of eight parliaments since 1860 but rarely took his seat, sending messages via friends instead; disability as well as lack of interest were factors, and when he was carried in with arthritis to vote against the cession of Nice and Savoy he remarked that in Uruguay it had been he who had been able to carry his injured soldiers. He did, however, retain an interest in southern Italy and Sicily, already suffering from the poverty which has been a running sore in Italian history. From 1871 until his death in 1882 he was living in retreat on Caprera.

Although he fell out with Mazzini, both in the Roman Republic and because he was willing to compromise with monarchy, Garibaldi remained an optimist about the possibilities of insurrection and revolution, which was why King Victor Emmanuel and Cavour were always suspicious of him and sometimes obstructive. They were especially worried after his conquest of Sicily and Naples, when he seemed to have his own fiefdom, and were relieved when he supported a plebiscite by which the population of the Bourbon kingdoms voted overwhelmingly to join the northern monarchy.

Yet a key part of his attraction, and central to the principles he represented, was the way in which the idea of potential victory could be conjured from the reality of defeat. He was telling a story that resonated with optimistic, better educated young men, and which was also to be exploited by less lofty adventurers who joined his colours later. Other countries in the twentieth century witnessed similar conjuring. Six years after 1916, the profound impact of the Easter Rising, defeated in Dublin, made independence possible for an Irish Free State; in 1940 de Gaulle said that France, overrun by Nazi Germany, had lost a battle but not the war and, in the same year, Britain saw this alchemy at work as the defeat and withdrawal from Dunkirk were converted into a story of survival.

In Garibaldi's case, the Italian Legion's remarkable performance as unconquered heroes at the battle of San Antonio in February 1846 had a similar quality. It was not a victory. But, grossly outnumbered, their survival and fighting retreat to Salto became legendary. The defeat of the Roman Republic only three years later, in 1849, had an impact altogether greater. The courage of the defenders was witnessed by people from many countries living in Rome as well as by those beginning to call themselves Italians. It turned Garibaldi into an international symbol of liberalism and progress—so that Abraham Lincoln invited him to fight for the North in the Civil War—and his cause into one that was bound to triumph in spite of setbacks.

Garibaldi himself was handsome, bearded and a showman, with his long hair, fine singing voice, and attraction to women which Anita had found so threatening in Montevideo. Female admirers cut locks of this precious hair. He ran his own public relations, and used this—and the scale of his wider reputation throughout Europe and North America—to build morale among the Redshirts.

Just prior to the invasion of Sicily there were three different support groups for Garibaldi in northern Italy—the Million Rifles Fund, the more radical committee under Dr Augusto Bertani, which recruited some of the best soldiers for The Thousand, and Cavour's more conservative and monarchical National Society. Garibaldi's personality expanded as he was able to engage with the struggle for Italy. In South America, though his self-confidence and insubordination led to problems and were factors in the brevity of his time as commander-in-chief in Montevideo, he could not be such a dominant figure.

Music had been important in South America and was a valued feature for the Redshirts in Europe. The *Farroupilhas* had a hymn and the Italian Legion sang along in Uruguay. A roll call of the legion's band in Montevideo listed forty-six names, and Garibaldi saw singing and music as valuable in building morale.

A key lesson which he brought across the Atlantic was the induction and use of completely untrained volunteers to create an effective army. There had been guerrilla fighters earlier in the nineteenth century, in Spanish sharpshooters picking off the troops of Napoleon I in the Peninsular War, and in the break-up of the Spanish empire in South America. But the Italian Legion in Uruguay represented a step-change. Largely organised by Francisco Anzani and overseen by a commission, this force was put together on the basis of enthusiasm for ideals, a charismatic leader and a willingness to suffer death and casualties for two causes—Montevideo and Italy. Tactics relied heavily on charges at the double, to wear down an enemy, with volunteers fearlessly thrusting the cold steel of their bayonets into the bodies of their opponents.

This approach inevitably led to tragic losses in Europe, when volunteers came up against disciplined troops using their rifles and gunnery to good effect. Some of his officers, during the siege of Rome, thought Garibaldi was throwing lives away needlessly, mown down by the firing of French regulars. There was, in his thinking at that time, some of the ruthless commitment to victory at all costs that led Stalin to ordain that there should be no Soviet retreats from Leningrad or Stalingrad in spite of enormous losses in the Second World War. In the Sicilian and Calabrian campaigns Garibaldi showed a more developed genius for generalship, and more care for his soldiers' lives. However, the Redshirts were often ill-shod and ill-equipped,[14] lacking the most modern rifles.

The discipline imposed on the volunteers in Italy was usually strict, a carry-over from experience in South America, and although

Garibaldi permitted the unhappy to leave, for instance on the retreat from Rome, the defection of Inácio Bueno seems to have been a relative rarity. The forced march on Naples, at speed and under a hot sun, was a real test of endurance. Trevelyan recorded that five members of the English Regiment—most of whom were Sicilians, led by a group of English *Garibaldini* who had attached themselves to the victorious Thousand—"were condemned to be shot for plundering on the north bank of the Volturno, where they had been left on the usual Garibaldian short rations, an intolerable torture to the hungrier Saxon race". In fact, their sentence was commuted to imprisonment. The loyal and competent Nino Bixio was one of Garibaldi's most violent commanders, having thirty-three "counter-revolutionaries" shot one morning in a Sicilian village.

Feeding the volunteers was a major problem, as it had been in Uruguay, for Garibaldi ignored the Napoleonic nostrum that an army marches on its stomach. There was little in the way of an organised commissariat and although the theory was that municipalities would be paid for the provisions taken by his troops—sometimes cattle were lassoed in the *gaúcho* style, butchered, and the beef grilled or boiled— farmers and peasants who were not his supporters could feel aggrieved. On the pampas Garibaldi said that he only ate "meat, meat, meat", which may have aggravated the arthritis which so disabled him in Europe. Not everyone in Italy could manage on his minimalist diet of fruit, bread, cigars and a dream of liberation.

A contemporary account, by Commander Charles Forbes of the British Navy, gives a picture of the Redshirts at the Battle of Milazzo, a victory in July near the end of the extraordinary Sicilian campaign:

> ... but these red-shirted, ragged-looking scarecrows, under this far from prepossessing exterior, were endowed with many of those sterling qualities which have often enabled impromptu levies to triumph over more elaborate organisations. A musket or rifle, sixty rounds of ammunition, a water bottle, and, for the most part, an empty haversack, and you have the *impedimenta* of a Garibaldian.

> Of commissaries in gorgeous uniforms there are none, yet of beef and bread there is an occasional supply—of discipline there is the merest shadow; all, however, are animated with unbounded confidence in their chiefs and especially Garibaldi who may be said to exercise an individual power over his followers wholly without parallel amongst mod-

ern commanders, who are too apt to lay influence on one side, and place their trust in fear. With this imaginative race, their faith in their chief almost amounts to a superstition: whatever he says, is—wherever he appears, victory follows as a matter of course.[15]

The Thousand, when they reached Sicily, numbered 1,089 in reality, and nearly all came from the north, chiefly from the towns of Bergamo, Brescia, Milan and Pavia. There were only around a hundred Sicilians and Neapolitans. But while many professions and trades were represented, the bulk were educated people, and a quarter were doctors or lawyers.[16] These were on the whole young men who had been inspired by the idea of Italy, the drama of the Roman Republic, and by Garibaldi's reputation.

As the campaigns in Sicily and Calabria progressed, the army swelled in numbers but was declining in quality. Cavour, worried about Garibaldi's popularity and revolutionary propensities, put a stop to recruitment from the north. Men in the south joined for many reasons, and not just from idealism, or because they hated the Bourbons. Garibaldi at the Volturno, outnumbered as usual, was commanding some 20,000 volunteers against 50,000 Bourbon troops. When the *Garibaldini* were paid off at the end of November there were 50,000 names listed, but their leader said that only a third had ever come near the front line.

Trevelyan commented: "thousands of ne'er-do-weels drew pay for trailing rifles and sabres in the cafes of Naples and parading themselves along the streets in uniforms of many colours".[17] There were also far too many officers, over 7,000, promoted in the field by Garibaldi for some act of heroism which had nothing to do with their ability to command. Nevertheless, while many were happy to go home and resume civilian life, several thousands of the Redshirts joined Victor Emmanuel's army, and sixteen of The Thousand became generals.

The South America in which Garibaldi had fought was far from democratic. Although there might be cosmetic gestures towards representation, usually limited to those with property, the reality was that *caudillos*, or warlords in modern parlance, ruled thanks to the militias, often poorly disciplined, at their disposal. Might tended to be right. Their regimes could be arbitrary and cruel. How far was Garibaldi, who styled himself dictator after the capture of Sicily, actually dictatorial himself?

During his unsatisfactory final period in Montevideo, when he was briefly commander-in-chief, he was disillusioned with politics. Whereas he had been a friend of Fructuoso Rivera earlier, he fell out of sympathy with him. He talked about favouring brief periods of dictatorship, and in later life commended a benevolent dictatorship. But his political thinking was naïve and ill-formed, mixing beliefs in socialism, European federalism and the positive virtues of popular insurrection. When he called himself dictator in Sicily and Naples he was a poor administrator, and he was sceptical about politicians, not least the devious Cavour. He was an idealist and a general, capable of exhorting enthusiastic volunteers to heroism and sacrifice, but day-to-day management was not his forte.

His Freemasonry, progressive ideas about national determination and libertarian attitudes to sexual relations would always have been opposed by the Catholic Church. In South America, however, this underlying anticlericalism did not stop him from marrying in a Montevideo church, and he had appealed to the apparently progressive Pius IX before returning to Europe. But in Rome, when the republic forced Pius IX to flee, he came out as more strongly anti-Catholic and was strongly opposed to the pope's temporal government of the Papal States. This did not stop him from cooperating with individual priests, like Ugo Bassi, chaplain to his Italian Legion, who was executed after the fall of Rome.

He was not an atheist, yet was highly critical of the role of the priesthood and of Pope Pius. In Sicily a conservative population watched him attend Mass, including one in Palermo Cathedral.[18] This was not just an exercise in public relations. Credulous peasants treated him as a second Messiah. But his Italian campaigns left him with a reputation, never entirely shaken off, as remorselessly anti-Catholic.

He has been labelled in retrospect "the hero of two worlds". His heroism, wherever he fought, is not in doubt. But his significance grew. In southern Brazil he was not unimportant for the *Farroupilhas*, in capturing Laguna and leading pinprick attacks with his tiny navy. But although this part of his career was crucial for his romance with Anita—it was where she helped him to ride like a *gaúcho*—and for his apprenticeship in amphibious warfare and warfare on land, his military contribution was marginal. In Uruguay it was more important, both in command of the navy, in raising and leading the Italian Legion, and in helping safeguard the defence of Montevideo and the country's independence.

Rightly, though, his historic reputation rests more on his inspirational military role in unifying Italy. This was achieved sometimes with and sometimes in spite of the king, Cavour and Mazzini, the others who can chiefly claim credit. He was a prickly character, conscious of the role he played. The insubordination he had showed in Salto, and the independence with regard to his British and French naval allies that he had demonstrated in Uruguay, were a foretaste of his performance in the peninsula. But the spirit of the times was with him in Europe, where nationalism was bubbling in Germany, Poland and the Balkans, and enlightened young Italians wanted a liberation from feudalism, and to make a new nation.

Napoleon 1 had said that he liked his generals to be lucky, and along with the other attributes that Garibaldi brought with him at the age of forty-one, after more than twelve years in South America, was the luck of the survivor. Always in the midst of the fray, he could have been cut down or shot a thousand times in South America. In Italy he almost courted death. At his headquarters in the Villa Savorelli during the siege of Rome, French sharpshooters would give him special attention when he went out onto the roof. "He seemed, in fact, almost to enjoy being under fire, even to be amused by his extraordinary escape from serious injury," comments Hibbert.[19]

Much is written of the guilt of the survivor, the depression of the man who is lucky to be alive and who suffers when he remembers the death of so many fellows hit by a bullet or cut down by the sword. The nearest Garibaldi seems to have got to this state of mind was in southern Brazil after the shipwreck where his Italian friends were drowned. He says that a sense of loneliness may have predisposed him to look for a female partner, just before he spotted Anita. His own frequent good fortune may have strengthened his sense of the providential, that he was being spared for the great work of Italy, and he knew its value for his troops.

The impact of this quality on his less heroic followers could hardly be overstated. Others before and since have shared this vital ingredient.

For instance, Winston Churchill, born eight years before Garibaldi's death, shared the luck of the survivor in the face of death. As a twenty-two-year-old subaltern shot at on the North West Frontier, he "rode on my grey pony all along the skirmish line when everyone else was lying down in cover. Foolish perhaps, but I play for high stakes and given an audience there is no act too daring or too noble".[20] He took part in a cavalry charge at Omdurman in 1898, lived dangerously in the Anglo-Boer War in South Africa, crashed planes when trying to learn to fly, and spent time in the trenches on the Western Front when in disgrace after the failure at Gallipoli. He could have died, or been killed in action, many times.

The galvanising power of a man who has himself survived was illustrated not only by Churchill but by his friend, President Franklin Roosevelt, imprisoned in a wheelchair after polio, who told the people of the United States in the depths of the depression that the only thing they had to fear was fear itself. The historian A.J.P. Taylor noted an intriguing parallel between Churchill and Garibaldi.[21] In retreating from Rome on 2 July 1849, Garibaldi told his followers: "I offer neither pay, nor quarter, nor provisions. I offer hunger, forced marches, battles and death." On 13 May 1940 Churchill told the British House of Commons: "I have nothing to offer but blood, toil, tears and sweat."

Garibaldi, so committed to Italy, retained a whiff of the exotic and an admiration for the freedom and courage of the *gaúchos* of the pampas when he returned to Europe. Just as he could never forget Anita, there was a part of him indelibly marked by his experience as a younger man in his thirties in South America.

8

AFTERMATH IN BRAZIL

Although the peace agreement at Ponche Verde in 1845 was supposed to be a peace with honour, in reality it recognised the final defeat of the *Farroupilhas* and the reincorporation of the Republic of Rio Grande do Sul into the Brazilian empire. But such a lengthy war, lasting for almost a decade and involving thousands of troops and hardship and disruption for civilians, could not be forgotten quickly. The economy and people were exhausted. Controversy began with the convention and peace treaty itself. A willingness to resort to force persisted in the DNA of the southernmost part of Brazil.

The *Farroupilhas* have had a lasting impact on the politics, identity and culture of Rio Grande do Sul. Garibaldi, whose fame in Europe was at its apogee in the period of Italian immigration, became a symbol of hope and triumph for arrivals struggling in a new world. The story of Anita, romantic, heroic and the most famous female warrior in Brazil, became the subject of fiction, films and television.

There were twelve clauses in the Ponche Verde agreement, negotiated by the Barão de Caxias on behalf of the empire and accepted by Davi Canabarro, as commander of the *Farroupilhas*. The new president of the republic, Gomes Jardim, did not sign it; his predecessor, Bento Gonçalves, had been pushed aside on the grounds of ill-health—he was already seriously ill, and would die two years later.

On the surface the agreement was extremely generous to the defeated republicans. Article 1 enabled the *Farroupilhas* to choose the next imperial president for the province of Rio Grande do Sul. Article 2 guaranteed that there would be no prosecution of republicans for any act committed during the war. Public debts for the former state would be guaranteed, subject to approval, and laws passed would be respected so long as they fitted in with the laws and constitution of the empire. Significantly, Article 7 stated that the imperial government guaranteed freedom to all slaves who had fought for the republic, or were currently in their ranks. This issue is discussed further in Chapter 10, recounting contemporary traces of Garibaldi and the *Farroupilhas* in southern Brazil.

On 28 February 1845 Canabarro told citizens in a proclamation that, with the agreement of his fellow officers, the war was over. Their property and personal security were safe, "guaranteed by the sacred word of the monarch". But in addition to treachery toward the black fighters, some of whom were massacred and others sold back into slavery, the empire's actions led to other grievances. The republicans were not allowed to choose their provincial president; many did not get monies they said they were owed; there was a scramble for funds among former republican officers; and Antônio Vicente de Fontoura, who had helped to negotiate the deal for the *Farroupilhas* and was then in charge of compensation payments, was an opponent of Gonçalves, who was murdered fifteen years later.

Some of the young men who had fought for the republic, like João Simões Lopes whose life is described in Chapter 10, made peace and new careers in the empire. José de Almeida, the republic's minister of finance, built up a business and became a local leader in Pelotas. Others took part in the oligarchic politics of the empire. But there remained residual bitterness. The sense of an unsettled frontier region, a contested borderland between Lusophone and Hispanic America, continued throughout much of the nineteenth century. In 1851 the deal with Montevideo at the end of the Guerra Grande, following Brazil's intervention on behalf of the *Colorados* and Urquiza, took a slice of northern Uruguayan territory into Brazil.[1] This included a small part of the old Misiones region, from which the Jesuits had been expelled in the late eighteenth century. The Brazilian empire also took the right to intervene in Uruguayan affairs whenever it wished. It did so in 1855 and again in 1864.

The economies and families of Uruguay and Rio Grande do Sul were intertwined, and both regions had suffered badly from the wars. There had been active collaboration between the *Colorados* of Montevideo and the defeated republic, and sympathy persisted, although the empire took over the role of ally to the *Colorados*. It was therefore in 1864, less than two decades after Ponche Verde and thirteen years after the end of the Guerra Grande, that the Brazilian empire and the republics of Argentina and Uruguay were at war again, fighting the eccentric Paraguayan *caudillo*, Francisco Solano López. This was a major and bloody convulsion on the borders of Uruguay and Rio Grande do Sul.

The origins of this terrible war, which led to the decimation of the people of Paraguay, lay in continued turbulence in Uruguay where a *Blanco* president, Bernardo Berro, faced an armed rebellion led by Venancio Flores, the *Colorado* leader. Berro had been a minister in Oribe's parallel government during the civil war. In a neat reversal of the start of the Guerra Grande, when Oribe had been an Argentine general, Flores was in the Argentine army when he launched his *Cruzada Libertadora* (Crusade of Liberation). This brought Brazil in on the side of Flores, for Berro took the chance to tear up the treaty which entitled Brazil to intervene in Uruguay, while Solano López was an ally of President Berro.

By early 1865, with Brazilian military assistance, Flores was ruler of Uruguay. On 1 May 1865 the Brazilian empire, Argentina and the new government of Uruguay signed a triple alliance against Paraguay, which was by then invading the Brazilian state of Mato Grosso. Rio Grande do Sul was in the front line of a war which lasted until 1870, when Solano López was killed by Brazilian troops at Cerro Corá; this was in the same year as the Battle of Sedan, which made possible the final unification of Italy.

Early in the war, in 1865, Rio Grande do Sul was invaded, with Paraguayan troops reaching São Borja and Uruguaiana, where the allies forced them to surrender after an occupation lasting six weeks. The province gave more than its share in a struggle which lasted far longer than was expected, not least by Bartolomé Mitre, Argentine president, who said it would all be over in a few months.

Armed *gaúchos* and cavalry, initially formed from the National Guard of Rio Grande do Sul, were important for Brazil. General

Antônio de Sousa Neto, a strong abolitionist who had taken his black lancers into Uruguay after Ponche Verde, and who had raised volunteers from Rio Grande do Sul to fight against Rosas in 1851, brought his own private army into the Paraguayan War; his cavalry flew both the old *Farroupilha* flag alongside the imperial pennant when they crossed into Paraguay in 1866.

Yet the Brazilians took heavy casualties in the war, both from death in battle and from wounds, which killed Sousa Neto, for example, and also from disease. Around a quarter of the Brazilian troops and many of the officers were recruited from Rio Grande do Sul. Caxias, the commander who had ended the *Farroupilha* war, was a key Brazilian general in a triple alliance that was always uneven, with disputes between the three governments and their generals. General Osório, a *gaúcho* who had joined the army at fifteen and briefly flirted with the *Farroupilhas* before rejecting their secessionism, was one of the bravest commanders in Paraguay. The empire granted freedom to black slaves who joined up, and a large part of the army was composed of Afro-Brazilians.

The Brazilians provided the largest contingent in the alliance, and they occupied Asunción for six years after victory, looting, raping and generally taking advantage of a defeated and depopulated capital. The sense of unsettlement across the extensive Plate region, with undercurrents of lawlessness, was palpable. Venancio Flores had pulled off a successful rebellion in Uruguay. Urquiza, the perennially powerful *caudillo* in Entre Rios, had turned against Rosas to make possible the final victory of Montevideo with Brazilian help, and had then backed President Mitre, whom he had earlier opposed, in the war against Solano López. There was a sense that might was always right, that boundaries could be altered by force.

Towards the end of the century a new figure came to dominate the politics of Rio Grande do Sul—Júlio de Castilhos. He was the enemy of Gaspar de Silveira Martins, who represented the old order in the state, a monarchist and parliamentarian who was a senator from 1880 to 1889 and briefly the empire's finance minister until he resigned in protest at a measure that would have discriminated against non-Catholics. He was exiled to Europe after the republican coup which ended the empire, as he was seen as the one monarchist capable of mounting a counter-coup. He was physically big—"the Samson of the empire"—and a brilliant orator.

Castilhos, (1860–1903) was younger, and abrasive. He was an energetic journalist and propagandist, combining a positivist republicanism with a vehement commitment to states' rights, along the lines of the *Farroupilhas*. He was a disciple of the French philosopher, Auguste Comte, the French pioneer of sociology who also influenced Henri de Saint-Simon, in turn an influence on the young Garibaldi. Positivism was a powerful intellectual current in Brazil at the time of the fall of the empire by military diktat in 1889, and was immortalised in the new republic's motto, "Order and Progress".

Castilhos had a *gaúcho* upbringing. He had been born on an *estancia* and then studied law in São Paulo, becoming editor-in-chief of *A Federação*, the new republican paper in Porto Alegre, at the age of twenty-four. He was against the empire, against Silveira Martins, against slavery, and unbendingly ideological. By 1890 Castilhos, who was already the power behind the scenes, had become governor of his state, the provinces of the empire having become states in the republic. He introduced a positivist state constitution which included a single chamber responsible for the budget, appointment of the vice-president by the president, direct election of the state president with potential for re-election, the exercise of all professions without qualifications, and free education. He remarked: "The state has neither its own science nor religion."

Castilhos took his positivist republicanism as far as he could. While introducing a directive constitution at the state level, which Silveira Martins described as a "Comtist dictatorship", he also demanded enormous freedom for the states as against the centre. In a constituent assembly for the new Brazilian republic in 1891, he and ultra-federalists sought to prevent a standing army, to maximise the states' sources of revenue and enable them to print their own currencies, to introduce universal franchise and even to have their own navies (shades of Garibaldi). The states still levied their own customs duties.

Castilhos had some support from other states, and some influence on the final Brazilian constitution that was adopted. But most of his delegation's amendments in favour of the autonomy of states were defeated, and crucially it failed to get rid of the words "a perpetual and indissoluble union of states" in the preamble. By 1892, with the military president, Floriano Peixoto, trying to consolidate the new republican regime in Rio de Janeiro, Castilhos had split the republican forces at state level. Rio Grande do Sul was slipping into another civil war.

Starting out from Uruguay, an anti-Castilhos coalition, which came to be led by Silveira Martins and was nicknamed the *Maragatos*, launched an uprising the following year. *Maragatos* was an insult, implying that its forces comprised Spanish-speakers from the province of Maragateria in Uruguay; on their side they dismissed Castilhos' followers as *Chimangos*, named after a bird.[2]

There was unrest elsewhere in Brazil, with the rebels marching through Santa Catarina and Paraná, and a naval mutiny against Floriano Peixoto. But the civil war in Rio Grande was of a different order. It lasted thirty-one months and was excessively bloodthirsty. It included torture and beheadings, notably of defeated loyalists after a rebel victory at the Rio Negro. There were some 10,000 victims in all. Guerrilla *caudillos*, backed on both sides by Uruguayan and Argentinian volunteers, laid waste to much of the countryside. This was an unwelcome introduction to local culture for the new Italian and German colonists, hacking out homesteads for agriculture in a sometimes roadless wilderness.

Families and clans were divided by this war, and it was not always clear what were the issues at stake. The *Maragatos* said they were fighting for a more liberal, parliamentary tradition, but Júlio de Castilhos argued that Silveira Martins remained a monarchist at heart, and would get rid of the new republic if he could. Castilhos shared with Floriano and the young positivist officers who had overthrown the empire a ruthless, dictatorial approach which they thought was justified if the republic was to be secure.

There were several echoes of the *Farroupilha* wars. When the *Castilhistas* won a battle at Inhanduí their commanders wrote to Castilhos: "The glories of Inhanduí, made famous by the Farrapos, were revived yesterday. Revolution strangled. Long live the Republic."[3] The brutal way in which this war was fought was similar. Yet there was no clear alignment in the goals of the two sides with those of the earlier combatants, for the *Maragatos* were described as federalists while the *Castilhistas* were even more passionately in favour of states' rights.

The Brazilian historian, José Maria Bello, has argued that this was, in various ways, a repetition of the drama of the *Farroupilhas*: "In their struggle for local freedom or for federation, the revolutionists of 1835 could have gone as far as secession. In taking up arms against Castilhos's extreme presidentialism and for republican parliamentarism, the revolutionists of 1893 could have been driven to a restoration of the monarchy or to a vast and dangerous national convulsion."[4]

What did happen, certainly, is that Júlio de Castilhos, who ruled his state from 1893 to 1898 and died in 1903, embraced the *Farroupilha* myth as foundational for Rio Grande do Sul. The flag of the old republic had become the state flag in 1889 after the end of the monarchy. While the loyalty of Porto Alegre was recognised by the empire after the end of the *Farrapo* civil war, Desterro, the capital of Santa Catarina, became Florianópolis in 1893. Victory by Floriano and Castilhos at the end of the nineteenth century was decisive in embedding the *Farroupilhas* in the southern psyche.

The sense of Rio Grande do Sul as a semi-independent state of what was now described as "the federative republic" of Brazil was reinforced by the lengthy rule of Antônio Augusto Borges de Medeiros, who succeeded Castilhos as head of the authoritarian state Republican Party. He had studied law in São Paulo, where he had joined Castilhos' republican club, and succeeded him as governor; his last term concluded in 1928. He was responsible for the grand Palácio Piratini, the state government building in Porto Alegre, constructed between 1909 and 1921. But the endless re-elections of Borges de Medeiros, and his dictatorial approach, caused revulsion.

In 1922 the opposition in the state came together to back a distinguished diplomat, Joaquim Francisco de Assis Brasil, in an alliance against Borges. Assis Brasil had negotiated a boundary dispute with Bolivia, negotiated a deal with Portugal, and served in Argentina, the United States and Mexico. He had also built a modern castle and raised herds of pedigree Jersey cattle at his home in Pedras Altas. His Liberationists of the Aliança Libertadora were campaigning against dictatorship and re-elections on a dubious franchise, and were reawakening the sense of liberalism of Silveira Martins and the *Maragatos*. Assis Brasil had belonged to a republican club as a law student in São Paulo, and stressed more liberal aspects of the *Farroupilha* heritage.

A fast-rising deputy in the Republican Party, Getúlio Vargas, satirically described as "the mathematician of the party", had been given the task of chairing the commission to oversee the election results. Unsurprisingly, it gave the election to Borges once more. At this point the Liberationists took up arms. There was a vicious eleven-month civil war. Borges was commanding the state militia, the Brigada Militar, and these were assisted by the *provisorios* (provisionals), troops of *gaúchos* raised by sympathetic ranchers. Assis Brasil's supporters were also calling out their workers and adherents. Vargas, in the uniform of the Brigada, raised 250 men from around São Borja, his home town, and made a night march to rescue besieged *Chimangos* in the town of Uruguaiana.

Once again Rio Grande do Sul had shown its penchant for settling disputes by arms. In this case the federal president, Artur Bernardes, insisted that the two sides should make peace, sending down his minister of war, himself a *gaúcho*, to arbitrate. The 1923 agreement of Pedras Altas, named after Assis Brasil's mock castle, ended automatic re-election, made the office of vice-president elective, and stripped out other undemocratic aspects of Castilhos' constitution.

But the subversive, disputatious, independent-minded and fighting traditions of the *gaúchos* lasted well into the twentieth century. After the military overthrow of Emperor Pedro II and a period of turbulence throughout Brazil, the country settled into what became known as the Old Republic, where regional oligarchies took turns to rule—a phase known as "Milk and Coffee" after the economies of the two most powerful states, Minas Gerais ("Milk") and São Paulo ("Coffee"). Here, Rio Grande do Sul, partly because of its situation on the southern border and partly because of its private feuds and the iron rule of Borges de Medeiros, was only an occasional player. Dissatisfaction with the Old Republic became widespread, particularly among young army officers, *tenentes*, who staged uprisings in São Paulo and Rio Grande do Sul in 1924.

The *tenentes* were rebelling against poverty, corruption, unemployment, feudalism in agriculture and the habit of federal presidents of resorting to rule by emergency decree whenever a major problem occurred in one of the states. The *tenentes* did not share the *Farroupilha* belief in states' rights, or any desire to rejig the southern boundaries

96

of the republic, and the ideologies of their leaders were varied. Nonetheless their actions, only two years after the latest war in the state, maintained a sense of insecurity.

Nationwide their message was that the Old Republic was rickety, and should go. In Rio Grande do Sul they briefly occupied São Borja, along with dyed-in-the-wool *Maragatos*, and some of the rebels then met up with others who had escaped by train from São Paulo. Led by Luís Carlos Prestes, "The Cavalier of Hope", they launched an extraordinary long march from the Paraguayan border to the northern states of Piauí and Maranhão before turning westwards to cross the border into Bolivia in 1927. Prestes had been born in Porto Alegre, and there were *gaúchos* who marched 25,000 kilometres with his column.

But Rio Grande do Sul really burst onto the national scene in 1929–30, in the person of Getúlio Vargas, born in 1883. First as presidential candidate of a country-wide Liberal Alliance, then as leader of a successful revolution, Vargas represented in himself the history of frontier warfare that was a timeline for the state. His brothers had killed a man in a feud, cutting short his education in Minas Gerais, and he spent a couple of years in the army when he was only fifteen. In the *gaúcho* civil war of 1893–4 his father had been the *Castilhista caudillo* in São Borja, while his maternal uncle, Dinarte Dornelles, was the *Maragato* commander in the district.

Trained as a lawyer, the younger Vargas became a state deputy for the *Castilhistas* but fell out with Borges de Medeiros between 1912 and 1917. He was too talented for Borges to ignore, rose fast in the state Republican Party and led the *gaúcho* bloc in the national Congress, becoming briefly minister of finance; he was then called back to be elected president of Rio Grande do Sul since, after Pedras Altas, Borges could not run again. Vargas then put together the so-called Liberal Alliance, designed to take him to power by means of an election on 1 March 1930. Within his own state he had even gathered the old *Maragatos* behind him, illustrating a talent for conciliation that served him well in future. His presidential opponent was Júlio Prestes from São Paulo, and according to the government's figures, Prestes won by almost two to one; even opposition leaders recognised that Prestes had won.

Yet by October 1930, Vargas was in Rio de Janeiro as provisional president after a successful revolution. The spark that got the conspiracy off the ground lay in the murder of his vice-presidential running-mate, João Pessoa. The country was fed up with the Old Republic and the Wall Street crash had shattered world trade, damaging the Brazilian economy. In his manifesto Vargas cried, "Rio Grande, arise for Brazil" and, in a tidal wave of patriotism, both teenagers and old men in the state joined up. Vargas, wearing his uniform of the Brigada Militar, made a stately journey north by train. Key fellow conspirators and former *Castilhista* warriors in the *gaúcho* civil wars, like Oswaldo Aranha, who became his foreign minister, and João Neves de Fontoura, who had an up and down relationship with Getúlio but supported his democratic election as president in 1950, came along too.

On 31 October, Vargas entered the Catete Palace in Rio de Janeiro, seat of the president, where he would commit suicide twenty-four years later. In a 1974 study of this leader, who dominated Brazilian politics throughout a lengthy period, I wrote about that October day: "The acclaim was tumultuous. Persons alive today, subsequently disillusioned with Vargas as president, can remember the heady feeling that a new era was dawning. *Gaúcho* troops tied up their horses at the obelisk in the federal capital, bringing a breath of the violent pampas into the sultry, subtropical city."[5]

Vargas was a chameleon figure who changed direction several times in his political life, a sphinx of the pampas whose real purposes were inscrutable, concealed behind an easy manner with associates. From the vague liberalism of the Liberal Alliance which he led in 1930 he moved, as provisional president, to intervene in the states; then, bypassing a new constitution and elections, he declared himself dictator in 1937, heading a fascist-style *Estado Novo* (New State), complete with censorship, a propaganda department and the arrest and torture of opponents; in 1943 he joined the Allies in the war against the Axis and sent troops to Italy;[6] overthrown by a military ultimatum in 1945, when Brazil was preparing for elections, he withdrew to São Borja. He had tried to promote a sense of nationalism, *Brasilidade*, reducing the powers and symbols of states, and ensuring that the children of Italian, German and other colonists should speak Portuguese.

In São Borja, at the end of the war, he reinvented himself as a democratic politician. He promoted two parties, the more centrist Partido Social Democratico (Social Democratic Party), the PSD, and the more radical Partido Trabalhista Brasileiro (Brazilian Labour Party), the PTB, which was built on the corporatist labour movement set up by the *Estado Novo*. These parties had him elected president in 1951, but by 1953, when the head of the presidential guard was tried for the murder of an air force officer and the attempted murder of an opposition politician, Carlos Lacerda, time had run out for Vargas.

His suicide provoked a wave of national mourning for the "father of the poor" in what became known as a bitter August. Although he had crossed swords with the United States in setting up Petrobras, the nationalised oil company, President Eisenhower sent condolences to his widow, Darci. Into the twenty-first century there remained diametrically opposed views of Vargas, with students from Rio Grande do Sul noting that the output of São Paulo publishers stressed his dictatorial rule, while southerners dwelled more on his role as statesman and nation-builder.

Prior to and just after declaring the *Estado Novo*, Vargas had had to put down at least three significant rebellions. The first was in 1932, led by a "Constitutional" campaign in São Paulo for an end to the provisional presidency—in reality a dictatorship—and the restoration of individual and states' liberties. This had had sympathy from Rio Grande do Sul but, in a crucial development, José Antonio Flores da Cunha, one of the military interventors imposed on states by the provisional president, came out for Vargas and sent troops from the Brigada Militar to fight the *Paulistas*; Getúlio's younger brother, Benjamim, raised some *provisorios* from round São Borja, including Gregorio Fortunato, a black bodyguard who would later be the head of the presidential guard, arraigned for murder.

The two other rebellions reflected the ideological battles of the 1930s. One took place in 1935, promoted by the communists and their sympathisers in the military. Luís Carlos Prestes had joined the Brazilian Communist Party and organised risings in Recife and Rio de Janeiro. These were put down without too much difficulty, offering Vargas a justification for his move to the *Estado Novo*. But Brazil also had a fascist movement, the Integralists, for which Vargas had little use, although he had found them helpful in creating the conditions for his own coup; he reviewed the "march of the 50,000 greenshirts" just prior to declaring the *Estado Novo*. In May 1938 the Integralists, who had been double-crossed and had had to turn themselves into a socio-cultural body, attempted a putsch in Rio and imprisoned Vargas for a few hours in his residence, the Palácio Guanabara.

But what was Vargas like for Rio Grande do Sul? He was tough on the state, and its avowed regionalism. Although he acquired a favourite son status in some quarters, he used the anti-communist campaign which led up to the *Estado Novo* as a way of putting an end to the regional militias, of which his own state had the biggest and most battle-hardened. During the Old Republic the state militias had outnumbered the underpaid federal forces, to the anger of the *tenentes*. But by 1937 the federal troops were approximately twice as big as the militias.

Nonetheless the *gaúcho* Brigada Militar, with the *provisorios* included, still amounted to 26,000 men, and was an efficient private army. It was under the command of Flores da Cunha, the interventor turned *gaúcho* governor who had become a thorn in Vargas' side. Vargas plotted against Flores da Cunha with guile. His personal relations with him had deteriorated sharply. Staying with him in Porto Alegre to celebrate the centenary of the *Farroupilha* Republic, he suddenly departed to his home in São Borja, complaining to his brother that Flores da Cunha had been violating his cyphered correspondence.

This centenary of the republic had been a major event. A meadow in Porto Alegre was labelled the Farroupilha Park, and a commemorative exhibition with seventeen pavilions lasted for five months from September 1935; while five of these reflected Rio Grande do Sul there were also those from Santa Catarina, Paraná and others from as far away as Pará in the north and Pernambuco in the north-east.

In the end the power and influence of Flores da Cunha, who had bought a newspaper chain and was orchestrating the *gaúcho* bloc in Congress, were destroyed over a weekend. Vargas had been ruling by emergency decree and in late 1937, just before the launch of the *Estado Novo*, a state of war commission insisted that the Brigada Militar be integrated into the federal army. Flores da Cunha saw that the game was up and took a commercial flight into exile in Uruguay.

Vargas was determined to promote a national identity, *Brasilidade*, and this was not good for his home state. All the state flags were burnt in 1937. Colonies of Italian and German settlers were required to speak Portuguese and join the national endeavour. The states' rights aspect of Castilhos' and Borges de Medeiros' republicanism was discarded, while the "Comtist dictatorship" of liberal critics was given a semi-fascist and corporatist makeover at the federal level.

It was during this period that a notable history, *Garibaldi e a Guerra dos Farrapos*, was written by Lindolfo Collor, a *gaúcho* associate of Vargas who became an opponent. The book appeared in 1938[7] and was one of a series for the publisher, José Olympio, overseen by the pioneering Brazilian sociologist, Gilberto Freyre. It was dedicated to "Rio Grande do Sul, a land of simple and good people, suffering and heroic, my land and my people." Significantly, Collor also thanked his daughter Leda for helping him with research for the book.

In Portugal, not long before he died in 1942, Collor witnessed Leda marry a journalist called Arnon de Mello from the traditionally violent north-eastern state of Alagoas. De Mello went on to be governor in Alagoas and Lindolfo did not live to meet their son, Fernando Affonso Collor de Mello—usually known as Fernando Collor—born in 1949 and later also a governor of Alagoas. Half a century after Lindolfo's death, President Fernando Collor, the first president elected after the end of the military dictatorship, saw his term aborted after only two years, impeached for corruption.

Lindolfo wrote his account in a literary Portuguese during a period of exile, when he was contemplating *gaúcho* history. He had been close to Vargas and drafted the manifesto he read as leader of the Liberal Alliance just before the 1930 revolution. He came from a German family in São Leopoldo, near Porto Alegre, where there was a large German colony. His mother married again after Collor's father's death and, unusually, he took his stepfather's surname, which was a Lusophone rendering of Koehler. His background was religious—he had been in a seminary and wrote religious poetry as a teenager—before becoming a journalist and active in the state Republican Party alongside Vargas, led by Borges de Medeiros.

As a journalist in Rio de Janeiro during the First World War he wrote a column for *A Tribuna* under the positivist title, *Pela Ordem* (For Order), and responding to the war and the Russian Revolution, he argued that it was necessary to give workers their legal rights. He put a promise of labour legislation into the programme of the Liberal Alliance and, when

Vargas prevaricated after the 1930 revolution, he made it clear that he would not join the government unless he was given the Ministry of Labour. Grumbling, Vargas is alleged to have remarked: "Very well, I will pay for a Ministry of Labour, to shut up the German."

Collor was only at the ministry for fifteen months, from December 1930 to March 1932, when he left to join the constitutional rebellion designed to end the dictatorship of the provisional government. But, overcoming much opposition, he introduced labour legislation—albeit without fully free trade unions—which was advanced for Latin America, the basis of his abiding reputation and critical to Vargas' political rehabilitation as a democratic politician after the Second World War. He was exiled twice, became hostile to dictatorship and dictators, and the *Estado Novo* censorship prohibited some of his articles which he sent from Hitler's Berlin just prior to the outbreak of war. After the Second World War the southern states became more prosperous and, thanks to the labour and welfare reforms of the *Estado Novo* and Vargas' last government, an urban working class shared some of the gains. Vargas had pursued policies of industrialisation with a strongly nationalist tinge, setting up the Volta Redonda steelworks and the Petrobras oil monopoly. This was followed by two of his political heirs, both from Rio Grande do Sul—Jango (João) Goulart, who had been minister of labour in his last government and became president in 1961, and Jango's brother-in-law, Leonel Brizola, who was elected governor of the state and nationalised US-owned utilities and spoke of land reform.

The early 1960s were when the Cold War hit South America hardest. Fidel Castro had come to power in Cuba and was keen to spread his revolution. The US president, John F. Kennedy, had launched the Alliance for Progress, a US-funded programme designed to keep Latin America on the side of the West. In October 1962, at the height of the Cuban missile crisis, it looked as though there might be a nuclear world war. It was only defused when the Soviet Union withdrew its missiles from Cuba, the US withdrew its missiles from Turkey, the US promised not to invade Cuba, and a nuclear hotline was set up between Washington and Moscow to limit the risk of war. The British and Americans were concerned at suspected communist influence in Guyana, the former British colony on Brazil's northern border, where

Cheddi Jagan was overthrown by the British in 1953 and was manoeu-vred out of power for a second time in 1964.

Brazil, as the largest state in Latin America, was at the apex of con-cern in Washington, as it was showing increasingly radical tendencies. Goulart was pushing an agrarian reform bill allowing for expropria-tion, while generosity to his labour supporters in the unions was stok-ing inflation; meanwhile his brother-in-law Brizola, with fiery rhetoric, was promoting a more extreme leftism. Army generals were angry that the PTB was recruiting rank and file soldiers and non-commissioned officers into the party. When Goulart announced a constitutional revi-sion, nationalisations and agrarian reform by decree, conservatives feared a leftist dictatorship was on the way.

Stimulated by Washington and by state governors in Minas Gerais, São Paulo and Rio de Janeiro, the generals launched a coup on 31 March and 1 April 1964. The government collapsed with little seri-ous opposition, and Goulart flew to Uruguay on 2 April. This was the start of a military dictatorship headed by successive military presidents which lasted until 1985. Although these presidents boasted of eco-nomic miracles, the reality was harsh for much of the population; civil rights were restricted and opponents fled, lost their rights, were imprisoned and sometimes killed and tortured.

Was this another version of the "Comtist dictatorship"—the idea that Brazilians needed order and discipline, and to take what was good for them? What was striking was that so many key figures in the mili-tary regimes were *gaúchos* who were roughly contemporaries of each other. They carried with them their family memories of civil wars, of violent acts, of *caudillos* and *provisorios*; they were coming of age and entering the army when *tenentes* were challenging the Old Republic and military discipline; they were climbing the ladder during the Vargas dictatorship when the army was greatly strengthened; some had received military instruction in the USA in the Second World War, or had served with the Allies in the expeditionary force in Italy. From the overthrow of Vargas in 1945 and into the Cold War, the army had been politicised, and their background may have predisposed them to make revolution.

Rio Grande do Sul produced three military presidents, starting with the second after the coup—Artur da Costa e Silva, the most hardline, who served from 1967 to 1969 until removed by illness. He had been born in Taquari, was trained in the USA in 1944 and was responsible for Institutional Act no. 5 which closed Congress and introduced the harshest period of the dictatorship. He was followed by General Emilio Garrastazu Médici, president from 1969 to 1974, who built roads across Amazonia and oversaw the highest growth rate in the era. He was born in 1905 in Bagé, Rio Grande do Sul. He in turn was followed by Ernesto Geisel, born in 1907 in Bento Gonçalves, who faced strikes and introduced a modest liberalisation from 1974 to 1979. These three all started their careers in the military school in Porto Alegre.

Arguably as important as the presidents themselves were two other generals who provided the brains behind the military regimes. Probably the cleverest was Golbery do Couto e Silva, born in Rio Grande in 1911. In 1955 he wrote an influential book outlining a national security strategy involving military, industrial and political collaboration for the good of the nation. It chimed with the anti-communist mood increasingly dominant among senior officers who had been exposed to US ideology.

Yet although he was part of the successful conspiracy in 1964 he was out of sympathy with the hard line of Costa e Silva and Médici. Seen as Machiavellian, he became extremely powerful as chief of staff to successive presidents from 1974 to 1981 as he tried to navigate a way out of the dictatorship. Although the military had defeated pockets of leftist guerrillas, resistance was growing in the trade union movement, and Jimmy Carter, US president from 1977 to 1981, was prioritising human rights and democracy. During Geisel's presidency another key *gaúcho* was the president's older brother and minister of war, General Orlando Geisel. He manipulated key military appointments to get rid of hardliners.

By the twenty-first century it seems as if Rio Grande do Sul was no longer a major source of military recruits. The role of the army had changed. It was more professional. Overseas tours, as part of the UN force in Haiti for example, became attractive. Democracy was becoming embedded, so that Fernando Collor and Dilma Rousseff were removed by Congress rather than by a military coup. Economic growth in the southern states meant that there were other careers available to ambitious young men. In the 1960s by contrast, the Third Army, based in the state, was the biggest force in the country, supposedly because of rivalry with Argentina.

It was therefore a throwback when the dictatorship-loving President Bolsonaro chose as his running-mate in 2018 a retired general, Hamilton Mourão, who had been born in Porto Alegre in 1953. Mourão was the son of a general, of indigenous origin and proud of it, and had become an officer in 1975 when Ernesto Geisel had just taken over as president from Garrastazu Médici. Arguably as hardline as Bolsonaro, with whom he had served as a parachutist in the army, he disagreed with his president over China and other issues in a dysfunctional government. He was a strong Catholic at a time when evangelical Protestantism was rising throughout the country, providing Bolsonaro with an important bloc of voters.

A surprising echo of the Piratini republic is recent—the creation of a campaign for autonomy or independence in the three southern states of Rio Grande do Sul, Santa Catarina and Paraná. It is called *O Sul é o Meu País* (the South is my Country) and has run two unofficial referenda, in 2016 and 2017. It originated in a 1992 conference in Laguna, and the instigator was Adílcio Cadorin, an activist who went on to be *prefeito* of the town for the conservative Partido da Frente Liberal from 2001 to 2004 (see Chapter 10). By 2001 it claimed 200 support committees in towns throughout the region.

Rather like the *Farroupilhas* themselves, the campaign has been dogged by divisions between those who would like the creation of a separate nation, and those who want a different federalism in Brazil, with most powers in the hands of the component states and the minimum possible left to Brasília. But those who are separatists are up against Article 1 of the "federative" post-dictatorship 1988 constitution, which talks of the "indissoluble union" of the states and federal capital territory, making such a breakaway unconstitutional. Júlio de Castilhos had lost the battle against this wording almost a century earlier, and independence-minded Catalans have faced a similar obstacle in the post-Franco constitution of Spain.

Cadorin, now no longer involved, had managed to get legal status for *O Sul é o Meu País* on the basis of freedom of speech and dissemination, and the right to defend ideas. But the movement was accused of xenophobia by its opponents, while supporters argued that there were cultural differences between the more Europeanised and whiter states of southern Brazil and the blacker, poorer, semi-tropical north; behind all this lay concerns that the wealthier south was paying more than its share of taxes, was under-represented in Congress, and there were clear hints of racism.

In the early years of the twenty-first century, with independence movements in Scotland and Catalonia and new states emerging in Eastern Europe, protagonists saw the campaign as part of a wider international upsurge of submerged identities; there were also less striking pressures for autonomy elsewhere in Brazil. Celso Deucher, a journalist who was one of its leaders, suggested that the capital of the new southern state would be Lages in Santa Catarina, and that its unit of currency would be called the *pila*. The ancient cry of Sepé Tiraju, a Guarani Indian in the eighteenth century, that "this land has an owner", was invoked in prayer in support of the cause.

The referenda brought the movement down to earth, however. Only a tiny minority of the population wanted the three southern states to break away. In a plebiscite organised by the *Sulistas* in 2017 only 350,633 voters out of a registered electorate of 21,217,328 voted in favour. This was down from the 590,664 who had voted in favour the previous year. Only in Paraná had there been any increase. It looked as though the movement had hit a brick wall. The work of Vargas, the military and the democratic dispensation of the last thirty years—as well as such intangibles as culture and the victories of Brazilian football teams—had increased southerners' perceptions of *Brasilidade* and their ownership of the polity. Pride in a *gaúcho* heritage was one thing, to cast aside Brazilian nationality was quite another. The failure contrasted sharply with the dramatic and continuing success of the cultural movement for *gaúcho* traditions, discussed later.

It is impossible to separate the long-term impact of Giuseppe and Anita Garibaldi from the reality of Italian migration. Nineteenth-century awareness of Brazil in Italy was obviously stimulated by knowledge that it was the scene of the first feats of Garibaldi, hero of the Risorgimento. As described in the later chapter on southern Brazil today, the towns of Garibaldi and Anita Garibaldi were named in their honour by Italian migrants. But it was ironic that the wave of Italian migration, between around 1860 and the end of the century, took place just as Italian unity was consolidated. Although Garibaldi had sailed westwards to escape a death sentence and in search of adventure, he might not have expected that his lifetime's achievement would be to see nationals of the new state of Italy leaving it in droves.

In reality the new nation created opportunities for movement. Improving health and education in a unified Italy, as well as continued frustration as large families subdivided their plots, encouraged young people to emigrate. In southern Italy the loss of the capital status of Naples, along with endemic poverty throughout the former Bourbon kingdom, were strong push factors. Whereas thousands of Irish went to the United States, and British settlers went to the USA and English-speaking countries of the British Empire, Latin America was an attractive destination for Italians. Many Italians did travel to the USA, but similarities of language, religion, culture and climate meant that Brazil, Uruguay and Argentina had certain advantages.

The first arrivals in southern Brazil opened up land for agriculture in the Serra, the highlands, where transport was difficult and clearing the bush was slow work. German colonists had arrived earlier and were farming the lower levels and easier terrain. Some of the first Italians came from Veneto, and it was they and others from the north who in 1875 established Caxias do Sul, north of Porto Alegre, now the second largest city in Rio Grande do Sul. They brought with them the vines which, by the twentieth century, had created a major wine industry in the state.

The amount of help that these early colonists received from the Brazilian empire was nugatory, but migration was put on a more organised basis later in the century as coffee planters in São Paulo saw impoverished peasants from southern Italy as a valuable source of labour. They subsidised their passages. But the planters were used to slave labour, only abolished in 1888, and did not treat these free workers much better. They were poorly paid and abused, and after publicised scandals at the start of the twentieth century the Italian government put a temporary stop on more migrants going to Brazil.

Nonetheless it is reckoned that some 70 per cent of Italian migrants went to São Paulo and, in the south, Santa Catarina was the state with the highest number; in all, 60 per cent of the people of Santa Catarina in 2000 were estimated to have Italian ancestry. Migration statistics are contested but it is thought that 10–15 per cent of Brazilians today can claim Italian heredity. When the republic was declared in 1889, all the Italians who had come before that date, and those of other nations, were given Brazilian citizenship.

Garibaldi was a link between their two countries for Italian migrants in the nineteenth century. A few knew him personally, and more had seen the Redshirts passing nearby as they marched through the peninsula. His romance with a feisty Brazilian, added a sentimental connection for newcomers to southern Brazil, building a life amidst the hardships of an untamed country. With the passing of time these immediate memories faded, and for the broader Brazilian population it was Anita who was more of a star. The Atlantic divided Italian and Brazilian portrayals, in films and television, of the hero and heroine of two worlds. But the magnetism of their story attracted good directors and actors. In 1952, for instance, Anna Magnani as Anita and Raf Vallone as Giuseppe took part in an Italian film about the 1849 campaign against the Austrians. In 1961 Roberto Rossellini directed a film about the campaign of the Redshirts in Sicily, and in 1987 the state broadcaster RAI televised a series called *Garibaldi—Il generale*.

In Brazil the powerful TV network Globo put out in 2003 a popular mini-series, *A Casa das Sete Mulheres* (The House of Seven Women) based on a novel by Letícia Wierzchowski. The director was Teresa Lampreia. It ran daily for fifty-three episodes and used a surviving *charqueada* near Pelotas as the house where the women, chiefly members of Bento Gonçalves' family, were imagined to be living. It was a fictionalised version of the *Farroupilha* war, with actors playing the roles of Davi Canabarro and Bento Gonçalves as well as Giovanna Antonelli as Anita and Thiago Lacerda as Garibaldi.

This *telenovela* in the Brazilian tradition is widely remembered, although a film that came out two years later, *Anita e Garibaldi*, has had its critics. This movie, directed by Alberto Rondalli, focused on the first meeting of the couple in Laguna and their involvement in war before they became recognised as heroes. Gabriel Braga Nunes was Giuseppe and Ana Paula Rosário, thought to be less good than Giovanna Antonelli, was Anita.

Commemoration of the *Farroupilha* war, billed as the "Heroic Decade", is now a major cultural and tourist event every September in

Rio Grande do Sul. Tourism is, of course, a growing industry, with visitors from the rest of Brazil, Argentina and Uruguay providing significant revenue. Adventurous younger travellers from Europe and North America join them so that, for example, *The Guardian* travel pages in August 2017 plugged the commemorations. The key date for the anniversary is 20 September when, in 1835, Gomes Jardim and Onofrio Pires led a group of armed men into Porto Alegre in a relatively short occupation which started the war.

Events are spread over three weeks throughout the state, with music, dancing, horse riding and dressing up in faux nineteenth-century costumes and a "*Farroupilha* Camp" in a park in the state capital. Numbers are large. In 2014 over a million people passed through the camp. Every year a different theme is chosen. In 2018 it was the *tropeiro*—the drover, or merchant in his horse- or bullock-drawn wagon who linked isolated communities in the trackless wilderness. In 2019 the theme honoured the heritage of an actor and writer, João Carlos D'Avila Paixão Cortes (1927–2018), who helped to initiate the traditionalist *gaúcho* movement in the 1940s.

If Júlio de Castilhos had adopted the *Farroupilhas* as part of a political strategy for his rule over the state at the start of the twentieth century, the end of the *Estado Novo* made possible a new regionalism. This took a folkloric and cultural turn, described by two academics, Jocelito Zalla and Carla Menegat in an article in *Revista Brasileira de História* in 2011.[8] They wrote of the "invention of traditions" and an idealised social hierarchy on the nineteenth-century *estancia*, with its boss and cowhands. Radio and films helped to promote these images, linked more to the state's pampas lowlands than to its Serra highlands, suggesting a generosity of landowners and democracy of rugged cowboys rather distant from reality. This imagined past included "the invention of a model of traditionalist women, the *prenda*, whose clothing did not have any historic correspondence with the dress of female *gaúchas* of yore". The *prenda* was the female companion of the *gaúcho* cowboy, unlikely to have been able to afford the fancy clothing available to their modern descendants.

Between 1947 and 1948 the traditionalist *gaúcho* movement (Movimento Gaúcho Tradicionalista) was created by a group of students, including Paixão Côrtes, at the Júlio de Castilhos College in

Porto Alegre. In September 1947 Paixão Côrtes organised the transfer and reburial of the remains of the *Farroupilha* general, Davi Canabarro, in a procession that became a major demonstration. Horsemen were dressed in wide trousers, *bombachas*, wearing ponchos, scarves and knee-high boots and spurs. The old flag of the Piratini republic was carried with pride.

This led to a cultural revival which has been astonishingly successful. By 2012 there were 3,000 centres of *gaúcho* tradition in Brazil and abroad, and 1,680 of them throughout the state; the movement had 190,000 members by then, enabling them to take part in a huge range of activities from cavalcades to beauty pageants. The majority of these participants were young. The movement adopted a charter of principles in 1960, but the real take-off was quite recent, and has involved far more citizens of the state than just the activists of the traditionalist movement.

In 1995, thanks to a state decree and also a federal law instigated by Jarbas Lima, a conservative deputy in Congress for Rio Grande do Sul, the *Farroupilha* anniversary was given state-wide support by government. Events take place in many towns every September. A sacred flame, comparable to the Olympic torch, is carried from place to place. State governors and local *prefeitos* take a prominent part in the celebrations. Big national companies, such as Bradesco bank and the brewer of Schin beer, have provided sponsorship. Unbothered by the regionalism, Bradesco's supporting ad in 2018 announced: "A people who cultivate their traditions will always get ahead."

While this *Farroupilha* nostalgia was insufficient propulsion, as seen above, for the separatists in *O Sul é o Meu País* and has had limited impact in education curricula, it has nonetheless had a widespread influence. Informants claim that the iconic date of 20 September is more widely recognised in the state than Brazil's independence day a fortnight earlier, on 7 September, the date when the country broke with Portugal in 1822. In schools, children are taught the state anthem, the old *Hino Farroupilha*, which a few sing every day, and others on special occasions. There were three versions of the words and it was in 1966, two years after the military coup, when it was approved by law. Significantly, a second verse referring to standing up against the "shadow of tyrants" was then deleted; but the anthem retains words going back to 1839 which talk of valour in an unjust war and exploits that can be a model for the whole country.

There is an uneasy relationship between this *Farroupilha* ideology and the leftist PT, the Workers' Party, which ruled Brazil at the federal level from 2003 to 2016. Two prominent PT figures were state governors in the Palácio Farroupilha—Olívio Dutra from 1999 to 2003, and Tarso Genro from 2011 to 2015. Both of them made use of *gaúcho* regalia and symbols of the heroic *Farroupilhas* in their electoral propaganda. But there has been caution at a deeper level.

This caution derives from the suspicion that the *Farroupilha* memories have been captured by opponents and more conservative forces. This was epitomised by the fact that in Laguna in the neighbouring state of Santa Catarina it was Adílcio Cadorin, a *prefeito* opposed to the PT, who was pushing the memorialisation of Anita Garibaldi. Other factors may be at work. The PT, a product of a coalition led by the urban labour movement in São Paulo in the 1980s, saw itself as a new party. Some versions of history were something it wished to move beyond and set aside, and the *Farroupilha* episode, in particular, as reinterpreted through rodeos and dress, seemed part of a world of ranches and large estates inimical to the PT, with its links to the landless campaigners of the Movimento dos Trabalhadores Rurais sem Terra who were occupying some of them.

There seem to be few real connections between the modern take on the *Farroupilhas* and more recent radical traditions in southern Brazil. Curitiba, state capital of Paraná, has been lauded for its experiments in participatory democracy and public transport. Rio Grande do Sul elected a gay governor, Eduardo Leite, in the same 2018 elections during which Jair Bolsonaro, openly homophobic, was voted in as president of Brazil. Progressives and *Farroupilhas* are estranged.

This is particularly relevant to the treatment of Giuseppe and Anita Garibaldi at the start of the twenty-first century. Giuseppe's values, internationalist, fraternal, freethinking and profoundly liberal, were those with which progressive Brazilians might identify. If he was anything he was a socialist, and his own life, which he put on the line for a republican cause that was not really his own, was austere. Some of his views, such as his attachment to Freemasonry, were of his time.

Anita, too, could be seen as a liberated woman, an equal partner in courage, of continuing significance in a Brazil where women's equality is still to be attained and sexism remains pervasive. Her capacity for self-education, and her willingness to break away from a loveless marriage, could make her a standard-bearer for contemporary feminists. But outside Laguna, where Anita is remembered annually in August— the month of her birth and her death—and the two towns named after her, her story is left to the efforts of handfuls of enthusiasts and erratic depictions in visual and print media.

9

AFTERMATH IN URUGUAY

The reputation of Garibaldi in Uruguay was in the ascendant in the nineteenth century, but came under strong attack from revisionist scholars in the second half of the twentieth. This had much to do with the continuing struggles between the *Colorado* and *Blanco* parties. The victory of the Gobierno de la Defensa at the end of the Guerra Grande created a triumphalism on the side of the *Colorados* which was balanced by a sense of victimisation among the *Blancos*, descended from the Oribe government of El Cerrito. The joy in 1851 at the end of the war, with people from either side of lines surrounding the besieged city embracing and celebrating, did not last.

Although convulsions persisted at intervals, the result of the war had confirmed the boundaries of this part of South America. The 1851 boundary treaty between Brazil and Uruguay settled a frontier at the Cuareim river, though this did not stop immigration from Rio Grande do Sul into Uruguay's north-eastern departments. The fall in land prices as a result of the war enabled Brazilian ranchers to buy Uruguayan land on the cheap, and some frontier districts had Brazilian majorities.[1]

However, the idea of a federation of states which would include Rio Grande do Sul, Uruguay, Corrientes and Entre Rios—promoted by Rivera and supported by the *Farroupilhas*—was now buried. Uruguay and Argentina were open to trade with and investment from Britain and

France. European migration, especially from Italy as the century went on, changed the demography and culture of the wider Plate region.

The *Colorados* had another, home-grown hero in Fructuoso Rivera, forgiven for earlier financial questions and his attempt to do a deal with Oribe. Expelled to Brazil by the Gobierno de la Defensa, he retained a Gaullist sense that "I am Montevideo" and was called back as one of three *Colorado* triumvirs with Juan Antonio Lavalleja, who led the thirty-three against Brazilian occupation, and Venancio Flores, who went on to overthrow a *Blanco* president at the start of the war against Paraguay. But Rivera died on the way to Montevideo, where he was accorded a funeral Mass in the cathedral. Rivera was also hailed at the time as the conqueror of the Churrúas, the most warlike of the Amerindian tribes occupying what is now Uruguay. In 1831 he authorised a massacre of Churrúas at Salsipuedes on the Rio Negro as part of a genocidal campaign that lasted three years, and saw the Churrúas gain some revenge by killing his nephew, Bernabé Rivera. Women and children who survived the campaign were transported to Montevideo, to be slaves and domestic servants.

But if the *Colorado* side welcomed European ideas of freedom of thought, liberalism and internationalism—which did not extend to indigenous peoples—the *Blancos* (officially the Partido Nacional) saw themselves as nationalists and "Americans". They noted the heavy dependence of the Gobierno de la Defensa on outside help and foreign troops. They did not see the Argentinian forces, which made up a large proportion of Oribe's army, as foreign in the same way. There were economic distinctions too. The *Colorados* were more commercial, more closely linked to the port of Montevideo, while support for the *Blancos* was more rural, linked to the cattle interests in the countryside. A Wikipedia entry in 2019, clearly submitted by a *Blanco* sympathiser, emphasised that the Gobierno de la Defensa was the result of the illegal overthrow of Oribe.

The sense of victimhood was exacerbated by the experience of Bernardo Berro, a *Blanco* who was briefly acting president in 1852 and then elected president in 1860 at the head of what was supposed to be a fusion of *Blancos* and *Colorados*. However, in 1863 Venancio Flores led a rebellion against him, supported by Brazil and Argentina, and the *Colorados* broke away from Berro to take part in another civil war which

Flores won, but at the cost of triggering the terrible War of the Triple Alliance against Paraguay.

The reputation of Garibaldi as a proto-*Colorado* took a step forward in 1868 when General Lorenzo Batlle became *Colorado* president for four years. He was of Catalan origin and his family had known riches and then expropriation by Artigas, the hero of Uruguayan independence, after which they returned to Spain for a while. Lorenzo had fought with Garibaldi and the Italian Legion in the capture of Colonia in 1845; he was briefly a minister of war two years later in the Gobierno de la Defensa, and later over time had the same ministry and the Ministry of Finance after the war was over.

As president, Lorenzo represented a personal link to Garibaldi, by now an international celebrity following the Sicilian campaign. Significantly, this president founded a *Colorado* political dynasty. His son, José Batlle y Ordóñez, was president from 1903 to 1907 and from 1911 to 1915. Nicknamed Pepe, he defeated a *Blanco* uprising in a short war in 1904, introduced a welfare state and tried to imitate the Swiss-style collegiate government system, getting away from an executive presidency. His nephew, Luis Batlle Berres, was president from 1947 to 1951 and his grand-nephew, Jorge Batlle Ibáñez, was president from 2000 to 2005.

Uruguayan history in the second half of the nineteenth century was turbulent, with divisions among *Colorado* factions, strong military influence and attempts by the dominant *Colorados* to co-opt the *Blancos* with power-sharing, offering them control of parts of the country where their greatest support lay. It was during the presidency of Maximo Santos (1882–6), a *Colorado* military ruler, that the Senate and Chamber of Representatives voted to erect a statue of Garibaldi.

This was an important moment in the process of Garibaldi's recognition, a year after his death. In July 1883 the joint houses of parliament allocated 10,000 pesos to the city of Montevideo "to perpetuate the memory of the illustrious General of the Nation, don José Garibaldi". They authorised statues of General Zabala, founder of Montevideo, and of José Artigas, father of independence, in the same session. He had joined a pantheon.

The debate about the statue brought out strong feelings. Ortiz, one of those who supported the project, used the expression "a hero of two worlds", which was becoming a common description among South

American admirers. He criticised opponents who saw a statue of an Italian as an example of servility. He was attacked by another deputy, Arozteguy, whose father had fought with Oribe: he said that a third of the population would be totally opposed to it, as it affronted their Catholicism, and claimed that only five Italians would back it.

Indeed, this was a persistent criticism during the period, as Garibaldi was seen as someone who had fired on the Vatican, chased the pope from Rome, ended the pope's rule over the Papal States, and was of questionable faith himself. One of the opponents said that he had uttered the ultimate blasphemy—that man had created God, not the other way about. The old criticism, that he was just a pirate, was repeated. Other speakers in parliament defended Garibaldi's religion and denied that he was a proto-*Colorado*. He had come to the aid of Montevideo because he believed in liberty, equality and fraternity, and the rights of small nations. It was pointed out that Uruguay would not be the first country to erect a statue; he already had one in England. In the end the project was approved in the chamber by twenty-seven votes to five. In a related debate in the Senate, Senator Fajardo said: "Garibaldi had no homeland. He was like the wise Socrates, a citizen of the world, a man who did more for humanity."[2]

This statue, erected so soon after his death, coincided with the wave of Italian migration to the Plate region and southern Brazil. In the 1870s and 1880s the Uruguayan economy was booming, at a time when large Italian families were looking to emigrate to survive. It is estimated that about seven million Italians, out of a population of 24 million, left the peninsula between 1861 and 1900.

Statistics are uncertain, but Uruguay was the South American country most affected, with more migrants arriving from Italy than from Spain. Whereas earlier in the nineteenth century most arrivals had come from northern Italy, and were better educated, there was a balance of south and north later in the century, when there were schemes for subsidised crossings. Southern Italians from Sicily and Naples were often illiterate at this time. Italian arrivals landed in Montevideo, and many stayed there. Migration continued well into the twentieth century, and there have been lasting impacts on culture, cuisine and even the Spanish language. A census of 2011 revealed that a third of

Uruguayans have Italian surnames, and possibly a half have some Italian ancestry, which became useful when families sought passports for the European Union.

In the latter part of the nineteenth century the Italian community became more diverse, filling churches, setting up businesses and establishing societies for mutual support like the one in Salto referred to in Chapter 11 where Garibaldi was proclaimed "perpetual president". The community had, for example, its own bank, El Banco Italiano del Uruguay, which issued a ten-peso banknote in 1887 known as the Garibaldi. Circulated five years after his death, this currency included a picture of the hero. An elegant building for community purposes in Montevideo, the Casa de los Italianos, was opened in a Garibaldi Street. In the 1920s, 20 September, the date when troops entered Rome and sealed the unification of Italy, was a public holiday in Uruguay.

By the early twentieth century intermarriage with others was beginning to reduce the separateness of those of Italian descent, although immigration continued. But Garibaldi's mythic status for *Colorados*, matched only by Fructuoso Rivera, was still held in high regard. José "Pepe" Batlle y Ordoñez was the dominant *Colorado* politician in the first decades of the twentieth century and made the Gobierno de la Defensa the spiritual foundation of the party.

After his government defeated and killed the *Blanco* leader, Aparicio Saraiva, at the battle of Masoller in 1904, Uruguay entered an era of peace and reform. The era of *gaúcho caudillos* was over. The economy did relatively well, in part thanks to exports of processed beef. Pepe Batlle overshadowed the country for more than thirty years. He pushed for secularisation and divorce laws, social security and a greater government role in the economy. Under his Swiss-style collegiate system he was prime minister for two years twice, in 1921–3 and 1927–8.

Like many Latin American politicians, Batlle had started as a journalist, launching *El Día* in 1886 to promote his agenda. His paper regularly celebrated anniversaries related to the Gobierno de la Defensa and Garibaldi, and in that context his emphasis on secularisation was significant. References to God and the gospel were removed from public oaths during his pre-eminence, and his campaign for divorce had to overcome opposition from the Catholic Church. However, in an extraordinary throwback to the country's turbulent past, in his sixties

Batlle killed a *Blanco* deputy, Washington Beltrán Garbat, in a duel. The two had been exchanging journalistic insults between *El Día* and *El País*, the *Blanco* newspaper.[3]

Changes in Europe after the First World War, and specifically Mussolini's rise to power in Italy in 1922, created new perspectives. His was a toxic and aggressive nationalism, and Mussolini was looking for Italian heroes as he sought to build his new Roman empire. Gabriele D'Annunzio, war hero and poet who ran a proto-fascist state in Fiume, wrote a poem about Garibaldi in Caprera, evoking a retiring dictator who had handed over Sicily and Naples to Victor Emmanuel. The reality that Garibaldi was as much an internationalist as a nationalist, that he believed in liberty and freedom of speech, and that he might well have fought for Abyssinia (Ethiopia) against Mussolini's invasion in 1935, did not trouble *Il Duce*.

Garibaldi was memorialised throughout Italy, but the most dramatic statue was his large equestrian sculpture on the Janiculum Hill, overlooking Rome from the Trastevere quarter, close to where he had held off the French troops for weeks during the defence of the Roman Republic. It was created in 1895, after a design by Emilio Gallori. It described him as the hero of two worlds and included his slogan, "Rome or death". Busts of other patriots nearby included those of Nino Bixio, Giacomo Medici, Gaetano Sacchi, Ugo Bassi, Menotti and Ricciotti Garibaldi and two of Ricciotti's sons.

Yet the fascists did not like the fact that there was also a Masonic crown by the statue, to recognise Garibaldi's role in Italian Freemasonry, and they replaced it with fascist symbols in a gesture of appropriation. Their line was that the fascist Blackshirts represented a heroic continuity between Garibaldi, with his faith in Italy and the Redshirt struggles of The Thousand in Sicily, via the sacrifices of the First World War, to the fascism of the twentieth century.

Mussolini proclaimed this version of history in celebrations for the fiftieth anniversary of Garibaldi's death, when he inaugurated a statue of Anita on the Janiculum on 30 May 1932. She was also on a horse, looking rather like a cowgirl from the Wild West, and holding the baby Menotti in her left hand and a pistol in her right—quite possibly an accurate portrayal of her appearance as she fled from Moringue soon after the baby was born.

Mussolini had rejected a request from the pope in 1929 that the Garibaldi sculpture should be moved because the pontiff did not like Garibaldi glaring in the direction of the Vatican. The inauguration of Anita's statue, which included the interment of her remains, was a three-day affair, and *Il Duce* was welcomed by Ezio Garibaldi, a son of Ricciotti, who fell out with other *Garibaldini* over his support for the fascists. The sculptor was the elderly Mario Rutelli, personally selected by Mussolini, who had rejected another artist. *Il Duce* had admired Rutelli's *Nymph of the Oceans* in the Piazza della Repubblica, erected over thirty years earlier.

Anita never had the same appeal in Uruguay, but all this enthusiasm for Garibaldi was relevant there, especially when the financial crisis precipitated by the Wall Street crash led to a dictatorship with fascist overtones. José Batlle y Ordóñez, father of the collegial constitution and the Uruguayan welfare state, had died in 1929 and Gabriel Terra, seen as an economic expert but a more conservative *Colorado*, was elected as president the following year. He was firmly opposed to Batlle's constitution, which dispersed power at the centre, and in March 1933 took over in a coup. He was supported by the police, the uniformed firemen and a majority of the *Blancos*, enjoying the benevolence of the army and richer sectors of society. There was not much opposition although, in a dramatic suicide, the former *Colorado* president, Baltasar Brum, shot himself in protest at the coup.

Terra was a dictatorial president until 1938, when he was succeeded by his brother-in-law, Alfredo Baldomir, who was in charge of the police during the coup. He changed the constitution, creating a clearly presidential system, broke relations with the Soviet Union in 1935, recognised the Franco regime in Spain the following year and was sympathetic to Mussolini and the Nazis in power in Germany. This was a conservative regime, which only began to change direction when the United States entered the Second World War after Pearl Harbor in December 1941. Uruguay joined a US-led pan-American system the following month, breaking diplomatic relations with Germany and Italy on 25 January 1942, along with twenty other Latin American states; Argentina ended relations only two years later.

Terra's dictatorship was friendly with Mussolini's Italy, but it is not clear that the large population of Italian origin shared this view. Many were unconvinced that the Blackshirts were heirs to the Redshirts, and Garibaldi's liberal, socialist and internationalist beliefs did not chime with fascism. The most significant external investment in the Terra era came from Nazi Germany, not fascist Italy, with the building of a massive hydroelectric dam on the Rio Negro, the Rincón del Bonete. The dam was built by Siemens, the German construction firm, and Hitler sent President Terra a telegram at its opening in May 1937, wishing him all success with the project.

Uruguayan politics were dominated, for over a hundred years, by the contest between the *Colorados* and the *Blancos*, and the competing factions within each. In 1958, at last, the *Blancos* won a presidential election. Whereas Fructuoso Rivera has been celebrated as a father of the *Colorados*, with statues and his houses in Montevideo and Durazno now museums, Manuel Oribe had to wait until 1961 for a statue in the capital.

It was part of a de-escalation in the partisan disputes which went back to the Guerra Grande, and a recognition that there was some right on both sides in the civil war. At the same time, the *Blanco* government awarded pensions to elderly survivors of *Blanco* uprisings in 1897 and 1904. *Blanco* historians in the first half of the twentieth century had been arguing that Oribe was not just a tool of the tyrant Rosas, but had been neutral as president between Argentina and Brazil before he had been overthrown by Rivera.

A principal advocate for Oribe was Luis Alberto de Herrera, who led the Partido Nacional from the 1920s until his death in 1959; he had inherited an archive from his father, who had been foreign minister in the Berro government which was overthrown by Venancio Flores. Garibaldi only came into this historiography insofar as he represented that external European influence in the Montevideo government that "Americanists" attacked, and his participation in the civil war was only for five years.

A rather weird footnote to the Garibaldi story, between the 1940s and 1960s, was the hunt by two Mazzilotti sisters from Italy for a so-called "Garibaldi treasure". This involved them excavating between tombs in an area set aside in 1853 as the Central Cemetery of Montevideo. The sisters had the idea that he had left a treasure in the city. An Uber driver who took me on one of my journeys recalled that his father had helped them in the search.

Dismissed by many as an urban myth, the notion that he would have deposited gold or other valuables must seem wildly implausible to anyone who has researched the historical figure. The austerity in which he and his family were living is well authenticated and was the subject of anecdotes during the siege. Raiding by his ships, and pillage by the Italian Legion as in Gualaguaychú, was intended either to help the straitened finances of the Gobierno de la Defensa, or to provide sustenance for his men. Any savings he might have had were badly needed for his expedition to Europe on the *Speranza* in 1848.

The backstory here, however, was that Garibaldi was being characterised once more as a corsair. If there was any basis in the theory, it may have rested in his affection for his daughter Rosita, who died at the age of two, and who had been buried at first in the Central Cemetery.[4] He certainly saw her as a treasure. Her death hit him hard when he was in Salto, and Anita came to join him after the child died.

More positive memories of the Italian were kept alive by a successful campaign to preserve his simple home in Montevideo, and the establishment of a Garibaldi Association in the capital. The house, in a street now named 25 de Mayo, had been in the hands of a Spaniard up until 1862. Then, in a curious coincidence, it was owned by a Dr Juan Garibaldi Heguy, named after the warrior, from 1905 until his death in 1932. It was his family that sold the single storey building to the campaigning Casa de Garibaldi association in 1940. This campaign among Italian descendants had raised money from outside Uruguay, including from Argentina as well as from supporters inside the country.[5]

The Garibaldi family rented one room of a house with four rooms, sharing cooking and washing facilities and a well for water with their neighbours. Their three Montevideo children were born in this room. The house had stairs to a flat roof from which, at the time, Garibaldi could have looked out on Admiral Brown's fleet blockading the city and, to landward, on Oribe's threatening army at El Cerrito. The building was owned by Ildefonso García, a merchant who had crossed over to El Cerrito during the siege.

According to a census in October 1843, there were actually eight other people in the same house: Manuel and Juana Pombo, who were Spanish, with their four children, and a Genoese single woman of twenty-five and a twenty-year-old Frenchman, both of whom were servants.[6] French people, and Argentine refugees from Buenos Aires, were in adjoining houses. Stefano Antonini, Garibaldi's friend who had the contract to supply rations for the legions and the garrison from May 1846, lived in a neighbouring block.

There was bureaucracy to overcome, and further fundraising necessary, before the Casa Garibaldi was donated to the state of Uruguay in 1957, to be managed by the Museo Histórico Nacional. When opened to the public there were four rooms to visit, not just the one in which the family had lived. The first included pictures of both Giuseppe and Anita and the flag of the Italian Legion; a second focused on Garibaldi's battles in the River Plate region and contained objects related to the defence of Montevideo and the Guerra Grande; a third displayed his medals and other objects, including a bedspread and a portrait of Alexandre Dumas; and the fourth showed what a home in the middle of the nineteenth century looked like, with typical items and objects attributed to the Garibaldi family.

This house, which had become a museum, was for several years the location for annual commemorations on 20 September by the Asociación Cultural Garibaldina de Montevideo. This association, with its journal simply titled *Garibaldi*, is the main flag-bearer for awareness of Giuseppe and Anita in modern Uruguay. The slogan on the journal's cover quotes his remark when he was fighting for Montevideo, "*Infelici i popoli che aspettano il loro benessere dallo straniero*"—"Unhappy are a people who depend for their well-being on a foreigner". It was both a description of the dependence of the Gobierno de la Defensa on its foreign legions and a more modern slogan for the virtues of independence and nationalism.

The journal has not been able to maintain a run of annual publications, but copies over the years have covered a wide range of Garibaldi material, from articles about the Italian Legion in Uruguay to The Thousand in Sicily, the Roman Republic and Ugo Bassi, the padre who supported Garibaldi in Italy and was executed after the fall of the republic. An inspiration for the association was the late Carlos Novello, whose widow remains its president. He was immensely proud that in 2004, as a result of the association's lobbying, 20 September was declared by law to be the Day of Freedom of Expression and Thought (*Día de la Libertad de Expresión de Pensamiento*). It had first presented this proposal to a Senate commission in 1999.

Significantly, the association had been born in 1985, just as Uruguay was emerging from a decade of harsh military dictatorship. Julio Maria Sanguinetti, a *Colorado* enthusiast for Garibaldi's memory, had been freely elected the previous November and took office as president on 1 March 1985. Key founders of the association, with Carlos Novello, included activists who had fought for the Spanish republic against Franco, and partisan veterans from Italy who had fought against the Nazis and Italian fascists. The launch of the association was, therefore, in part a recognition that Giuseppe's struggles for liberty were still relevant at the end of the twentieth century.

Sanguinetti, from an Italian migrant family, had two periods as president, from 1985 to 1990 and from 1995 to 2000. He was a journalist and lawyer. He had had a long career in factionalised *Colorado* politics and was minister of education for Juan María Bordaberry in 1972, resigning just before Bordaberry's coup which opened the era of dictatorship. Deprived of his rights for five years, he was part of the campaign which brought back democracy in the 1980s. In 2007 he and his wife wrote a book about Garibaldi and the *Colorado* Party,[7] and was interviewed by Mauro Gavillucci for a 2016 book in which this Italian writer was following the Garibaldi trail round South America.[8]

The former president told Gavillucci that it was not surprising that the heirs to Oribe, the *Blancos*, saw Garibaldi as a partisan figure. But he was really just a fighter for liberty, he added, and that was why he had fought in Brazil, in Uruguay, in Italy and in France, and had been offered command of a corps by Abraham Lincoln during the US Civil War. "Every battle, every shot or bayonet charge was always made in the name of liberty, and not for the purpose of conquest or oppression of another people."[9] He was unlike Che Guevara, who was hero only of Marxism. He did not share the unpredictable behaviour of a *caudillo*, like Fructuoso Rivera, since as a seaman he needed the crew to work together in confronting dangers at sea. Sanguinetti claimed that Garibaldi had respected the individual, had personally freed hundreds of slaves, and was a forerunner of emancipation. For *Colorados* he embodied, to the maximum extent, a romantic and libertarian struggle, and would always be a preeminent figure.

My own findings as to how Garibaldi is now regarded in Uruguay are recorded in Chapter 11.

PART 3

REPORTAGE

10

TRACES OF GARIBALDI, BRAZIL, OCTOBER 2018

I started my search for the traces of Giuseppe Garibaldi in Brazil in the shadow of an impending political convulsion. Jair Bolsonaro, a retired paratroop captain who had been an unimportant congressman for Rio de Janeiro for twenty-seven years, was about to win the presidency in elections in 2018. He would do so as an unashamed admirer of the military dictatorship which lasted from 1964 to 1985. He had electrified the country in April 2016 when he dedicated his vote for the impeachment of the then president, Dilma Rousseff, to the memory of Carlos Ustra, the colonel who had run the feared torture unit, Doi-Codi, in São Paulo in the 1970s. Rousseff, who had been captured as a guerrilla, had herself been tortured.

Everything about Bolsonaro reeked of the populist ultra-nationalism displayed by Donald Trump in the United States, Narendra Modi in India and other leaders who react noisily against globalisation to put their countries first. Bolsonaro was also anti-gay, racist, *machista* if not misogynist (though he had been married three times), wanted the police to shoot on sight, and was threatening to run opponents out of the country if elected. He was hostile to environmentalists and wanted to open up the previously protected Amazon rainforest to ranchers, loggers and miners. He was supported by the rich, the evangelical churches, the army and police, the powerful agricultural lobby, and many ordinary Brazilians.

How could it be that ordinary Brazilians would see Bolsonaro as a saviour? They were feeling desperate. There had been a recession for four years. There was a feeling that crime was out of control—particularly in the *favela* shantytowns in all the big cities, often ruled by drug lords. And there was a reaction against corruption in the political class, especially the PT, the Partido dos Trabalhadores or Workers' Party, to which Rousseff and her charismatic predecessor, Lula, belonged. Whether Bolsonaro, and especially his key backers, were quite as clean as they claimed remained to be seen. They mounted an effective social media campaign for their newly-invented Partido Social Liberal, bombarding WhatsApp users, and their TV ads denigrated the *corruPTos*.

While opponents of Bolsonaro talked of leaving the country, two of his wealthier supporters told me they would head off to Portugal if the PT won. The politics had become sharply polarised and Bolsonaro, as erratic in his programme as Trump, was promoted as a breath of fresh air. Rousseff was out of the picture and Lula, who might well have beaten Bolsonaro, was sentenced to twelve years in jail in January 2018 on the back of a massive corruption scandal in Petrobras, the national oil company. A short-lived conservative government, led by Michel Temer after Rousseff's departure, had failed to get the economy going: Temer had the lowest polling figures in the short history of Brazilian democracy.

Walking round Rio de Janeiro, a city I have known and loved since I first visited on a Brazilian government scholarship in 1965, I was struck by the sense of insecurity. So many blocks of flats were now gated communities. This was true of the Rua Anita Garibaldi in the famous upscale district of Copacabana, where I decided to ask who knew what about Anita, Giuseppe's brave and formidable partner.

The answer was, not a lot. The first person I spoke to, running a paper stall on a corner, said he had no idea why the street had this name, or who Anita was. However, a youngish couple were somewhat more aware: the girl knew nothing, but her man had heard about the *Farroupilhas* and associated Anita with their rebellion. Finally I spoke to a woman running another paper stall who said she did not know about Anita, but I could find out about her on the internet!

I always like to get my bearings when returning to Rio, so had checked in for three nights at the Novo Mundo, an old hotel in the

Catete district, round the corner from the flat where I first stayed in 1965. My room had a fine view of the Sugarloaf and, if I craned my head, I could just make out the Corcovado with its towering statue of Christ. The internet connection was spasmodic when I was asked to comment on a conference report which was forwarded to me from London, but there was a lovely rooftop restaurant where I was able to lunch an old friend who lived nearby. She was someone who was worried about crime in the city, and I took care to walk home with her.

A more political discussion followed later with my compatriot, Professor Leslie Bethell, the United Kingdom's most eminent Brazilianist, who now resides in Rio. Over drinks in a historic wine bar patronised by writers and artists and then over dinner, he was profoundly depressed at the rise of Bolsonaro. How far was this the result of the failure of the PT and the Brazilian left, or were the causes more deep-seated? Were the centrists and orthodox conservatives also to blame? Given the opposition to the Brazilian dictatorship from 1964 onwards, and the relief and revulsion after it ended in 1985, it was a challenge to analyse how someone as nostalgic as Bolsonaro was on the verge of the presidency.

I flew from Rio to Porto Alegre, state capital of Rio Grande do Sul, the southernmost state where the *Farroupilhas* declared their republic. Both rival candidates to be governor were saying they supported Bolsonaro, hoping to ride on his tidal wave. This was even true of Eduardo Leite, who had been a successful young mayor (*prefeito*) of Pelotas, who was gay. When he was elected in the second round on 28 October, he became at thirty-three the youngest governor in the country.

Arriving at Porto Alegre airport I was greeted by a driver, Henrique Nunes, who took me at once to the substantial town of São Leopoldo, not far from Porto Alegre. São Leopoldo was originally peopled by German immigrants and it was a family of German origin who welcomed me with a classic *churrasco*—the Brazilian version of the barbecue—with lightly salted beef grilled over charcoal. Accompanied with beer and wine this was a hospitable occasion and an opportunity to get to know Henrique, who would be my driver around southern Brazil.

Wandering round the centre of Porto Alegre later, one could suppose that the *Farroupilhas* had won. The governor's mansion was called the Palácio Piratini, after the first capital of the revolutionaries. The legislative assembly building is the Palácio Farroupilha. The state flag includes the flag of the rebels, and the date the defeated republic was born. And every year, on 20 September, the Day of the Farroupilhas, there is a huge *gaúcho* cavalcade, with people dressed up as cowboys and cowgirls on horseback. In 2018 a crowd of over 10,000 turned out to watch.

But my first cautionary reaction to this piece of historical appropriation came from a ninety-year-old scholar, Sergio da Costa Franco. A student of the history of Porto Alegre who spent three years compiling a historical gazetteer of every street in the city, he thinks there should be statues to the defenders of Porto Alegre, not to people like Garibaldi. Although the rebels occupied the city briefly at the start of the uprising, they then failed to capture it in a siege which, on and off, lasted for four years. It was bombarded from 1836 to 1840, and was defended not by a wall but by a ditch of only some four metres in depth. The citizens ran short of provisions, and the imperial defenders organised raids into neighbouring *fazendas* (farms) to find supplies.

Sergio argues that the revolution was defeated here and in Pelotas, the two key ports in the state. Without ports the *Farroupilhas* could not establish an effective state. Furthermore, he considers that the rebel economy was not viable. Much of the energy behind the uprising lay in the complaint of the *charqueadors*, the owners of the processing plants that converted beef into dried jerk or *charque*, that their sales were being undercut by cheaper imports from Uruguay and Argentina. But their market was with the slave owners of Rio and Bahia, for whose workers the *charque* was the staple food. An independent Rio Grande do Sul would still need these markets to the north. The revolution did not make economic sense.

My guide in Porto Alegre was Eduardo Bueno, a local celebrity, humourist and TV pundit who had made money translating Jack Kerouac's *On the Road* and American beat poets into Portuguese, as well as writing a history of Pedro Cabral's discovery of Brazil in 1500, which was anything but a fluke. He has proved that the Portuguese Crown knew exactly what it was doing in organising the expedition which "discovered" Brazil.

He was a huge fan of Gremio, one of the two premier league football clubs in Porto Alegre, currently top of the table. It was Eduardo who led me to a plaque on the wall near the Ibis hotel where I was staying. This commemorates the Black Lancers, eight companies of which, or possibly over 400 men, were massacred by the empire's troops after the peace of Ponche Verde of 14 November 1844, which ended the war.

Controversy, still alive, surrounds this episode. The *Farroupilha* leaders were divided in their attitude to slavery. Some felt that for a republic whose slogan was "Liberty, Equality and Humanity", slavery was wrong. Others, conscious that the *charque* industry depended heavily on slave labour, thought it was essential.

In 1836, after the defeat and surrender of Bento Gonçalves and his army on 4 October at the island of Fanfa, a dramatic decision was taken. Fanfa was a massive setback for the revolution. Gonçalves and other captured leaders were shipped to Rio, and the *Farroupilhas* were short of troops. Commanders who remained decided to free black slaves as recruits, to make up the numbers. In the course of the war the Black Lancers, cavaliers armed with long spears and protected only by their ponchos, became one of the most effective and feared units in the Rio Grande army. By the end, at the battle of Porongos, which led to a so-called "honourable peace", it was reckoned that the black troops amounted to a third to a half of the *Farroupilha* force. Article 4 of the peace treaty guaranteed their continuing liberty.

However, the Duque de Caxias, overall commander of the imperial forces, ordered that the captured Black Lancers should be killed. The government feared that the survival of a group of freed slaves experienced in warfare would provide a dangerous threat to a system of slavery which, in spite of continuing pressure from the British and a growing abolitionist movement in the empire, continued in Brazil until 1888. What happened next is a subject of dispute. Were the *Farroupilha* leaders complicit in this betrayal by disarming their black troops so that they could be easily murdered, or was this the action of the imperialists alone?

What is clear is that General António de Sousa Neto, a principal Rio Grande commander who refused to sign the peace treaty, led some sixty black troops south to Uruguay, where he had properties and where they could continue to enjoy their freedom, though there is some suggestion that Brazil pressed for their repatriation. Sergio da

Costa Franco thinks that the *Farroupilhas* were not complicit in this crime, as their military leaders continued to enjoy respect after the war. He also points out that the empire, too, had black troops; many of them, coming from Rio and Bahia, found the winters in southern Brazil too cold, which led the imperial generals to suspend fighting for a while when they went home. Nonetheless now, with a greater awareness of race in Brazil, this episode has led to theatrical and other commemorations.

The main square in Porto Alegre, a prosperous, hilly city, contains not only the governor's and the assembly buildings but also attractive old buildings—the cathedral, a theatre and a Partido Progressista headquarters, now bedecked with posters for Eduardo Leite. But the central statue, which lacks any explanation, is of Júlio de Castilhos, the key political figure in the state in the second half of the nineteenth century. In 1884, aged twenty-four, he became editor-in-chief of *A Federação*, the republican paper campaigning for a positivist constitution in the dying days of the empire. In 1891 he was elected president of the state and introduced the positivist constitution giving wide powers to the president which opponents described as dictatorial. Removed later in the same year as the result of a coup in Rio, he came back the following year as state president once more. In 1893–4 Rio Grande do Sul was the scene of another civil war, pitting the opponents of Castilhos against his supporters, backed by Floriano Peixoto, the military president of Brazil who had come to power after the fall of the empire. The *Castilhistas* won, and Júlio ruled the state with a firm hand from 1893 to 1898.

It was Júlio de Castilhos who entwined the modernity of his state with the history of the defeated *Farroupilhas*. It was a brilliant and lasting piece of myth-making. Garibaldi was an addendum. I visited the Praça Garibaldi, some distance from the centre, where there was a statue of the great man in Carrara marble. It was designed by an Italian sculptor and unveiled in 1907, the centenary of Garibaldi's birth. The explanatory plaque on the edge of the square was covered in graffiti and hard to read.

Throughout my strenuous tour in southern Brazil I was ferried around by an intelligent and untiring young professional driver, Henrique Nunes. He drove for long hours, fixed places for us to eat on

his smartphone, confirmed arrangements for my interviews and toler-
ated my ropy Portuguese. Sometimes I sat in the front with him, sometimes in the rear. Without his assistance my inquiries about places of
significance to Giuseppe and Anita, and how they are remembered
today, would have been impossible.

From Porto Alegre we went inland to the town named after
Giuseppe, an hour and a half's drive away, in the foothills. A friend of
mine, whose brother had recruited Henrique Nunes to help me, had
remarked that she never thought of Garibaldi as a person, only as a
place. Keen Garibaldi historians in southern Brazil tend to ignore the
town on the grounds that he never went there. But that is to overlook
an important perspective. Garibaldi the town was a centre for Italian
immigration in the late nineteenth century, and the name was a homage to his role in unifying the peninsula.

Garibaldi is now a charming small town of some 30,000 people,
with cobbled streets and good shops, and it is the centre of sparkling
wine production in Brazil; some of the sparkling wine is of the highest
quality. Bento Gonçalves, not far away and named after the *Farroupilha*
leader, is the main production centre for still wine. I visited the wine
cooperative in Garibaldi, started by forty wine growers of Italian origin
in 1930, and now owned by 400 growers; it has a museum attached,
and I bought a bottle of pink and a bottle of brut. A wine trail, the
Estrada de Sabor (The Highway of Flavour), takes in various attractions
for tourists, and a steam train does a twenty-three-kilometre run
which includes Bento Gonçalves.

Garibaldi is honoured in the town on the main road leading in, with
a statue on a roundabout near the centre, and a bust unveiled at the
bicentenary of his birth. The town museum, in a building originally
opened in 1878 by the Società Italiana de Mutuo Socorrso (Italian
Society of Mutual Aid) explains the connection. The town was originally settled by German, French Swiss and Italian migrants, starting in
1870. Transport links were difficult. Migrants cleared the bush for
agriculture in lots ranging from twelve-and-a-half to fifty hectares. Life
was hard. This was at first called the Colony of the Conde D'Eu, named
after the son-in-law of Emperor Pedro II, whose daughter Princess
Isabel finally freed the slaves. By 1878 the population of Conde D'Eu
was 3,000, and the majority were Italian speakers who had come from

the Tirol, then occupied by Austria. The state of Rio Grande do Sul gave them little support.

It was in October 1900 that a decree of the state gave the town municipal status, with the title of Garibaldi. This was very much thanks to Abramo Canini, who with his parents had arrived as a migrant in 1882 at the age of thirty-two. An active Freemason, he had been involved in the Garibaldi movement in Italy, and served as regional Italian consul from 1894 till his death in 1926. When the town acquired his name, Giuseppe had been dead for eighteen years but was at a peak of his renown as "hero of two worlds". The town museum has a few mementos and pictures of Garibaldi and Anita, but it is not exclusively focused on them.

We drove for some four hours from Porto Alegre through flat terrain to Camaquã. Along the way, we passed directions to two or three "indigenous villages"—a reminder that in Garibaldi's era this was still a contested geography, and that Amerindians were bystanders if not participants in the war between the republic and the empire. Camaquã was where Garibaldi had built his boats, though no relic of his primitive shipyard has survived. My arrival coincided with a book fair where Elma Sant'Ana, a one woman industry for the memory of Anita and her family, was giving a talk about them. In 1992 she founded the Instituto Anita Garibaldi, open to women only but not, as she carefully explained, a feminist body. Her Anitas have taken part in cavalcades, the week of the *Farroupilhas* in Rio Grande do Sul, as well as acts of social service in their communities.

In *A Mulher na Guerra dos Farrapos*, 2017, she has rescued the memories of women who, like Anita, played a courageous role in a rebellion which other historians have largely defined as a masculine affair. These include Maria Francisco Duarte Ferreira, nicknamed "the Little Parrot" (*A Chica Papagaia*), who was the girlfriend of General Davi Canabarro, a leading *Farroupilha* commander. A pretty nurse and wife of the chief medic to the revolutionary troops, she had caught the general's eye and was blamed for a collapse in discipline towards the end of the war. He was said to be canoodling with the Little Parrot on the eve of the disastrous battle at Porongos, emerging underdressed as commander at the final defeat.

Elma Sant'Ana has written books about towns with *Farroupilha* associations as well as people like Menotti Garibaldi, the *gaúcho* son of

Anita and Giuseppe, born in Mostardas. She has supported the twin-ning of Mostardas with Aprilia, in Italy, where Menotti died. She tries to reach children in order to awaken a sense of history, and complains that school curricula in both Rio Grande do Sul and Santa Catarina contain very little about the *Farroupilhas*. Talking to her one realises that her interest now is in international exchange rather than in dressing-up, horse-riding or social work among the young, the women and the old; this is where many of her "Anitas" find their satisfaction. But she would like to see an international Institute of Giuseppe and Anita Garibaldi. She is in touch with the descendants of Garibaldi in Italy, who do not always get on with each other.

In 2019 she flew to Italy to take part in a series of events to remem-ber Giuseppe, Anita and Menotti. On 28 May she attended a pro-gramme on the Janiculum Hill in Rome at Anita's statue, organised by her great granddaughter, Costanza Ravizza Garibaldi. The next day she was at Aprilia, where Menotti is buried, and on 2 June she went on to Caprera for further Garibaldi events involving students, academics, descendants and others, 137 years after his death. Her commitment is unrivalled, almost exhausting.

Elma has won some recognition herself. The history of her Institute has a preface from the coordinator of women's affairs in the cabinet of the governor of Rio Grande do Sul. But her frustration is similar to that of many enthusiastic outsiders to school systems throughout the world, who would like to see their particular hobby horse recognised and taught in classrooms. Pageants and re-enactments can transmit ideas to those who see them, but lack the solid grounding of a history curricu-lum which can reach all the children.

My next stop was Pelotas, Brazil's southernmost large city which has fine squares and a historic market building. Getting near I saw huge rice granaries, and was reminded of the agricultural wealth in southern Brazil. Walking in the city, I watched as a mother endlessly circled a water tower in one of the squares, holding the back of a bike which her son was learning to ride. Her husband was less patient—letting go and then showing less sympathy when the boy fell off and tears flowed.

From my viewpoint the real interest of Pelotas lay in its *charqueadas*. Three of these buildings, whose produce of *charque* beef was so impor-tant in the *Farroupilha* era and long after, have survived in a district named Charquadas. One, open to the public with a guide, is the Charqueada São João. Now a rambling single-storey building built round a courtyard, it dates from 1810. The abattoir and land where hundreds of carcasses were dried in the sun are no longer visible, but the guide explained that at its peak there were forty *charqueadas* dotted along the Rio Pelotas, and the heavily polluted river ran red with the blood of cattle.

The *charque* could stay good and edible for up to a year. The business had begun after the 1777 Treaty of San Ildefonso settled the boundaries between the Portuguese and Spanish possessions in southern Brazil. A Portuguese entrepreneur who had been making *charque* in the more difficult terrain of north-east Brazil found that the climate and potential for rearing cattle in a southern region, which was now safely Portuguese, was optimal.

Slavery was critical to the operation of the *charqueadas* in their heyday, though the *charque* cycle only came to a final end with the Wall Street crash, over forty years after emancipation in Brazil. The family of four who owned São João, and operated the *charqueada* had 200 domestic slaves. In addition to the cruelty and loss of humanity within the system, it was incredibly wasteful of labour. A plaque in the courtyard and a whipping post and statue of St John in the garden gave sidelights on this bitter reality. The plaque recounted the massacre of the Black Lancers after the peace agreement at Ponche Verde, though giving different numbers from those in the plaque in Porto Alegre.

Here it was stated that the Duque de Caxias had ordered Colonel Francisco Pedro de Abreu, the ruthless Moringue who was imperial commander, to surprise the *Farroupilha* soldiers after they were disarmed; over 100 were killed and 300 taken prisoner. Many of these were taken to Rio, where they were sold again into slavery. But the São João plaque also recorded what I had learnt in Porto Alegre, that General Sousa Neto, who had not taken part in the surrender, retreated to Uruguay with his sixty black troops.

The little statue of St John with a lamb in the garden testifies to another intriguing aspect of the time. It may be that St John had particular significance as a protective saint for the owners of the property. But he was also seen as a patron saint of Freemasonry, and so influential in the early nineteenth century, particularly among republicans in

Europe and South America. Furthermore he was also syncretised as an *orixá* in the *candomblé* religion developed by enslaved Africans in Brazil, for St John the Baptist is venerated as *Xangó*, god of thunder. St John had many devotees, black and white.

This was not the only *charqueada* I visited, as through a friend I was lucky enough to see round Estancia de Graça, an extensive ranch of some 5,000 square kilometres out in grassland described as the middle of nowhere, but actually not that far from Pelotas. It had 2,000 head of cattle—European breeds such as Aberdeen Angus and Friesian—as well as significant areas producing rice and soya. It was still in the hands of the Simões Lopes family whose ancestors had founded the ranch and *charqueada* in the nineteenth century. Below the hill on which the old building stands, now with a modern pool and office alongside, one can see a tributary of the Rio Pelotas down which the *charque* was originally shipped. Here, too, I was offered a delicious *churrasco* in a historic dining room, and generous hospitality.

The story of the most celebrated early owner, João Simões Lopes, gives a classic picture of Rio Grande do Sul in the imperial epoch. Born in 1817 he was married at nineteen to a girl of fourteen who came from Piratini, the first capital of the rebels. Although most of the *charqueadors* were with the empire, he threw himself into the *Farroupilha* cause as a young man, and was captured several times. It is from this period in his life that, hanging in an honoured place on a wall in the house, a *Farroupilha* scarf is still on display. Large numbers of these scarves were originally imported from the United States and worn by fighters and supporters, but only half a dozen have survived.

However, his rebellious youth was not an obstacle after the war ended in 1844. Then, still under thirty, he was able to develop a career as a businessman and politician. He was running his *charque* business, helped start the gas and light company of Pelotas and carried out various public services, including cleaning the canal and establishing a public library in Pelotas. An active member of the Conservative Party he became president of Rio Grande do Sul in 1871 and was made Visconde de Graça in 1876.

His son pioneered rice farming in Rio Grande do Sul and the family has carried on a tradition of political activity and public service. The visconde's grandson, Luís Simões Lopes, was one of the *gaúcho* politicians who came to Rio with Getúlio Vargas when the president of Rio Grande do Sul led the successful revolution of 1930. Although trained as an agronomist and engineer, and initially working in the Ministry of Agriculture, he was picked by Vargas in 1938 to reform and shake up the sleepy and corrupt civil service machine in Brazil. He set up DASP, the Departamento Administrativo do Serviço Público (Administrative Department for Public Service) and instituted entry by exam, promotion on merit and a rational salary structure.

His passion for better public administration helped persuade President Vargas to launch one of the most influential institutions in the country. In 1944 Vargas set up a foundation in his own name, the Fundação Getúlio Vargas. From 1945 until 1993, the year in which Luís was ninety-three, he was its president. The reputation of Vargas himself—sometime semi-fascist dictator, latterly a democratic president who committed suicide in 1954—has had huge ups and downs. But the foundation, a respected institution, has doggedly carried out research, training and an increasing range of activities designed to improve the performance of the Brazilian state. Few would quarrel with its quality and non-political record.

From Pelotas, and its *charqueadas*, we drove westwards into the hills to Piratini. Mauro Gavillucci, in his 2011 book about Garibaldi, compared the countryside here with Umbria. To an English visitor passing green fields broken up by stands of woodland in rolling hills, it is reminiscent of Salisbury Plain. Only the sight of large numbers of cattle being fattened up in enclosures is a reminder that this is *gaúcho* country.

The first *Farroupilha* capital now has a population of some 20,000, with a historic heart surrounded by new buildings. There is a *Linha Farroupilha*, a walk round significant places, and the *Semana Farroupilha*, the Farroupilha Week in September, aims to bring tourists into the town. There are enterprises named after Garibaldi. When I was there the Garibaldi house, where he sometimes stayed and Rossetti edited *O Povo*, was being partially renovated with the sponsorship of CORSAN, the state water utility in Rio Grande do Sul. But the first grant had run out after the roof was retiled. It was probably more important historically as regards Rossetti and *O Povo* than for the fact that Garibaldi occasionally lodged there.

Shortage of funds for the municipality, including development of tourism, was a persistent theme of the *prefeito*, the mayor, Vitor Ivan

Gonçalves Rodrigues, when we met. The town, which has two museums, would like to make more of its history but only has two hotels; one, naturally, the Hotel Garibaldi. Transport is difficult, and funding has not yet come through to replace an old bridge over the River Piratini which has seen several accidents and cannot accommodate high buses. The private sector refuses to invest without more money coming in from the state and federal governments. There is an impasse.

Rodrigues was elected on behalf of the Partido Democratico Trabalhista, a centre-left party which opposes Bolsonaro, and he blames politics for some of the problems he faces. He points out that ruling governors do not get re-elected in Rio Grande do Sul, which means that in the first year of each governor's term municipalities have to waste time building links with new people. In Brasília, where there have been separate ministries for culture and tourism, it is harder to get support for programmes which should involve both.

The context, too, is one of relative poverty, with young people leaving the town in search of work, and the nearest university being some distance away in Pelotas. Regional investment, in shipping and docks at the ports of Pelotas and São José do Norte, could lift the wider economy. Rodrigues would like to see a combined tourism push by local towns, but lack of money is the obstacle.

There is, however, quite a lot for a tourist to see. The Barbosa Lessa museum is in the two-storey building which housed the offices of the rebel republic. From an upstairs lookout one could watch for imperial forces threatening the town. The collection inside includes *gaúcho* trousers and boots and relics of the war, and the less interesting municipal museum houses mementos of the wife of Bento Gonçalves, the republic's president. When it can be renovated the Casa Garibaldi, a rambling, low-lying building, shown to me by Fladimir de Moura Gonsalves, secretary for culture, tourism, sports and leisure, has the potential to be a major attraction.

Although it has given its name to the breakaway republic, it is arguable that Piratini has been unlucky. The revolutionaries raised it to the status of a city in 1837, as the Most Loyal and Patriotic City of Our Lady. But two years later the rebel capital was transferred inland to Caçapava following military setbacks, and, after the empire won, it returned to not much more than small town status. Piratini has never recovered its fleeting grandeur. The high-flown Argentinian sister-in-law of my friend, Eduardo Bueno, once visited it and exclaimed: "Wow, Buenos Aires it ain't!"

Our plan was to drive south from Piratini and Pelotas, to cross a narrow neck of water from Rio Grande to São José do Norte. I wanted to get to Mostardas, where Menotti, the Garibaldis' first baby, was born nearby. São José, where Garibaldi and the *Farroupilhas* suffered a strategic defeat in 1840, is at the southern end of a long and rather desolate isthmus where sheep and cattle graze. Mostardas is a good two hours' drive north, just beyond a national park, the Parque Nacional da Lagoa do Peixe, attractive to ecologists. Cars and lorries need to take a ferry—a *balsa*—to get across, and in Piratini we were told that the last *balsa* went at 5 p.m.. In fact, it had gone at 4 p.m., so we had to stay overnight in a hotel by the waterfront and get into an early queue the next morning.

But one reason why we ran late for the ferry was that I had stopped by the roadside for a fascinating phone conversation with Professor Cesar Guazzelli, one of the leading scholars of the *Farroupilha* period. He confirmed that the *Farroupilhas* provide the key foundational myth for Rio Grande do Sul, and that this became entrenched around the start of the twentieth century largely due to the influence of its positivist leader, Júlio de Castilhos. It is a reason for the strong identity of the state.

However, the earlier revolutionaries had never succeeded in their aim to make Brazil a federation of republics when the monarchy was overthrown in 1889. Although its formal description today is the Federal Republic of Brazil (República Federativa do Brasil) the central government in the capital, Brasília, holds most of the power. Brazil, which has had various spells of military and authoritarian rule, is less of a federal state than the United States or Germany. It is possibly more like Nigeria.

Guazzelli compares Rio Grande do Sul with Texas, which enjoyed a temporary independence between 1836, when it seceded from Mexico, until 1845, when it was annexed into the United States. Rio Grande do Sul played an important security role on Brazil's southern flank, for the territory might have been swallowed up by Uruguay or Argentina. The symbolism of the state flag, incorporating the name of the Republic of Rio Grande and its declaration of independence on 20 September 1835, goes further. The yellow and green, the colours of Brazil, are divided in Rio Grande do Sul by a red stripe. Red signified liberty, autonomy and federalism and had meaning in the River Plate republics.

Garibaldi was important in his own research, Guazzelli said, as the cause of diplomatic friction between the empire and Uruguay when he was sailing off the coast of Uruguay. For the empire, Garibaldi was a pirate who could and should be shot on sight. But for the *Farroupilhas* he was a corsair, licensed to attack and raid as commander of their ships, entitled to consideration should he be caught. In reality he was well treated initially when he was put under house arrest in the Argentine province of Entre Rios; he was only tortured by Millan following his escape attempt.

Finally, Guazzelli said that the treaty of Ponche Verde, which ended the war in 1845, should not be regarded as a humiliation for the republic, even though its army was by then reduced to some 1,500 and it had just been defeated at Porongos. He thought Ponche Verde was more like a tie. After a decade of war on Brazil's southern border, the Duque de Caxias needed a settlement. The empire might find itself in wars with its neighbours and needed pacification in the state. In fact, Brazil was to be involved in the conclusion of the civil war in Uruguay, and then the extremely bloody War of the Triple Alliance two decades later, fighting the Paraguayan dictatorship of Francisco Solano López.

When I reached Mostardas the *prefeito* was having lunch, so I and my driver did the same. Moisés Batista Pedone de Souza, the *prefeito*, is a youngish man, representing the Partido Progressista, which he told me controls more local authorities in the state than any other. But like other local authority leaders, he complained about limited resources. Mostardas, a small town in the middle of a long and rather desolate peninsula, has an air strip but its access road is of variable quality; we had to change a tyre after picking up a nail. Since 2009 there has been a programme to develop culture and tourism, and there are seven hotels.

The Garibaldi connection is seen through the lens of Menotti, son of Giuseppe and Anita, who was born nearby in São Simão in September 1840, and died in Italy in 1903. A general in his own right, he fought alongside his father in Italy and raised a Garibaldi Legion of volunteers to join a Polish uprising in 1863. But his early days were fraught. Garibaldi had left Anita to obtain supplies and she had to escape from Moringue, raiding with an imperial force. Menotti was born with a dent in his head, the result of a fall from her horse by a pregnant Anita, probably on her escape from Curitibanos.

Menotti died in Aprilia, a town forty-eight kilometres outside Rome, and Mostardas is now twinned with Aprilia. Rather as Garibaldi is often thought of in Brazil as a town rather than a person, Aprilia in Italy, like Kawasaki in Japan, is known chiefly as a make of motorbike. Out in the countryside near Mostardas is what is described as "Anita's stone", where Menotti was born in Christ-like simplicity; the 1996 plaque bears the coat of arms of both Aprilia and Mostardas. But Moisés, the *prefeito*, told me that there has been no great influx of Italians on treks of historical tourism, and the attempt at twinning has yet to yield results. More important currently is ecological tourism, stimulated by visitors to the national nature park close by. From 15 to 18 November 2018, for example, the town was hosting the 14th Brazilian Festival of Migratory Birds.

This part of Rio Grande do Sul, quite cool in winter, is suitable for rearing sheep. Eduardo Bueno, my friend in Porto Alegre, told me that Mostardas is the best place in Brazil to buy a woollen poncho. I badly wanted to buy one for my wife, who had suffered a shoulder injury and who found it easier to put on a poncho than a coat. But could I find a woollen poncho in an artisan shop? Not in the short time at my disposal, so I found her a thick woollen jersey instead.

This was one of the longest days of my tour searching for traces of Garibaldi in southern Brazil. In seven hours we drove up the peninsula and then beside a series of lakes to Laguna, the home of Anita, where the short-lived Julian Republic of Santa Catarina was declared. I went close to the point between Imbé and Tramandaí, which was the scene of Garibaldi's celebrated overland transport of his *Farroupilha* and *Seival* vessels. There has been a re-enactment of this epic with modern oxen, but having seen a photo of an unkempt concrete memorial on a bridge, unveiled in 1989 to celebrate the 150th anniversary, I could easily have missed it.

In Laguna, however, we were lucky to be guided by Adílcio Cadorin, a lawyer and *prefeito* of Laguna in the first years of the twenty-first century. Author of *Anita: A Guerreira das Repúblicas* (1999), he is one of the greatest experts on Anita and Giuseppe. He has written several books, and with his partner and volunteers he runs an Instituto Cultural Anita Garibaldi in a small building behind his legal office in the historic centre of the town. He tried unsuccessfully to persuade Elma Sant'Ana to name her Instituto Anita Garibaldi the Instituto Menotti Garibaldi, to respect Menotti's *gaúcho* birth, and there has been some confusion between the two heritage bodies.

We arrived in Laguna before the summer season, when visitors from inland Santa Catarina and further afield come to enjoy the beaches in a part of the town with apartment blocks, shops and restaurants, which was only developed in the last decade. Adílcio has a house overlooking this new quarter and I and Henrique Nunes, my expert driver, stayed in a large hotel which was virtually empty.

Adílcio is not a native of Laguna, but arrived from further south in Rio Grande do Sul and has soaked himself in the town's history. He has written a book about its origins going back to the megalithic era. He points out the mysterious similarity of the Stone of Frade (*Pedra do Frade*) by one of the beaches—a vertical hunk with what looks like a stone hat on top—to the standing stones of Stonehenge. He has thrown himself into researching and disseminating Anita's heroic story over more than thirty years.

During his time as *prefeito* from 2001 to 2004, elected for the PDT with support from a more conservative party, the Partido da Frente Liberal, he managed to get the Julian Republic and Anita's role included in the town's primary school curriculum. He also obtained national publicity for Laguna, and coverage on the Globo network's *Fantastico* programme, with an annual re-enactment of Garibaldi's capture of the town. This led to an influx of Italian tourists for the occasion, and Laguna was twinned with Ravenna, the Italian city closest to where Anita died.

But his time in office was clouded with allegations of fraud, and he lost his political rights for five years after a judge ruled that he should not have used a symbol of a dolphin, being used by a political party, as a symbol for the municipality. When he was succeeded by Célio Antônio, a leftist PT mayor from the Workers' Party, he says that the Julian Republic and Anita lost their place in the local school curriculum. He finds it ironic that an iconic revolutionary woman should not be a leftist symbol, and claims that the PT is not interested in history.

He told me he thought Bolsonaro would be a good president for Brazil, and the fears of his extremism were overblown. He himself was the founder of the movement *O Sul é o Meu País* in the 1990s, designed to stimulate a regional identity in the three southern states of Paraná, Santa Catarina and Rio Grande do Sul. Discussed earlier, this movement subsequently split between those who sought to break away from Brazil, and those like Cadorin who wanted a properly federal constitution with much more power for its twenty-six states and Brasília, the federal capital.

Adílcio has had other battles, too. In the early 1990s he was involved in controversy with a Uruguayan who, extraordinarily, claimed that Anita was Uruguayan. Adílcio obtained copies of church records and a declaration from the Brazilian justice authorities in 1992 that she was undoubtedly Brazilian. She was in fact born at Morrinhos near Tubarão in Santa Catarina, where there is a monument to her, before she moved to Laguna. Not long after, during the presidency of Fernando Henrique Cardoso (1995–2003), he was less successful in a campaign to bring Anita's remains back from Rome to Laguna. This became stymied in a wrangle between the Italian government and Brazil over Italian claims for post-war compensation. So the Cardoso government never made a formal request.

His own perspective on Garibaldi is that he was a good strategist, he was brave, and he was lucky. From a hill overlooking Laguna, Adílcio showed how, in a cunning manoeuvre from the sea, Garibaldi organised its capture after the *Farroupilhas* had been besieging it without success for a couple of years. It was in Laguna, too, that as well as courting Anita he became a better horseman under her tuition, so leading to his transfer from naval to land-based command after the loss of the republican navy.

Adílcio is also aware of Giuseppe's flaws. He points out that, after the defeat at Curitibanos in January 1840 when Anita was captured, he retreated with the surviving republicans. He abandoned her to her fate, and must have thought he was unlikely to see her again. During a period of six months in the Uruguayan civil war, when he was away from Anita, he had a liaison with another woman which resulted in the birth of a daughter, of which Anita was aware. And in 1847, when he was unsure how he would be received back in Europe, he sent Anita and the children in advance to test the water. When she was celebrated on arrival in Nice as the wife of a hero, he followed her in April 1848 with his shipload of volunteers.

Parades and events in Laguna take place every August to mark the birth of Anita, on 30 August, 1821 and her death on 4 August, 1849. Adílcio Cadorin, his partner Ivete Scopel and their Instituto are now gearing up for ambitious commemorations of the bicentenary of her birth. The aim is to have committees and activities in all towns with a connection to her in Brazil, Uruguay and Italy. He worries, however, about the impact of local politics in Brazil. There will be local elections in 2020 and many *prefeitos* will change, so he is keen to lock in the municipal commitments in advance.

One idea is to plant roses in her memory—"*uma rosa por Anita*". Sra Scopel emphasises that, although poorly educated and first married at fourteen, Anita was an intelligent woman who spoke Portuguese and then learnt to speak Spanish, Piedmontese, Italian and French; she became a skilled nurse in Uruguay, helping the wounded on both sides in the civil war. Probably illiterate as a teenager, she learnt to read and write, and a number of her letters survive. Sra Scopel promotes recognition of Anita in primary schools, even though she has dropped out of the formal curriculum. A large Anita doll is taken into children's homes and used as a stimulus for their project work.

Anita is widely acknowledged in Laguna. The town's museum, the Museu Histórico Anita Garibaldi, is in the old building where the short-lived Julian Republic was declared, and nearby is a bust of her husband. It was unveiled in 2002 thanks to the Italo-Brazilian Association of Laguna, when Adílcio was *prefeito*. The Casa Anita Garibaldi was closed for refurbishment during my visit, but in fact she lived in various houses in the town, including the small building, now painted blue, in my photograph (see Plate 10). Her name lives on in enterprises including hairdressers and the ANIPA pale ale, a brew which is a sideline of Marcio Rodrigues, president of the cultural foundation of Laguna.

Today's Laguna is in many ways a tourist and holiday town, with fine beaches and a historic heart. Adílcio drove me round with pride, pointing out the sights from the top of a hill which overlooks it. He would dearly like to increase the significance of *Farroupilha-* and Anita-related tourism, but this does not have the wider resonance in Santa Catarina that applies in Rio Grande do Sul, to the south.

More immediately attractive to visitors is the sight of fishermen, standing waist-deep in the sea as dolphins herd mullet fish towards them. The bottle dolphins, intelligent mammals, signal to the fishermen with an abrupt dive or a slap of the tail when they can fill their nets. This inherited cooperation between humans and dolphins only exists in Laguna and on the coast of Mauritania in North Africa, and is a wonder to behold.

From Laguna it was a short trip north to Imbituba, site of early heroism by Anita where Garibaldi fought off a superior naval force and Anita was knocked over by a cannon ball and insisted on staying above deck, driving up more cowardly sailors who were hiding below by firing her carbine. There is, of course, no relic of this battle now, and the landward part is covered by the port area, now being developed to serve a commercially important region from Florianópolis to Curitiba.

Paulo Armando, secretary for culture, said that Imbituba regards its heritage as important, but shortage of funds makes it hard to create the necessary infrastructure for culture and tourism. He took me on a tour of the town, which included a beach which has six-metre waves used for a world surfing championship, and an abandoned electrical power station. The power station, which could have a second life like the Tate Modern art galleries in London, had run out of funds for restoration some years ago. A small corner was being used by an experimental theatre group. A large site nearby, which formerly housed ceramics factories on which Imbituba's economy used to depend, was lying idle. Ambitious plans for housing, shops and amenities on this site remained unrealised, in part the victim of Brazil's lengthy recession.

Armando explained that culture is a weak department in the local authority, with few professional staff and lack of power where it counts. Old buildings are theoretically safeguarded by preservation orders, for instance, but an attractive old chapel had recently been demolished, although it was supposed to have protection. He saw a positive opportunity in Anita's bicentenary in 2021, and would like to respond to Adílcio Cadorin's initiative. He thought it would be necessary to build support, involving politicians, business people and educators. This would be the only way in which a significant celebration could be made to happen.

From Imbituba we could have driven west to Anitápolis, a small town of less than 4,000, named in honour of the revolutionary heroine in 1961. But we didn't, for this is really a German town set up by the Brazilian government in 1907 as a nucleus for European migrants. Its houses look German, and the municipality belongs to a network of nine places linked in an association of towns of German migration. Set among hills, it is now known as a "paradise of rivers and cascades" and is a centre for outdoor adventures. It has annual cavalcades, in the tradition of the south. What is interesting is that, as late as 1961, the reputation of Anita was such that a newly recognised town should take her name.

Instead, from Laguna we drove up into the highlands, the Serra, which were major forested obstacles to inland penetration in Garibaldi's day. Our object was to get to the town of Anita Garibaldi, and slow-moving lorries, loaded with logs and towing second vehicles behind, made overtaking difficult. It was a day of eight hours of hard driving for Henrique Nunes. Garibaldi purists wondered why I wished to visit the town of Anita Garibaldi, with which she had not had a strong connection. But I am glad I went.

As with the town of Garibaldi, the name was really acquired thanks to nineteenth-century Italian migrants. A visitor, welcomed to "a city of lakes", cannot be unaware of its heroine. A huge mural portrait decorates the *prefeitura* (the council offices of the mayor) and outside it stands a large statue of Anita, carrying a sword in her right hand and what could be a torch of freedom in her left. The statue was erected in 2000–4 "in an act of homage to the immortal woman who passed by here in 1840, fighting for the ideals of the Farroupilha revolution". In fact, her precise route is not known, but it is a fair bet that Anita would have been riding not too far from the site of today's town.

A visit to the library provides more context. This is close to a statue of a *tropeiro*, one of the nineteenth-century traders who travelled these outback regions with their horse or bullock carts, buying and selling goods in isolated communities. *Tropeiros* were also drovers, driving their cattle over long distances to markets, the commercial backbone of the main business in the region. At a time when roads were rutted, unmetalled tracks, dried out or flooded and sometimes impassable, the *tropeiros* provided a crucial transport and information network.

In fact, Italian migrants reached the district, then part of the extensive Lages municipality, in the last quarter of the nineteenth century. It was originally called Baguais, after a semi-wild breed of *gaúcho* horse. Then a Captain José Maria Antunes sold lots of thirty hectares each to fifty Italian families, who did not occupy their land straightaway. But on 29 August 1900 the settlement was formally installed as the Anita Garibaldi colony, with nineteen families that had arrived from Rio Grande do Sul.

The colony did not keep her name for long. In 1912 the settlers renamed it the Colonia Hercílio Luz, in honour of the governor of Santa Catarina who was a long-lasting power in the state under what is known as the Old Republic. He was governor from 1894 to 1898, substitute governor for Lauro Muller (now another place name) from 1918 to 1922 and governor again from 1922 to 1924, when he died in office. He has a bridge named after him in Florianópolis, the state capital.

But Anita had not been forgotten. The town strongly favoured the revolt in 1930 which brought Vargas to power, and the new revolutionaries wanted her name restored. On 4 December 1930 the state's federal interventor, General Ptolomeu de Assis Brasil, signed a law creating the district of Anita Garibaldi, cut out of the municipality of Lages. The town's grasp of her history remains a little shaky. Whereas the inscription on her statue outside the *prefeitura* has her passing by in 1840, a school book kept in the library, *Conhecendo nosso municipio: Anita Garibaldi* (Knowing our municipality: Anita Garibaldi) states less accurately that she rode through the region in 1842, after escaping from capture in Curitibanos.

From Anita Garibaldi we drove to Curitibanos, the most moving part of my Brazilian exploration. It is now a substantial town in the Serra, and its significance lies in the battle which took place some twenty kilometres away in 1840, when Anita managed to escape after counting the corpses of the defeated republicans and realised that Giuseppe was not amongst them. Getting away on foot, at first, she was then given a horse by a sympathiser. She had to ride through nearly a hundred kilometres of dense scrub and woodland before reaching Lages, where she had a quick coffee before pressing on to be reunited with her lover in Vacaria. When the republican commander, Teixeira Nunes, asked how she had managed this terrible journey, pregnant and with only berries for food, she told him that she just kept on coming. She had crossed two wide rivers with her horse, the Canoas and Pelotas, and had at least one fall.

The Museu Histórico Antonio Granemann de Souza in Curitibanos retains a unique survival from the *Farroupilha* war. It is a battered wooden cross which used to mark the battlefield, shown to me with pride by a keeper in the museum. What one sees of the battlefield now, nine kilometres up a dirt road and in a private *fazenda* at the Capão de Mortandade, is understated and hardly a tourist attraction. A cross and an inscription lie in a small, unmarked woodland glade, probably rather different from the more open site of the original clash. There are warnings to respect nature and avoid litter, but little sign of visitors. The plaque remembers the "Farroupilha heroes" buried there, and Anita Garibaldi of Santa Catarina, "heroine of two worlds". There is no word about the empire troops who died in the same fight.

The throwaway, forgotten quality of this historic site seems to sum up the ambiguous nature of today's recollection of the *Farroupilhas*. At one level, they are seen as crucial to the identity of Rio Grande do Sul in particular and to the broader south of Brazil, with its small secessionist grouping *O Sul é o Meu País*; Laguna, as Anita's birthplace, makes much of her especially. But at another, the *Farroupilhas* seem like cultural cosmetics, dabbed on for anniversaries with a certain historical vagueness.

This sense of history as a consumerist art form was reinforced when I met Professor Fabricio Furtado, professor of journalism at UNIPLAC, Universidade de Planalto Catarinense (University of the Plateau of Santa Catarina), a relatively new university in Lages, who is also the information officer of the Fundação Cultural de Lages. An enthusiast for film and the *telenovelas* created from the lives of Anita and the *Farroupilhas*, he predicted with confidence that there will be more films of various kinds to mark her bicentenary. But he also told me that the past lives on in Lages in other ways. He lives in a district of the town that is still largely black, where there was a concentration of freed slaves after emancipation.

It had been a whistle-stop tour for me, travelling 3,000 kilometres in eleven days and ending up in Florianópolis, now a major centre and holiday resort which had been called Desterro in the nineteenth century. There, in pouring rain, I had supper with a British family who had made the bold decision to move for six months to Brazil, putting their two children into Brazilian schools. The mother had been born in Brazil and therefore had Brazilian as well as British citizenship. The father, an academic, was able to combine a sabbatical, writing a book, with attendance at a conference in Chile. Their children, temporarily uprooted from a state school in London, were thriving mightily in a different linguistic and educational environment. It reminded me of the Brazilian daughter of a friend who joined our sons at a London comprehensive for much of a spring term in the 1980s and who took to it like a duck to water.

My visit was not quite over, as I decided to spend three nights in São Paulo on my way back to London. This coincided with the second round of the Brazilian presidential election on Sunday 28 October, and gave me an opportunity to see my friend, Maria Laura Canineu, director of Human Rights Watch, Brazil. The prospect of a Bolsonaro victory would mean a great deal of pressure on Brazil's human rights defenders, for it was clear that he was hostile to gays and to the protection of Amerindian lands, and would encourage the poorly trained and often corrupt military police to fire on sight at alleged criminals. With a small staff, and in conjunction with other civil society and legal bodies, she was preparing to take up the challenge.

By Sunday evening, with an efficient electronic voting system, it was clear that Bolsonaro had comfortably beaten Fernando Haddad, the PT candidate who had only entered the race rather late after ex-president Lula da Silva was finally ruled out of contention by the courts. I went out onto the streets from my hotel and strolled along the Avenida Paulista, the central artery that runs along a ridge in São Paulo. There were crowds waving Brazilian flags, hooting horns, some young, most looking relatively well off. I had a momentary feeling that this was reminiscent of the fascist or Nazi demonstrators of 1930s Europe, with danger and vengeance lurking beneath the celebrations.

In fact, the turnout was small compared with the hundreds of thousands who came out onto the Avenida Paulista in 2002 for Lula's first presidential victory. Journalists, particularly from *Folha de São Paulo*, which had been critical of Bolsonaro, and TV crews were given a hard time by his more euphoric and aggressive supporters. Meeting Tom Phillips, *The Guardian*'s Latin America correspondent the next day, who had been up much of the night doing interviews and filing copy, was to exchange foreboding. He knows Brazil well. This was a victory for the rich, for deforestation, and for a Trump-style politics where key ministers would be generals and a dictatorship was to be recollected with affection. I flew home with a heavy heart.

So what had I learnt? I had met several people who knew a lot about the Garibaldis, and visited many sights which were significant in their story. Many of these make too little of the connection, and Adílcio Cadorin's plan for a "rose for Anita" struck me as the most significant initiative to shine a fresh light on this history. Inevitably, different aspects of history can become crowded out of public consciousness, and if the *Farroupilhas* mean more in Rio Grande do Sul, Anita means more in Santa Catarina.

It would take further reflection, and a subsequent visit to Uruguay, to judge how far the Garibaldis have meaning in South America now, nearly 200 years after Anita's birth. How far can their values, in addition to their courage and romance, now resonate with younger generations? This is an era when Trump and Bolsonaro dominate politics, not idealistic adventurers who believe in liberal values and go to the rescue of small countries.

11

TRACES OF GARIBALDI, URUGUAY, FEBRUARY 2019

The first time I visited Montevideo was in late November, 1971, so my second time there was almost half a century later. In 1971 it was a city of old American cars, like Havana. One felt close to the pampas; I was covering a presidential election as a reporter for *The Guardian* newspaper, and I remember *gaúchos* on horseback riding into the Uruguayan capital in a demonstration of support for the *Blanco*, or Partido Nacional, candidate.

But it was also a time of political excitement, with South America seen as a battlefield in the Cold War. The year before in Chile, Salvador Allende, the candidate of Unidad Popular—a left-wing coalition which included communists and socialists—had won narrowly and was elected president. Earlier that November he welcomed Fidel Castro from a Cuba which the United States sought to isolate on a state visit which I also covered, which included Chuquicamata, the famous copper mining town.

President Richard Nixon's administration was anxious about what might happen in Uruguay. That January a leftist guerrilla movement, the Tupamaros, had abducted Geoffrey Jackson, the British Ambassador. He was released in September following payment of a £42,000 ransom by the Conservative government of Edward Heath in a deal brokered by Allende. British governments, of course, always deny that they pay ransoms. The same month over a hundred Tupamaros prisoners had tunnelled free from the Punta Carretas jail in the middle of Montevideo in a public affront to the government.

A new leftist coalition in Uruguay, the Frente Amplio (Broad Front), was contesting the election. It was said to have covert support from the urban guerrillas. There were rumours that the Brazilian generals, running a right-wing military dictatorship since 1964, might intervene if the Frente Amplio won. But the worries were misplaced. Ever since the civil war in the early nineteenth century the country's politics had been dominated by the *Colorados* and the *Blancos*. When the results came in, the *Colorado* candidate, Juan María Bordaberry, had narrowly beaten his *Blanco* opponent, with the Frente Amplio coming third with some 18 per cent. Fraud was alleged, but the results stood.

Coming back in 2019, after such a long absence, Montevideo looked like a modern, European-style capital, safe, with clean streets, new cars and swept if sometime broken pavements. Tall apartment blocks somewhat oppressively overlooked the River Plate, replacing the low-rise housing of my previous visit. The old quarter, the part which had been besieged in the civil war of the 1840s, was relatively unchanged, and the Mercado del Puerto, the market opposite a still active port, had been transformed into a warren of bars, restaurants and shops, with staff touting for business. Intriguingly the Punta Carretas jail, closed in 1985, had been converted into a huge shopping centre with its own McDonald's.

The political cycle was turning again. In the 1970s the south of South America was entering a dark night of military dictatorships, human rights abuse and ineffective guerrilla resistance. In the 1980s the military dictatorships in Chile, Brazil and Argentina, where defeat in the Falklands/Malvinas in 1983 put paid to the Argentine generals, had given way to renewed democracy. In Uruguay, where an eccentric Bordaberry had launched a dictatorship in 1973 but was displaced by the military in 1976, a brutal military dictatorship lasted until late 1984.

At the start of the twenty-first century the process of gradual democratisation in Brazil and Uruguay led suddenly to more dramatic leftward changes. In Brazil in 2003 a charismatic former lathe operator, Lula Inácio da Silva, was elected president at the fourth attempt on behalf of the Partido dos Trabalhadores (PT, the Workers' Party). In

13. Portrait of Garibaldi, *Casa de los Italianos*, Montevideo

14. Casa Garibaldi, Montevideo, still closed in 2019

15. Entry gate to old Montevideo

16. With Milka Rappa, Secretary, Garibaldi Association, and Sergio Falchio-Arrigones, committee member

17. Dancers at *Candombé* carnival, Montevideo

18. Garibaldi obelisk, San Antonio battle site outside Salto, towers over author

19. Two masonic tributes to Garibaldi, foot of obelisk, San Antonio site

20. Bust of its Perpetual President, Italian Society (*Societá Italiana de Unione e Benevolenza*) Salto

21. Salto port, now disused, Rio Uruguay, with Argentina on right bank

22. *Casa de Haedo*, Garibaldi's brief HQ while looting Gualeyguachú, now Argentina

23. Cannon and defence wall, Colonia, Uruguay, which Garibaldi helped capture in 1845

Uruguay in 2005 Tabaré Vazquez, an oncologist, was elected president as the candidate of the Frente Amplio, the rebuilt and wider broad front. This coalition now embraced progressive members of the traditional *Colorado* and *Blanco* parties, socialists and communists, and former Tupamaro guerrillas.

Yet by 2019 the wheel had turned once more. Argentina and Chile had conservative governments. In Brazil, where PT presidents had lasted until the impeachment of Dilma Rousseff in 2016, the hypernationalist Jair Bolsonaro had just taken office, nostalgic for the military dictatorship. Brazilians I had met who were worried about Bolsonaro were thinking seriously of migrating south. Only in Uruguay, where Vazquez was completing a second term after another Frente Amplio president—an attractively anarchic former Tupamaro prisoner, José Mujica—had had a spell in between, was the left still in power. Could that last?

El País, the Montevideo paper, gave me a sense of some of these shifts. The day after I arrived in February I read that Lula had been condemned to a further twelve years and eleven months in prison, charged with corruptly benefiting from improvements by a construction company to a farm of his in the interior of São Paulo state. Odebrecht, the firm concerned, was at the centre of a web of corruption which had ensnared many Brazilian politicians, and some in neighbouring countries.

Jair Bolsonaro had sworn that Lula would "rot in jail". Ex-President Mujica had visited Lula in his prison in Curitiba. But the same issue of *El País* also reported that Flavio Bolsonaro, the senator son of a president who had made rooting out corruption his mantra, was now the subject of allegations relating to luxury flats in Rio. And the slow, drawn-out agony of Venezuela, where three million citizens had emigrated from a land of hunger and social breakdown, was a running sore for the Latin American left.

Uruguay and Mexico sought ineffectively to mediate between the socialist authoritarian Nicolás Maduro and Juan Guaidó, the right-wing opposition leader who had declared himself interim president. A conference of Latin American countries, along with the European Union and CARICOM, the Caribbean Community, was being held in Montevideo to try and find a peaceful way out. President Trump and

Bolsonaro wanted regime change, but were reluctant to put their troops at risk. Guaidó's ploy to send humanitarian relief convoys to the Venezuelan border was stymied by Maduro.

There was no point in trying to fit Garibaldi too tightly into contemporary politics, but one has to remember that Uruguay has not been the peaceful "Switzerland of South America" it is sometimes portrayed to be by guide books, and that its population is small. With around 3.4 million people, compared with some 45 million in Argentina and 212 million in Brazil, it ranks in world terms somewhere between Jamaica (2.9 million) and New Zealand (4.8 million), and even the Brazilian state of Rio Grande do Sul has nearly four times as many inhabitants.

Formally described as the "Oriental Republic", because it is on the eastern side of South America, it is wedged between the Atlantic and the Plate estuary. This is a country with a strong sense of identity and its own independence. It is quite distinct from its two large neighbours, Argentina and Brazil. Fortunately there were many who wanted to talk to me about Garibaldi's role in history, and the traces he has left in Uruguay today. His significance in Uruguay was much greater than in southern Brazil, though Anita's was less.

I was staying in a comfortable Mercure hotel, overlooking the Plate. The riverside road was named after Mahatma Gandhi, father of Indian freedom. His statue was a short walk away, in a reminder of the continuing international awareness in Uruguay's capital. When I went to a seafood restaurant opposite the hotel I found it was selling its meals by weight, a common practice in Brazil also.

My work began at the Biblioteca Nacional, an excellent library near the centre of the capital. Thanks to Professor Enrique Hernández, a professor of law and international relations at the Universidad de la República, the big public university in Montevideo, I had a reading list from books it holds. He was a mentor for me throughout my research. The national library is in an old building with helpful staff but only a few readers on the day I came. It was possible to see all the books that I needed. Montevideo is a city with parks and squares and yellow-flowering trees. In a lunch break from the library I had a *pancho* (hot-dog) from a roadside stall; I fondly remembered sausages, grilled in a square in the open air, in 1971.

The next day was especially fruitful, as it gave me a modern perspective on Garibaldi and on the Guerra Grande, the long civil war in the early nineteenth century. I learnt from academics and education-ists, and had an opportunity as well to meet the executive of the Garibaldi Association (Asociación Cultural Garibaldina de Montevideo) which campaigns to keep his memory alive.

At the Universidad de la República I met Ana Frega, dean of humanities and education sciences, and her colleague Nicolás Duffau. They explained that few students now are interested in the civil war period, even though it was so significant for the independence of Uruguay and its subsequent politics in the nineteenth century. They argued that even for supporters of the *Blancos* and *Colorados*, more recent heroes have taken centre stage. For the *Blancos*, for instance, Wilson Ferreira Aldunate (1919–88) is admired for his unswerving resistance to the recent dictatorship. For *Colorados* the role of an ear-lier figure, José Batlle y Ordóñez, credited with founding the welfare state, is more numinous.

However, historians are now asking new questions. They are getting away from the narrow *Colorado/Blanco* dichotomy, and looking at a more regional concept of state-building, affecting Argentina, Brazil and Paraguay as well as Uruguay. Different ways of organising the region were on the table in the early nineteenth century. Argentina was just a collection of provinces and Rivera, from Uruguay, had a relationship with Corrientes, one of the Argentine provinces, as well as Rio Grande do Sul.

More exacting scholarship was showing that in the first couple of years of the siege of Montevideo there was quite a lot of movement across the lines. Both sides were dependent on foreigners—Montevideo on the foreign legions which included Basques and even a Swiss legion, and Oribe on the Argentinians of Rosas. Rosas and Oribe relied heavily on the Irish-American admiral, William Brown, who had been fighting since 1814 for Buenos Aires against the Spanish and Brazilians, before blockading Montevideo in the civil war. Greater attention was also now being given to the Afro-Uruguayans like Andrés Aguiar, "Garibaldi's Moor", and although they did not have the warrior reputation of the Black Lancers of the *Farroupilhas*, there was a black regiment fighting for the Gobierno de la Defensa. Rivera, who had also used Amerindian Guarani to settle the frontier with Brazil, had Guarani fighting with him.

The academics pointed out that the *Colorados*, tracing their descent from the defenders of Montevideo, had ensured that Garibaldi was honoured throughout their period of dominance in the nineteenth century. They emphasised that in 1883 he was one of only four, including José Artigas, father of independence, recognised by publicly funded statues in the capital. It was not until 1960, by contrast, at a time of *Blanco* government, that Oribe was also honoured with a statue.

They also explained that Italian revolutionaries were moving freely round South and North America at a period of turbulence with the break-up of the Spanish and Portuguese empires, and when European soldiers and sailors, unemployed after the end of the Napoleonic Wars, were looking for pay, work and adventure. However, many members of the Italian Legion had actually been born here. While Garibaldi was sailing and fighting, his wife Anita, now with children, was having a hard time living in poverty. She was in only one or two rooms in a house shared with others, and friendship with Bernardina Rivera, Fructuoso Rivera's wife, was one of her lifelines.

From the humanities department, in a battered old central Montevideo building, I took an Uber across to the Ministry of Education. I used Uber a lot and one of my drivers on this day was a Venezuelan exile, living in Montevideo for five months; his home was near the Venezuelan border with Colombia and Brazil, and he wanted a better life. I asked him why he had come as far as Uruguay. He said that the neighbouring countries held little attraction. He chose Uruguay, as it was "more tranquil". In London I had never used an Uber, but a helpful student on the plane next to me from Madrid, returning from her marketing and publicity course, explained how easy it was.

At the ministry I met three key players: Rosita Angelo, director of education at the Ministry of Education and Culture; Ana Olivera, general director of the secondary education bureau at the National Administration for Public Education; and Monica Salandrú, National Inspector of the Teaching of History at Secondary School. Between them they gave me a thorough overview. They explained that the nineteenth century is covered, in history, in the third grade in junior high school; the half of students who choose humanities in senior high school will have to study the Guerra Grande. The approach at this higher level will link the civil war with the continuing political struggles between *Colorados* and *Blancos*. Simplistically, the *Colorados* were seen as the liberal, progressive party, open to European ideas; the *Blancos*, the Partido Nacional, were seen as more nationalist, concerned to prevent European imperialism and commercial dominance in South America.

Teachers may or may not mention Garibaldi in class. If they do, it will usually be to describe him therefore as a liberal, progressive hero. One of the problems for teachers is that his reputation has been captured by the *Colorado* party; this means that in the education system, and more widely, he has become a partisan rather than a national figure. Anita is unlikely to get a mention at all, even though the curriculum is making "baby steps" towards a more feminist perspective. These senior educators knew of the work of the Garibaldi Association and saw their enthusiasm, rather than the public curriculum, as the way in which knowledge is kept alive.

They also discussed the response of teachers to the recent dictatorship, as it had been suggested to me that coverage of nineteenth-century history had suffered from the need to explain—and prevent a recurrence of—this violent disruption in society and politics. But they said that it had been a struggle to persuade teachers to deal with this 1970s-1980s period, although the education system had worked hard to rebuild democracy and civic participation. There had been almost fifteen years of leftist government since 2005 and there was no nostalgia for dictatorship now. Indeed, it was "still an open wound", with bodies of the murdered being discovered and persons prosecuted for human rights abuse.

School curricula were now becoming more international, with more coverage of Latin America, Europe and Africa, and the Guerra Grande was approached not only through history, but via geography and citizenship. The civil war was looked at not only in terms of sovereignty and the creation of the state, but the human and material losses were acknowledged. Population declined. Uruguay was saddled with a war debt for years. Foreign influence increased. Continuing immigration in the nineteenth century, and the ideas that migrants brought with them, had blunted extreme nationalism.

From the Ministry of Education I went to the Casa de los Italianos (House of the Italians), in a fine old building with its portraits of

Garibaldi, to meet the executive of the Garibaldi Association. A choir was practising when I arrived, and there are regular community events. The executive included its president, Maria Sagario—widow of its energetic founder, Carlos Novello—and Milka Rappa, its secretary, who has provided me with much Garibaldi material. The association has thirty to forty members and runs an annual event with the Italian Institute of Culture on 20 September, the anniversary of the liberation of Rome and the Papal States in 1870, taken as the triumph of the Risorgimento.

The executive was frustrated at the closure of the Casa Garibaldi, the tiny home near the port, which Giuseppe and his family occupied during their time in the city. It was run by the Museo Histórico Nacional (the National History Museum), a government institution based in the former home of Fructuoso Rivera, not far away. But it had been closed for more than two years, and no date had been announced for its reopening. It was possible to learn more about this closure later, and in the meantime Milka Rappa was able to supply some pictures of the interior of the house. Another frustration was that the Association's painting of Anita—the only true and contemporary image of her that has survived, and authenticated by her son Menotti—had been loaned to an Italian body and had never come back.

More positively, the executive was delighted to hear that Adílcio Cadorin in Laguna is planning international celebrations for the bicentenary in 2021 of Anita's birth, with "a rose for Anita"; he subsequently planned to visit Montevideo to follow up, and did so. For me there were various stories of Garibaldi's poverty—he told an English diplomat that he always wore a poncho because he could not afford a shirt— and of his insubordination. At Salto, after the battle of San Antonio, he had arrested Anacleto Medina, the general who had arrived too late to help him when he was outnumbered, and sent him back to Montevideo. Technically Garibaldi was only a colonel at the time. The committee also celebrated the fact that after he had retired from the service of Rosas, Admiral William Brown had called on Garibaldi in Montevideo to salute a worthy antagonist.

After our meeting the treasurer of the Association drove me on a slightly hair-raising tour of the city to see a statue of Garibaldi overlooking the port; the exterior of his small house; and surviving walls from the defence of the city in the civil war. In the port he showed me guns from the *Graf Spee*, the German pocket battleship damaged by gunfire from British cruisers, which was scuttled in December 1939. This morale-raiser for the British so early in the Second World War was a reminder of more than a century of British involvement in the Plate region. The British in fact had briefly occupied both Buenos Aires and Montevideo early in the nineteenth century, and were major investors in and traders with the Plate countries until the 1940s.

That weekend, thanks to the kindness of Enrique Hernández, I saw a festive, multicultural side to modern Montevideo: *candombé*. *Candombé* in Uruguay, not to be confused with *candomblé*, the indigenous syncretic religion of the descendants of Africans in Brazil, is a series of street processions made up of dancers, drummers, flag-wavers and large *papier-mâché* models. Comparable to, but perhaps a little less commercial and professional than the carnival of Rio de Janeiro, it pays tribute to an Afro-Uruguayan past otherwise often forgotten. Only a small minority of the performers, who parade in a competition, are black. But these were some of the best dancers.

An overnight storm on the Plate, not unusual, had reduced the number of groups on the first night so on the second we were able to watch fifteen out of the twenty-four in the competition. The format was unvarying, in the more than a dozen groups we stayed for, in processions which were widely spaced down southern streets in the city: huge flags swirled over the crowds on either side; a banner announced the competing group, which sometimes came from outside Montevideo, with any sponsor (and a Catholic hospital sponsored three of the schools); large *papier-mâché* figures; then around a hundred non-stop female dancers in mini-outfits, perpetually smiling and sometimes taking water bottles or waving at boys in the crowd; then dancers dressed up like grandmas and grandpas; then two or three of the best and sexiest dancers; and then sixty-six drummers, for unlike other carnivals the Uruguayan *candombé* has no other instrument but the drum.

It was exciting, with audience delight, clapping and participation, and a slight whiff of cannabis by midnight. Children stayed up late and sometimes broke through the tapes to dance and turn cartwheels on the road, as gaps opened up between the troupes. There were seats for the audience, and some watched from windows. I saw no cannabis on sale at the carnival, though Uruguay was one of the first countries to decriminalise the drug; there are a small number of shops in every town, but few people are obviously high.

The African origins of the event were acknowledged, with troupes named Nyanza, after one of the Great Lakes, Samburu, after a Kenyan game park, and "The Day after Emancipation" where the banner was emblazoned with a quote from Friedrich Engels: "The nation cannot be free that oppresses other nations." More significantly, a troupe was named after Ansina, Joaquín Ansina Lenzina, the black lieutenant of José Artigas; Ansina raised a regiment of blacks and mixed-race fighters, who fought with Artigas in the struggle for independence and joined him in exile in Paraguay at the end of his career. But the festive and international quality was celebrated with the appearance of Anibal Pachano, a popular Argentinian actor, cheered as he processed along with one of the groups.

On a relaxed Sunday I took the chance to swim in the brown waters of the Plate, just before another storm broke, unaware until later that it is affected by pollution. In the evening I heard a jazz singer accompanied by a guitarist who looked like a child's image of Jesus in an eccentric building like a false castle overlooking the river. She was a scat singer, and her songs were in English and Portuguese as well as Spanish. Her small audience was older and more respectably middle-class than is normal among jazz aficionados in Europe.

My last working day in Montevideo before heading inland was to see Gianni Piccato, the Italian Ambassador. Ambassador Piccato was from Piedmont, well versed in the history of unification under Cavour and King Victor Emmanuel. He had also served as a consul in Curitiba, southern Brazil, so he was familiar with Brazilian enthusiasm for Anita and was aware of a failed campaign to bring her remains back to Laguna.

The ambassador said that he thinks that what Garibaldi learnt in South America was fundamental to his role in Italy. His promotion of the idea of Italy through the creation of an Italian Legion helped put an idea into practice. The volunteers in Montevideo were bourgeois and enlightened, and only some 20 per cent were common people; this was similar among The Thousand he took to Sicily, where it was a challenge to convert a conservative peasantry to the nationalist ideal.

At the same time Garibaldi's republicanism, demonstrated in South America, created problems when he returned to Europe and he reluctantly realised that only compromise with a monarchy could deliver Italian unity. The royal house of Savoy, with Victor Emmanuel and Cavour, had become a serious player in European politics. It was ambitious. In 1855 it sent 10,000 troops to support Britain, France and the Ottoman Empire against Russia in the Crimean War.

Ambassador Piccato stressed the importance of Freemasonry for Garibaldi, as a progressive, anticlerical set of beliefs linked to democracy and republicanism. The Masons had helped him in Brazil and Uruguay, and this was a matter of ideology as well as finance. Unlike in Europe, the Masons in Uruguay have maintained prestige and respect. The current president, Tabaré Vazquez, was a mason.

In Uruguay the ambassador thought that the impact of Garibaldi's adoption by the *Colorados* had worn off in the course of the twentieth century, so that he had become a more national figure. But he remained a symbol for the Italian community in a country where some 40 per cent of the 3.4 million population was of Italian descent. Mussolini had tried to make use of him. The equestrian statue on top of the Janiculum Hill in Rome had been inaugurated in 1895 with a Masonic crown, but this was replaced by fascist symbols. Mussolini had promoted him as a brave hero committed to *Italianità*, ignoring Garibaldi's commitment to democracy and his statement that if ever a united Italy attacked another country he would come to the aid of the other. As a mother and often deserted wife, Anita lacked the status in Uruguay that she enjoyed in southern Brazil, he added.

Milka Rappa and Sergio Falchio-Arrigone of the Garibaldi Association then took me to an exhibition upstairs in the old *cabildo* or city hall of Montevideo. This included a map of the city at the time of the siege, which showed tight lines of defence and the topographical advantage enjoyed by Oribe. He was able to look down on the city and its peninsula jutting out into the Plate from his camp at El Cerrito, only ten kilometres away. Quite close to the centre now, en route to the airport, one passes Oribe's old customs building; this was where ships were required to pay their dues to him when the port of Montevideo was blockaded by Admiral Brown and Rosas' fleet. Sergio explained the coat of arms of Uruguay, adopted in 1829—scales to symbolise justice, a little hill for Montevideo, a horse for freedom, and an ox for hard work.

Milka and Sergio invited me to a nineteenth-century Brazilian café in the old quarter patronised by intellectuals, and said they would like to collaborate with Adílcio Cadorin's plan to remember Anita's bicentenary with "a rose for Anita". A pedestrianised street nearby, Sarandí, featured metal plates dedicated to the Rolling Stones and Nelson Mandela in a walk of fame, and they explained that the *ramblas*, the wide pedestrian foot and cycle paths adjoining the Plate where hundreds walk, jog and cycle at the end of each day, were vital to the well-being of Montevideo. Exiles during the dictatorship—and there are communities as far away as Sweden today as a result—said they missed the *ramblas* more than anything else.

Sergio said that the father of independence, José Artigas (1764–1850), had learnt his warlike skills in fighting Amerindians, but he also had Indians fighting for him. In an illustration of the confusion of early Uruguayan history Artigas had been expelled to Paraguay in 1820 and lived through most of the Guerra Grande in exile. He died at the great age of eighty-six and had survived an attempt to assassinate him by Rivera, another hero.

My next stop, after a six-hour bus ride, was Salto, in northern Uruguay close to the battle site of San Antonio. Salto, with a population of over 100,000, is the second largest city in the country. The bus terminal from which I departed in Montevideo is large, busy, but well organised, adjoining a crossroads called Tres Cruces with a big cross and statues of Fructuoso Rivera and Pope John II who came in 2005. Buses arrive and leave with exemplary timeliness and my trip took me through rolling country without significant hills. I crossed the Rio Negro, with its major hydroelectric dam. Uruguay is a country with nearly four times more cattle than people but there were also some sheep, stands of commercial woodland with vertical pole-like trees and, nearing Salto, one or two vineyards. Although not promoted internationally on the scale of Chilean or Argentinian wines, some Uruguayan wine, using the Tannat grape, is of high quality.

Salto is a bustling, attractive town, but as a port on the Rio Uruguay it no longer has a significant role. Wider than the Thames below

London and with Argentina on the opposite western bank, the river's two inactive cranes testified to a lost strategic importance. My modern hotel, also including a casino, overlooked the expansive Plaza Artigas with an equestrian statue of the man himself in the middle, and I did a lot of walking in the town.

The battle of San Antonio, and the role of the Italian community, are alive in the memory. By the port are a fascist monument and flagpole dedicated to the "sons of Italy" in 1930, the same year in which the battle site was endowed with a towering monument designed by Giovanni Veltroni, an Italian-born architect, with lettering in a style that nods to Bauhaus modernism but with fascist and dominant proportions. The word GARIBALDI in large letters runs down the front of a kind of obelisk constructed of blocks of red granite. It faces downhill along an Avenida Garibaldi which turns from tarmac, as it leaves Salto, into a dirt road nearing the memorial.

Remains of the dead are buried in a crypt. Inscriptions and engravings from the Masons and "free Italians" adorn the base. One shows Giuseppe carrying a wounded soldier through the bullets, possibly Gaetano Sacchi; another quotes his message to Joaquín Suarez about fighting against despotism and concludes: "I owe nothing to your beautiful country. I humbly comply with my duty as a soldier of liberty and am proud of my title of citizenship of the republic." Although there are some trees there is open ground close to the monument, and it is hard to imagine the battlefield of nearly two centuries ago.

From this site I went to the Museo del Hombre y la Tecnologia (Museum of Man and Technology), which was about to make an unscheduled closure. However, Cary de los Santos Guibert, running the museum, kindly kept it open for me and showed me items of interest. These included a painting and lithograph of the battle of San Antonio, made in the nineteenth century in Genoa, and the skeleton of a Charrúa Amerindian.

Although the Guarani survived, some intermarrying with other Uruguayans, and Guarani is a national language in Paraguay, the massacres of the Charrúa between 1831 and 1833, led by Fructuoso Rivera and his nephew Bernabé, were genocidal. For many decades it was thought this people were pushed to extinction. They had been warlike and resisted white expansion and, as happened to the Xavante in Brazil whose name was given to an air force jet, their name has been expropriated by modern Uruguayans. The national football team is sometimes called *Los Charrúas*.

However, DNA research, and campaigns for indigenous recognition and self-determination in South America, are putting a different gloss on this story. In the last thirty years two different associations in Uruguay have been established representing descendants of Charrúa, and Charrúa have identified themselves in Argentina and southern Brazil also. After the Salsipuedes massacre, the worst in the 1830s, four surviving Charrúa were shipped to France as exotic specimens for examination by the National History Museum, where they and a child all died. In 2002 the remains of one of them, Chief Vaimaca Peru, were returned to Uruguay and buried with honour. DNA research on the chief has proved that many Uruguayans have Charrúa ancestry, since the women and children were not all murdered in the nineteenth century, and individuals are now using their own family histories to win recognition.

Cary de los Santos Guibert then pointed me towards one of my most interesting finds in Salto—a 2016 inscription on a bust of Garibaldi in the Avenida Barbieri, where he looks down towards the river. The bust shows him to be young and vigorous and was erected in 1948, the work of Edmundo Prati, a sculptor who was born in Italy but grew up in Salto. He had earlier been responsible for the monumental Plaza Artigas, the square in the centre of the city.

The recent 2016 wording celebrates the 170th anniversary of the battle of San Antonio. The inscription states that it is a tribute from "the citizens of Salto", not the Italian community, nor the *Colorados*, nor the Freemasons. It describes him as a hero of two worlds who fought for his ideals: absolute freedom of conscience; freedom of thought; freedom of expression; social equality; solidarity. "His example continues to guide us."

This was a unique example during my visit of the acknowledged contemporary relevance of the Italian adventurer. It tied in with something else I had noticed in the streets of Montevideo: posters put up by the *intendencia*, the city mayoralty, to celebrate the seventieth anniversary of the Universal Declaration of Human Rights, not something one saw on the streets of London. There is a post-dictatorship spirit that makes a Bolsonaro-style enthusiasm for generals who torture unimaginable in Uruguay.

Visiting the museum of the Rio Uruguay, in an old building by the river, was a reminder of how small the population of Salto was when Garibaldi was there. The 1833–4 census showed there were 1,315 people in the town then, and there were still only 9,500 by 1869. When Oribe's forces took Salto many fled, though foreigners stayed put, and when Garibaldi captured it he encouraged these citizens to return.

The centenary history of Salto, 1837–1937, confirmed that when General Anacleto Medina arrived there was constant friction with Garibaldi. Colonel Garibaldi overruled the general "against all order and military discipline" and: "In effect General Medina, a general in charge of an army, was expelled from Salto by Colonel Garibaldi." The whole episode, which after San Antonio saw Garibaldi recognised as a military commander and not just an admiral, was damaging for him later, leading to hostility and jealousy. It may have been one reason why his tenure as commander-in-chief of the Gobierno de la Defensa forces of Montevideo lasted for only a few days.

My final stop in Salto was the office of the Italian Association in a fine nineteenth-century building, originally the Società Italiana Unione e Benevolenza (Italian Society of Union and Charity) in Avenida Artigas. The society had started as a mutual support body for the Italian migrants, and that era of arrivals, coinciding with Italian unification and then Garibaldi's death in 1882, explained a portrait of him inside as "perpetual president" of the society and his bust facing the street. Officials of the society were meeting when I called in, but they explained that nowadays they do not commemorate either Garibaldi or the battle of San Antonio.

These mutual support societies are a feature of many of the towns developed by Italian migrants in the nineteenth century. Inspired by Catholic teaching, and linguistic and social solidarity at a time when Italy itself was a newly-born nation, it is a reminder of the fragile situation of these families starting out in the New World. Life was hard. Poor harvests could bring hunger to a farming family. Sudden accidents could be devastating, where doctors and medicines were unavailable or unaffordable. There were no pensions, sick or unemployment pay or state supports.

From Salto I took a four hour bus ride to Fray Bentos. The bus was full, with ten standing at any time and people getting on and off at small stops, sometimes met by friends in cars. There was a significant turnover at Paysandú, a substantial town and still an active port, but although the route ran southerly, parallel to the Rio Uruguay, the river was out of sight.

The series of unfenced vistas, with herds of cattle roaming free, was a reminder of how difficult it will be for Uruguay to adjust to plant-based diets, as recommended by ecologists concerned to halt climate change. Next to me for a while was one man making use of what is a staple plant—source of the *yerba maté* green tea drink which he was mixing. Regularly refreshed with hot water from a thermos, this kept him going throughout the journey: the drink is popular throughout Uruguay and neighbouring countries.

Fray Bentos, my destination, is internationally celebrated for its historic production of corned beef. Most recently in Britain, the company that bought the name has garnered publicity for its vegan "meat" pies. In fact, the industrial complex which launched a revolution in tinned food in the nineteenth century is now a world heritage site, and a friend at the Uruguayan Embassy in London said I should see it. The Liebig Extract of Meat Company was founded in 1863, only four years after the town itself, and the factory was making meat products under various owners until 1979; a local history museum and a technological university are nearby.

Justus von Liebig, the German chemist who also invented the Liebig condenser used in many labs, is seen as the father of inorganic chemistry. His discovery of a way of concentrating meat extract found a new export use for meat from Uruguayan cattle, hitherto only a source of leather. British and Belgian capital was invested in the new firm which moved into corned beef in 1873 and marketed the extract, used for flavouring soups and sauces, as OXO from 1899. Its corned beef, in easily transported tins, became a staple for the British Army in the Anglo-Boer war.

But my attraction to Fray Bentos was quite different. It was on the Uruguayan side of the wide Rio Uruguay from Gualeguaychú (pronounced *wallewashoo*) in Argentina, site of sacking and robbery by Garibaldi's men in 1845, an episode for which some have never forgiven him. It was important to visit Gualeguaychú. I consulted the staff at the Gran Hotel, overlooking the river, where flowers and candles had been put out for St Valentine's Day. They quoted a taxi price to cross a friendship bridge into Argentina that was unaffordable.

Fortunately, my friend Enrique Hernández in Montevideo had a contact who lived in Gualeguaychú who might be able to help. He was General Federico Anschütz, who had been an Argentine military attaché in London in the early 2000s, and had overlapped for a year with the then Colonel Hernández, representing Uruguay. He offered to pick me up on the Argentine side in his Peugeot. So the problem was simply to get across the bridge.

A taxi took me to the customs and immigration controls on the Uruguayan side of the river, where I was told I could not walk across— I had to go by car. Then I had a stroke of luck. A young Argentine family, returning from a holiday in Punta del Este, the great beach holiday attraction east of Montevideo, offered me a lift. There were two adults, with two children and an electric fan packed in the back already. The man had spent a year in the United States and spoke good English. Nobly they bunked up.

So I crossed this high, long bridge and, after a brief wait among a number of trucks, Federico collected me on the Argentine side. It was a good start to one of my best days in the footsteps of Garibaldi, as Federico took me on a tour and gave me fresh insight into what had happened. He explained that Garibaldi had fooled the defenders of the town by apparently bypassing it and sailing further up the Uruguay. A local pilot behaved treacherously, however, showing Garibaldi how he could navigate the tricky Rio Gualeguaychú, a tributary which ran into the Uruguay. He landed at the site of subsequent meat refrigeration, and the Argentine commander, Eduardo Villagra, was captured asleep, along with the other authorities in the town. Villagra was initially court-martialled, but ultimately vindicated when it was reckoned that he had not been at fault.

Garibaldi threatened to shoot all the captives, but was dissuaded. In the meantime some thirty-one shops and commercial establishments were pillaged, and innumerable private houses. We visited one of them, the Azoteo de Palma (the house with a roof of palm leaves); like many of the old houses it was painted red because the blood of cattle was used in the pigment. We also visited the Casa de Haedo (named after the family which occupied it) in the town centre, where Garibaldi placed a cannon on the roof and which he used as his HQ for the two days he was there.

This house is now a small museum and Raúl Ingold, in charge, showed me an article from a newspaper in 1918 in which an old lady had been interviewed and spoke up for the commander of the Italian Legion. Her family lived in the house. She had been twelve when the Italians arrived, her sister eighteen, and her parents were worried what might happen to them. They told the girls to lock the door to their room. But when a soldier tried to break down the door he was whipped by his officer.

The Italian writer, Mauro Gavillucci, in his *Seguindo o caminho de Garibaldi*, identified Gualeguaychú as the one place he visited where hostility to Garibaldi was still present. For Gavillucci he was "our hero", so it was with considerable irritation that he found a bust of Garibaldi hidden in a lavatory at the museum. But he also acknowledged that at various times in the town's past there had been serious friction between the Italian community and other citizens. As elsewhere in Argentina there had been significant Italian immigration in the late nineteenth century. Unfortunately, however, community celebration of the fall of Rome in Gualeguaychú in September 1870 coincided precisely with the anniversary of Garibaldi's raid on the twentieth of the month.

I talked more generally with Raúl Ingold and Federico Anschütz about the attitude of present-day Argentinians of Italian extraction. They suggested that there is a split today between those who see Garibaldi as a pirate, for his part in South America, and those who regard him as a hero, for his role in Italy. Federico also made an important point. He said that new nations need heroes. He instanced Garibaldi for Italy, and Abraham Lincoln for the United States.

My tour of Gualeguaychú concluded with a companionable beer with the general in a bar overlooking the river which gives its name to the town. Federico was rather pessimistic about the prospects for his country and particularly for his service, where soldiers are paid less than prison officers or customs staff. He remarked wryly that in the Malvinas/Falklands war around a thousand Argentine and British troops were killed, but that a thousand people every month die in road accidents in Argentina. "It is safer to join the army than to drive on our roads," he remarked.

He was, incidentally, critical of the lack of forethought by the Argentinian generals during their brief occupation of the Falklands in 1982. They had foolishly wanted to make Spanish the language of the islanders and force them to drive on the right of the road. As I heard this I thought of the follies committed by the Americans and British after the overthrow of Saddam Hussein in Iraq.

He had had an unfortunate recent holiday in Paraguay, Argentina's northern neighbour, where his passport and money had been stolen. He was struck to see what he described as a *favela*, a slum, in one of the main squares of Asunción, the capital, and remarked that Paraguay was a "smuggler's country". Situated in the heart of South America, there have always been easy opportunities to smuggle goods into and out of Paraguay, and there has been substantial Brazilian penetration in recent decades.

But it was a country I liked. I had briefly met General Alfredo Stroessner, its long-time dictator, at around 6 a.m. one morning in the 1960s and wrote a chapter about him in my *Political Leaders of Latin America* (1969) when my young wife and I spent a night in a *hotel familial*, which was almost certainly a knocking shop, and flew on to São Paulo in the one Líneas Aéreas Paraguayas plane that was still airworthy. This inspired me to join the Paraguay Committee for Human Rights in Britain. Later, I gate crashed a party on an island in the Rio Paraguay in the early 1980s after watching the first water flow from the giant Itaipú hydroelectric dam on the Brazilian-Paraguayan border. I had been hanging uncomfortably overhead in a helicopter with its doors open as Mike Goldwater, the photographer, took daring pictures for *The Observer Magazine*.

Federico gave me a lift back over the international bridge, since the formalities are on the Uruguayan side, and pointed out a large modern pulp mill downstream in Uruguay, owned by the Finnish company Botnia. This had been the cause of a huge international wrangle from 2007 to 2010, with Argentine activists blocking the bridge. Protestors claimed that the works would pollute the river, although a World Bank study showed no measurable harm before its International Finance Corporation made a loan of US$170 million to build the mill.

Successive Peronist presidents of Argentina, the husband and wife duo of Néstor and Cristina Kirchner, made a major nationalist and environmental issue out of the pulp mill. Activists thought the blockade might strangle Uruguay's tourist industry, as the bridge was a popular route for Argentinians driving to Montevideo and Punta del Este. The Uruguayan government, for whom 12,000 jobs were at stake, stood firm behind Botnia, and in April 2010 the International Court of Justice at The Hague ruled in favour of Uruguay.

The upshot was an agreement to update an existing Rio Uruguay treaty by the creation of the Comisión Administradora del Rio Uruguay (Administrative Commission for the River Uruguay) to monitor pollution. Traffic now flows freely over the bridge, and the Uruguayan government has approved another pulp mill near Conchillas, where the Uruguay turns into the Plate. Commenting on the controversy, Federico said he thought there were far more important environmental issues on the Argentine side of the border about which campaigners should protest.

My next stop was Colonia del Sacramento, another city on UNESCO's world heritage list, with a pretty cobbled centre and surviving walls, overlooking the River Plate. It had been founded by the Portuguese in 1680 and remained in their hands for almost a century. The Gulbenkian Foundation, which funds Lusophone heritage and culture around the world, has rehabilitated a small, simple, single-storey house dating from that era. But what I thought would be a two-hour bus ride to Colonia from Fray Bentos turned out to take four, and the hotel which I had chosen, though central, had a haywire internet connection and lacked a fridge, a lockable safe or a laundry service. Everywhere else in Uruguay the internet connection had been fine, but this coincided with a Skype call to a conference in Accra in which I had promised to participate, and there were several interruptions.

My plan was to chill out in Colonia. Garibaldi had taken the town with assistance from the British and French in 1845, although Oribe recaptured it three years later. It was possible that the municipal museum and the naval museum might have something about him. Both are sited in the old quarter. In fact, the municipal museum was supposed to contain a Garibaldi bust, but when I failed to find it in any of the rooms I was told that it was not on display because the displays are rotated. The small naval museum had no reference to the admiral of the Montevideo fleet. My attempts to make contact with the honorary consul of Italy, and Helena Corbellini, a romantic novelist who had written *El sublevado—Garibaldi, corsair del Rio de la Plata* in 2009, were both fruitless.

Corbellini, who lived in Colonia, had done serious research for her fiction. Gavillucci had been staying in a hotel next to her house and met her by chance. She told him that although Garibaldi is commemorated in street names and statuary, he had been written out of history books used for teaching purposes some years ago. This was partly for political reasons, and her own Italian grandparents hated him, probably because they were *Blancos*. It was more surprising that the Frente Amplio and the Uruguayan left were hostile to him, given his commitment to democracy and progressive causes. Corbellini told Gavillucci:

> In effect, Garibaldi was never either a *Blanco* or a *Colorado*. He was only interested in the freedom of the Uruguayan people, which was threatened by the interference of the Argentine dictator, Rosas. Garibaldi was like a cyclone that agitated the sky of the Uruguayan civil war. It was the Colorado Party which appropriated the 'Italian giant' and not the other way about, for he was not linked to any party.

Colonia is only around an hour away from Buenos Aires by fast ferry and I also saw the odd cruise ship. But its freight business collapsed when Uruguay and Argentina were linked by modern bridges crossing the Rio Uruguay. Another piece of transport history has been preserved in the Colonia railway station, close to the Plate. A few rails, the station building and the sign are all that remain of a service from Montevideo that began in 1901 and closed as late as 1985. While there has been talk of reviving Uruguay's rail network the hotel association of Colonia now uses the station building.

It is a town that lives today by tourism, and watching the sun going down over the Plate with a beer in my hand gave me a mellow feeling. Nonetheless, my arrival in early 2019 coincided with a plunge in Uruguay's visitor totals. The Ministry of Tourism reported that the number of foreigners coming to the honeypot of Punta del Este had fallen by 50 per cent in the first six weeks of the year, and hotels were cutting prices by 20 per cent. Much of this was due to a sharp reduction in tourists coming from Brazil and Paraguay, due to their economic stagnation. In consequence, almost three-quarters of all visitors were from Argentina, and they were insufficient.

In my short time in Uruguay I heard few American or British voices. Colonia offered two British exceptions—a Hooray Henry couple, lounging with drinks by the Plate, and a slightly travel-weary young family with two small children whom I spoke to in the lift at my hotel. They were returning from a day trip to Buenos Aires. They were near the end of an exciting couple of weeks, where they had stayed on an *estancia* and visited several places of interest, giving their children a trip they would probably always remember. One felt pleased for the children, and their parents.

Returning to Montevideo I could have taken the faster Colonia Express but my slower bus allowed me to take in the sight of a full-length statue of Garibaldi on the main road out of Colonia. Appropriately, for a former commander-in-chief of one of the armies in the civil war, it was just outside the barracks of an army battalion. On the road I passed the first group of wind turbines I had seen in the country. There were few solar panels either and, for a country lacking oil or gas, Uruguay relies considerably on hydroelectricity.

My last day in Montevideo, where my hotel upgraded me as a returning visitor, was especially useful. Milka Rappa of the Garibaldi Association came to see me and gave me various items of interest, including copies of its journal, *Garibaldi*, and of the wedding certificate of Giuseppe and Anita, which showed that while recognised as married by the Church, they did not receive its full blessing. She told me she thought that Giuseppe's love of freedom was born of his love of the freedom of the sea.

Argentinians, as well as Uruguayans, had supported the campaign to protect the Casa Garibaldi, where the family had lived, and turn it into a museum. Well into the twentieth century the building was being used as a shop. Milka's father had been part of the campaign to conserve it. The Association had been founded in 1985, the year of the first issue of the journal, but publication had become erratic and the last number came out in 2016. In the second decade of the twentieth century the 20 September date of the liberation of Rome was celebrated as a national holiday in Uruguay, but this had fallen into disuse by the 1930s.

Milka acknowledged that repair and management of the Casa Garibaldi would cost money: damp and humidity from the building next door had seeped through. A different perspective was given to me when I met Gabriella Galeotti of the Istituto Italiano di Cultura, the cultural wing of the embassy. She said that the real problem with the Casa was that there was not much to see there—a uniform, books, a sword, the flag of the Italian Legion. It attracted few visitors and there was a staff cost for the historical museum which had managed it.

She made the surprising suggestion that more people may remember Garibaldi in Uruguay than they do in Italy. She thought that Italians generally had an attitude of "Thanks, but no thanks", seeing him as running a private army and a bit player in the drama of the Risorgimento. She confirmed that, with the Association, the Istituto runs an annual event on 20 September. There are also new angles being explored. For example, in 2011 the national post office had put out a stamp of Andrés Aguiar on horseback, in its series on *Personalidades Afrouruguayos* (Afro-Uruguayan Personalities).

The Istituto itself is flourishing, teaching Italian to 300 students each year and running cultural events. She said that most adults wanting to learn the language do so for reasons of "the heart" because parents or grandparents had come from Italy. But there are practical reasons, too. People wanting to obtain European Union citizenship find the language valuable, and a recent law passed by the right-wing and populist coalition government of the Lega and the Five Star Movement now requires spouses who want citizenship to reach B1 language proficiency.

She confirmed that extreme right-wing politics have little appeal in Uruguay, where there are still marches for those who disappeared during the dictatorship, and bodies are still being dug up. Gabriella instanced Macarena Gelman, a deputy in parliament and human rights campaigner, who only recovered her identity in this century. She is the granddaughter of Juan Gelman, an Argentine poet who died in exile in Mexico. His son and daughter-in-law were killed—her remains have yet to be recovered—and Macarena was born in prison and then forcibly "adopted". President Jorge Batlle of Uruguay ordered an investigation in 2000 which revealed her true identity, and she regained her Gelman surname.

My final dinner in Montevideo was with Enrique Hernández, who had been my mentor throughout. He chose a restaurant called El

Berritín—The Hideaway—quite close to where I was staying at the Mercure, on the Rambla Mahatma Gandhi. The restaurant had a series of rooms but he had booked a remote one with a glass floor. This allowed one to look down into an earthen void which had housed a Tupamaro arms dump during the struggle of the urban guerrillas. For someone British it was contemporary history with a twist. Are there any restaurants in Belfast which allow one to look down to a hiding place to see where a former IRA or Protestant militia arms cache was kept? The Troubles in Northern Ireland were running at the same time as this guerrilla war.

My travels in Uruguay were not as extensive as they had been in Brazil, but it was obvious that the Garibaldi of Uruguay is not the same as the Garibaldi of Brazil. In Brazil he had been a sailor and fighter for the *Farroupilhas*, and had played a crucial role in the capture of Laguna and the attempt to challenge the empire's mastery at sea. But he was not that militarily important for the Republic of Rio Grande, and he is recollected more as the partner of Anita, dubbed the heroine of two worlds.

In Uruguay his status is different, more important and more contested. He spent twice the time in Uruguay that he had spent in Brazil. He tried to break the Argentine blockade of Montevideo, and his expeditions up the Paraná in 1842 and the Uruguay in 1845 had both practical and morale-raising implications. He was a serious admiral and general serving the Gobierno de la Defensa, which was why he was briefly made its commander-in-chief. His invention and leadership of the Italian Legion was a major contribution to the idea of Italian unity. It gave him the credit and experience which were necessary for his subsequent career in Europe.

Nonetheless, it is remarkable that while there is a town named after him in Rio Grande do Sul, Brazil, there is no municipality bearing his name in Uruguay. The impact of Italian immigration in the nineteenth century was not so different in the two neighbours. It is also a cause for reflection that in Argentina, with its strongly nationalistic historiography in a line from Rosas to the Kirchners via Juan Perón, the Irish-American Admiral William Brown is today celebrated as the founder of the Argentine Navy. He, too, had to overcome nationalist opposition at the beginning of his career. Now that the *Colorado-Blanco* hostilities are calmer, the time would seem ripe to reassess Garibaldi's contribution in Uruguay.

12

AN ITALIAN IN THE STEPS OF A HERO

It was thanks to Vitor Gonçalves, *prefeito* of Piratini, that I learnt that an Italian writer, Mauro Gavillucci, had visited Brazil and Uruguay only a few years before me, and on a related quest. Gonçalves had been the secretary for tourism at the time, being elected *prefeito* more recently.

Gonçalves gave me a copy of the Portuguese-language version of Gavillucci's book whose Italian title was *Sulle trace di Garibaldi*. It had first been published in 2011 in Italian, to tie in with the 150th anniversary of the unification of Italy. Its Portuguese edition, with a nod in the direction of the 125th anniversary in 2014 of Brazil as a republic, came out five years later as *Um Italiano seguindo o caminho de Garibaldi: José e sua Anita entre Brasil, Uruguai e Argentina*.[1]

Gavillucci's book, which is well illustrated, has a different origin from mine. He had had no prior interest in Brazil or Latin America. As he explains in the first chapter, he had first been attracted to the subject when he was staying for three years on the small island of La Maddalena, where he was running a literary festival. La Maddalena is linked by a bridge to Garibaldi's island of Caprera, just off Sardinia. He had also grown up close to the mausoleum in Aprilia, where Menotti Garibaldi is buried, and went to the state school named after him. When he decided he would try to retrace Giuseppe's path in South America his project was blessed in Rome by Anita Garibaldi, the warrior's great-granddaughter.

Born in 1961, he had had a varied career. He had started a magazine when he was under twenty-six, and had written for several journals and reviews. He was an active tourism promoter and had organised concerts, gastronomic and literary festivals. He had lectured on tourism marketing and event launches, and from 2000 to 2010 had published a marketing annual for fifty-five Italian cities from Rome to Naples. He was also personally fond of travel. In 1996 he had toured round the Balkans, writing an account with a title of 'Christmas in Sarajevo'.

He writes that he was worried about a feeling of pessimism in Italy at a time when the old political parties were losing support and the populist Northern League was changing street and other names that honoured Garibaldi. It had not helped that the *Azzurri*, the country's football team, had been knocked out of the soccer World Cup in South Africa in 2010. He was not a narrow nationalist, but wished to remember the heroism displayed by Giuseppe even before he returned to Europe. Throughout his book he constantly refers to him as "our hero".

He fell in love with the pampas and to simplify his account for readers he alternated chapters of travelogue with history. He spent rather longer on his tour than I did, getting to places like Gualeguay in Argentina and the island of Martín García, on the border of Argentina and Uruguay where the Paraná and Uruguay rivers flow into the Plate. For much of his journey he was driving round in a Chevrolet Celta, a small, Brazilian-built hatchback also known as the Suzuki Fun in Argentina. He advertised his purpose, that he was travelling in the steps of Garibaldi, with posters on the car in the three languages of Italian, Portuguese and Spanish, and made a point of calling on tourist offices and *prefeitos* wherever he could. But in Montevideo he was unable to see the Italian Ambassador.

His aim seems to have been to stimulate Italian tourism as well as to awaken Italian national pride. Because of the parallel to my own inquiries on the ground, and the fact that we were both challenging that European lens which reads backwards from his campaigns in Italy to Garibaldi's twelve years in South America, it is worth reflecting on what Gavillucci found, and comparing it with my own impressions. For what is too often written off hastily in Europe as an apprenticeship deserves more consideration, both for the past and the present.

He appears to have spent around sixty days in his research in the two countries, roughly twice as long as I did. Like me he started his travels in Rio de Janeiro, taking a coach from there to Rio Grande at the southern end of the Lagoa do Patos. He fought off a man armed with a knife who threatened him and tried to rob him of his camera in Rio's Copacabana district. He was concerned about security for tourists, mentioning that central Montevideo could also be dangerous. He spent a couple of days searching Rio's old port area before locating "the sacred quays" where he thought Garibaldi had tied up on arrival in the *Nautonnier*. He was caught up in Brazil's World Cup fever, as girls in Brazil T-shirts stopped traffic outside his hotel, and no one seemed to mind.

In Rio Grande he picked up his white Celta car and then followed a zig-zag route through Uruguay and southern Brazil: to Maldonado in Uruguay and into Gualeguay in Argentina; then back via Uruguay into Piratini and Camaquã in Rio Grande do Sul; then up the coast to Laguna in Santa Catarina, to the towns of Lages, Anita Garibaldi and Garibaldi, then São José do Norte and Mostardas; then to Montevideo, Buenos Aires, Gualeguaychú, Colonia and Salto. He then headed north to Rio and visited Salvador de Bahia, where Bento Gonçalves had been imprisoned on an island fort.

My own two-part investigation was less complex, beginning in Brazil. Starting from Rio and flying to Porto Alegre I had then gone by car to the town of Garibaldi, to Camaquã, to Pelotas, Piratini, Rio Grande, Mostardas, Laguna, Imbituba, Anita Garibaldi, Curitibanos, Lages and Porto Alegre, returning to London via São Paulo. My second exploration, in Uruguay, was simpler still—a series of bus trips from Montevideo to Salto and Fray Bentos, Gualeguaychú (by car courtesy of Federico Anschütz and an Argentinian friend), then buses to Colonia and back to Montevideo.

In Rio, Gavillucci was also struck by how little was known of Garibaldi. Someone told him it was a very good wine, the first he learnt of the significance of the town of Garibaldi as a wine producer. There was some knowledge of both Giuseppe and Anita from the *Globo telenovela* of 2003, *A Casa das Sete Mulheres*, which had given a stronger role to Giuseppe than in the original novel by Letícia Wierzchowski. But the fact that the Brazilian Senate had added Anita's name to the Brazilian pantheon in 2009, for example, had left no trace in public awareness.

Driving into Uruguay he called in at Maldonado, close to the luxury resort of Punta del Este, which he thought put the poorer housing of southern Brazil to shame. A hotel receptionist and someone in the tourist office told him where there had once been a mill and a quay. He saw an upper room, where Garibaldi had stayed in 1837, and had his photo taken with his arm around a bust, courtesy of the Italian circle of Maldonado.

Unlike me he crossed over to Gualeguay in Argentina, where Garibaldi was put under house arrest, escaped and was then tortured. He photographed a modern building, now a bank branch, which he thought was on the site of the house where he was held for at least six months. He stayed in the Gran Hotel, in a room opposite one occupied by the Argentine writer Jorge Luis Borges some twenty years earlier, and paid a visit to the little river port of Ibicuy, which had been Garibaldi's objective in his failed escape. The offices of the local Italian society contained various items including what is said to be the cross-beam from which Garibaldi was suspended when he was being tortured by Millan.

The author believes that it was in Gualeguay that his hero learnt to ride like a *gaúcho*, whereas I was told that it was Anita who trained him on horseback in Laguna. More romantically, he has written that this was where Giuseppe assuaged his powerful libido, bringing conquests to a damp cavern which he was welcomed to use in a general store outside the town. The general store is now a farmhouse, baptised *La Garibaldina*, and Gavillucci met persons claiming descent from Garibaldi and a young waitress named Pérez. He printed a genealogy over five generations. Their daughter, Angela Pérez, lived to be 105, well into the twentieth century, and the deputy mayor, when he visited, was a remote descendant.

Gavillucci pays attention in his book to the importance of Free-masonry for Garibaldi, the Italians in South America, the *Farroupilhas* and the Gobierno de la Defensa. In Italy in the late 1970s there had been a scandal involving the P2 Lodge of Freemasonry, said to be oper-ating a state within a state with powerful contacts both in the world of politics and the Roman Catholic Church. So he explains to his readers that in South America today, as in Garibaldi's era, the Masons are both widely spread and generally respected.

He pinpoints the wide reach of the Masons, publishing a pyramidal drawing in a Maldonado museum which illustrates the international structure of their rites, and listing people who helped him such as Vitor Gonçalves and Adílcio Cadorin as members of the brotherhood. Gonçalves and a friend took him to see their Masonic Lodge in Piratini and he wrote that while Italians think of Masons as a gang of acolytes with no sense of fraternity, "Vitor and others spoke to me of freemasonry as an association for mutual aid, formed by true brothers of different generations, social classes and educational level, with completely different economic and occupational status."[2]

Visiting Piratini he was struck by the quantity of *Farroupilha* memorabilia in museums, although a local lawyer told him that there was little documentary evidence of Garibaldi's visits. He then drove up beside the Lagoa dos Patos to São Lourenço do Sul, because he wanted to visit the Estancia do Brejo, the house of the seven women in Bento Gonçalves' family which had featured in the novel and *telenovela*.

Now known as the Fazenda do Sobrado, it was bought from the family of Bento Gonçalves in 1926, and Gavillucci was able to wander through rooms, imagining where his hero had walked, danced and broken the heart of the young Manoela, forbidden to marry him. The house and grounds are playing a role in the modern Farroupilha Way, when *gaúcho* riders pass through, and in 2009 the estate had hosted the sacred flame, the *Chama Crioula*, which is a feature of the annual cavalcade.

Beside the house he was shown some blood red flowers known as the flowers of St John, which were a Masonic emblem, and a few hundred metres away, by the small Rio São Lourenço, he saw a stone building where Garibaldi and his Masonic brethren met for Masonic rites. He was told that to meet in woodland close to a river meant that votaries were permeated by the divine, and nature rules all. Further along the lake he saw another house belonging to Bento Gonçalves, now being refurbished, near to the site of Garibaldi's shipyard.

He noted with approval that São Lourenço do Sul was investing heavily in its tourism industry. But its German links were the priority. German families had settled in the area in the nineteenth and twentieth centuries, and houses, guesthouses and public buildings showed their strong architectural influence.

People who helped him also helped me, and of course we had different contacts, too. Like me he had been impressed by the energy with which Elma Sant'Ana and Adílcio Cadorin were seeking to keep Anita's memory alive. Elma Sant'Ana had introduced him to Neliane Ereno, then with the secretariat of culture in Rio Grande do Sul, who had started a section of "Anitas" linked initially to a Piquete de Anita and a Círculo Menotti Garibaldi. The "Anitas" had combined long-distance riding on horseback, following cross-country tracks used by the *Farroupilhas*, with social and cultural projects for poor children. Sant'Ana saw the horse and riding as integral to *gaúcho* culture. While she told me that she did not conceive of her "Anitas" as precisely feminist, she explained to Gavillucci what had really attracted her about the young heroine. "Anita represents the emancipation of women. She left her home, her habits, her friends and her town to give herself totally to an adventurer from the old world, a corsair in command of a tiny fleet for a little state. Above all a young woman from Santa Catarina threw everything aside and embarked bravely on a new life, dedicating herself entirely to the republican cause," she said.[3]

Gavillucci himself thought that Anita should still be held up today as an example. He felt she ought to be an inspiration for those who work in social fields and with students, and for those who fight on behalf of the poorest and most deprived.

In Laguna his luck was in when he met Antônio Célio, then the *prefeito*, within ten minutes of turning up at his office without an appointment. Célio had been elected for the PT, the leftist party, and had succeeded Cadorin. He held this position for two terms, from 2005 to 2012, and though arguably not as super-enthusiastic as Cadorin, he told Gavillucci that the culture and history of Laguna were clearly marked by the importance of Anita and the Julian Republic. He took pride in the claim that the short-lived Julian Republic was the first government in the Americas to free the slaves.[4] The author handed him a letter from the Mayor of Ardea, an old commune south of Rome, who raised the possibility of a twinning between the two. When I visited later, it did not seem that anything had come of this.

Gavillucci found that the Laguna museum dedicated to Anita was closed for restoration, a frustration I shared later, but he came across one or two items of interest, including a letter of September 1877 in which Garibaldi said he would like to be cremated. His body was not cremated, however, as cremation was still illegal in Italy, and the author remarked that, even in death, he was frustrated by the great power of the Roman Catholic Church. He also saw one of Anita's houses, now a shop, where Garibaldi knocked on a boarded window when he wanted an assignation; he was told that young lovers still knock on it, swearing undying affection. A little Madonna, thought to have belonged to Anita, had been found under a floor during recent building works. He also met a seventy-nine-year-old, of Italian-Amerindian origin, whose ancestors had known Garibaldi and who told him that Anita had returned to live with her family after her husband deserted her, and before she met Giuseppe.

Gavillucci was, like me, impressed with the vigour with which Cadorin had promoted Laguna's Garibaldi connection when he was in office. He had run a worldwide campaign to boost tourism in the name of Anita. With a few friends he had followed "Anita's Way", starting in Curitibanos and travelling via Lages, Vacaria, São Gabriel, Mostardas and São José do Norte into Uruguay. He had visited Italy, where an Italian deputy had asked why Anita's remains had not been returned to Brazil, leading him to start a fruitless campaign which had even met opposition in Laguna.

Cadorin said that his push for tourism had been a great success, and there had been a growth in tourists from Italy in particular. Once people in Laguna could see a commercial return they began to take a different view of the value of the town's history. Interestingly, the town's coat of arms shows a reconciliation between *Farroupilhas* and imperialists, with a soldier from each of the protagonists standing on either side of a shield.

After Laguna the Italian drove up into the mountains of the Serra, anxious about the sharp drops beside the road. He did not stay long in Lages when he realised that there was a town named Anita Garibaldi, given the name in homage to the passage nearby of the escaping Anita after her capture at Curitibanos. He thought it auspicious that the town had been given the status of a *prefeitura* in 1961, the year of his birth. Anita with her horse had had to swim through the fast-flowing Pelotas and Canoas rivers, but the region had been transformed since the 1960s. There were now three huge hydroelectric dams on each of these

183

rivers and at the point where they join. As a result Anita Garibaldi was selling itself as a city of lakes, and it is a fishing paradise for visitors from throughout Latin America.

In Vacaria the secretary of tourism told him that the adventures of Giuseppe and Anita are studied in schools throughout Brazil, a line contradicted when I toured only eight years later, which suggests that he was being fed information that he wanted to hear. In the town of Garibaldi he had the satisfaction of visiting a place where 70 per cent of the population was of Italian origin. He noted that it prospered from the production of sparkling wine, which he adored, and chickens, which he detested. He waxed lyrical: "This enclave of 40,000 souls, different from typical Brazilian towns, is incredible. Almost everything here is Italian, even the architectural style. There is no poverty or unemployment. It seems to be a tiny, perfect world." He met Italians, as well as those of Italian origin, and someone he met at dinner was so impressed that he broke away to get hold of a copy of the Dumas biography and wrote in dedication: "Garibaldi was a man who lived fighting social injustice."

Gavillucci then drove south to Rio Grande at the southern end of the Lagoa dos Patos. He was impressed by this modern maritime city, a superport where large-scale oil rigs are constructed to service Brazil's offshore oil boom. He chatted up the secretary of tourism, Abdo Tafuik Nader, and discussed a "Garibaldi Tourist Route", in which he said that, including Rio Grande, eight municipalities were now interested.

He also visited São José do Norte, where he went into a craft shop selling ponchos and other *gaúcho* regalia, luckier with ponchos than I was in Mostardas. He saw the strategic importance of the twin ports on either side of a narrow strip of water which provided access to the Atlantic to ships going to and from the Lagoa dos Patos. Reinforcements from the empire had had to pass through to reach Porto Alegre and the other lakeside ports during the civil war, and São José was the scene of one of the bloodiest battles when the *Farroupilhas*, including Garibaldi, failed to capture it. They had taken three out of four of its forts, but the imperial defenders were saved when naval ships from Rio Grande came to their aid.

He remarked that in this defeat Garibaldi won his umpteenth victory by ordering the republican commanders to stop decapitating their captured enemies. He thereby saved the lives of hundreds of young men and was given a doctor by the imperial army in acknowledgement. Some had been killed already in this way, and he said that young men like these would be useful for their country in the future.

Gavillucci, who was taking photos of busts and statues of his hero wherever he went, found that the Italian colony had erected a bust in 1941. But a new museum of the *Farroupilha* war had closed two years before his visit, having run out of funds. He was pleased that a marble flagstone for the "hero of two worlds" had been inscribed on 16 July 1882, only just after a month following his death on Caprera. He thought it was the first recognition in Latin America following his demise.

In Mostardas, twinned with Aprilia where Menotti is buried, Gavillucci brought a letter of good wishes from Aprilia's mayor. His visit to the town started poorly, as he could not find the *prefeito*, arrived at nightfall and felt that he had reached the ends of the earth. His mobile phone was not working. But then he cheered up as he found the commemorative plaque from 1996, recording Menotti's birth on 16 September 1840 and the twinning of Mostardas and Aprilia. He located a legendary tree, said to be the site of Menotti's birth, and in a moment of fantasy he compared a hole at the base of the tree with the manger in Bethlehem, birthplace of Jesus. He was shown the registration of Menotti's birth and met red-shirted *gaúchos* who belong to the Centro Cultural Nativista Menotti Garibaldi. He had difficulty, however, in enjoying the *mate* tea, the drink so common in the pampas regions, but was delighted that the Centro Nativista laid on a rodeo and party for him. He believed that Menotti was known throughout Rio Grande do Sul, thanks to these performers.

While he saw many marks of recognition of Aprilia in Mostardas, he compared them unfavourably with the lack of attention to Menotti or Mostardas in Italy. Few people visit his mausoleum. Since 1996 the local authorities in Italy had done little to follow up the twinning. The public, in consequence, were uninterested. Yet Menotti was a figure of historical importance, and Aprilia does not have many others.

Gavillucci drove to Montevideo via the border town of Chuí. When he got there with the "Garibaldi-car" emblazoned with his quest in three languages, he raised a smile at traffic lights and from people standing in bus queues. Initially stopped from entering Garibaldi's house in Montevideo, he did manage to get inside with assistance from the National Historical Museum in the Casa Rivera. The tiny quarters, with shared bathroom, were an eye-opener. He noticed various plaques on the walls, including one from the northern Italian city of Bergamo, which had provided so many volunteers to join The Thousand in Sicily. There were plaques from the Garibaldi Association and the Association of Descendants of the *Farroupilhas*. He was not surprised to see a Masonic plaque from the Gran Logia de la Masonería del Uruguay on behalf of three lodges: Garibaldi, Libres Pensadores and XX de Setiembre.

In the offices of the Colorado Party he thought that Garibaldi, with a bronze bust, enjoyed more honour than Fructuoso Rivera whose image was almost hidden, perhaps because his career had ended in infamy. Garibaldi, by contrast, was as visible as the founder of modern Uruguay, José Batlle y Ordóñez. Having assumed that the *Colorados* were a leftist party, not least because of Garibaldi's militancy, he realised that in Italian terms they were closer to the Social Democrats, while the *Blancos* were more like the Christian Democrats.

His sense of adventure took him into the southern district of Montevideo, the poorer and traditionally Afro-Uruguayan streets where I later watched the *candombé* processions. He chatted to young layabouts, turned down an offer of cannabis, and was seriously worried that when he started filming he might be robbed. He thought that the local youth had been angry since birth, that the streets were a school for violence, and that they were currently depressed because the national football team had been beaten in the FIFA World Cup. Yet his capacity for friendship won them over. He bought them a drink, and distributed some cash. At a cost equivalent to eighty euros and being called "our yankee friend", he parted from them on the best of terms and had had an unforgettable day.

In Colonia, as described earlier, he had met the novelist Helena Corbellini. In addition to talking about Garibaldi she remarked that the Frente Amplio, now in power, did not share a regard for him. But she also criticised Fructuoso Rivera as a culturally inadequate *caudillo*, who could not draw up or elaborate the independence constitution. He was a poor commander, defeated at Arroyo Grande and India Muerta, and retreated into Brazil in a cowardly fashion after leading his troops to their death.

Gavillucci was delighted to interview the former *Colorado* president, Julio Maria Sanguinetti, known to be an enthusiast, who told him optimistically that the legacy of Garibaldi is intact in Uruguay. He was a prominent figure in the headquarters of the party. "He is still, today, a symbol for the *Colorados* and all South American liberals." He had a clear concept of the republic, respect for the individual, and was hostile to slavery. The author reflected that this Garibaldi spirit has become soiled and rusty in Italy itself, overtaken by local disputes of a kind that absorbed the *communes* in medieval times.

But he did not appear to have asked Sanguinetti about the attempts that Italian fascism had made to use the Garibaldi legacy for propaganda purposes. When he visited Salto he was impressed by this. The 1930 bronze monument on the esplanade by the River Uruguay had been presented by the fascist regime to the city of Salto to celebrate the centenary of the republic of Uruguay. When he visited the modernist, Bauhaus-influenced Garibaldi monument at San Antonio he recalled the political reality of Mussolini's fascism. The style was similar to buildings and public monuments in Mussolini's new towns near Rome, like Littoria, Sabaudia, Pontinia, Aprilia and Pomezia.

On 4 July 2011, the anniversary of Garibaldi's birth, there was a celebration of repairs completed to the Veltroni monument and the *prefeito* of Salto signed a twinning agreement with Cairo Montenotte. This is a town in the Italian region of Liguria, and the agreement was to honour soldiers from Cairo Montenotte who had died in the battle of San Antonio.

Gavillucci placed a lot of emphasis on the potential of town twinning, and it is worth stopping to consider this phenomenon. Town twinning is widespread in continental Europe, probably first as a local response to underpin Franco-German reconciliation in the 1950s, after three wars between the two nations. It took off more widely as the European community gained adherents and strength. In the United Kingdom, for example, it became a significant movement in the 1970s after the country had joined the then European Economic Community. Towns would twin with one or more places elsewhere in Europe. Grander cities would seek more prestigious partners, villages would link with villages.

But the content has varied enormously. Sometimes it would just be a matter of exchange visits between local worthies. Sometimes there were school visits, or an exchange between professional groups. Local authorities did not necessarily invest in these visits, leaving costs to be borne by individuals or sponsors. In the internet era it is uncertain that these links have been warm or close enough to provide frequent meaningful attachments.

More seriously, these twinnings have had to run the gauntlet of political change and the cost of travel. Two London boroughs illustrate these limitations. In the 1980s the borough of Lambeth, which had been twinned with Vincennes in Paris since 1955, was twinned with Bluefields, Nicaragua, an English-speaking, African Caribbean town on its Atlantic coast. This was at a time when the leftist Sandinistas had come to power in Nicaragua and Lambeth had a leftist Labour council. It was a political gesture, which respected the African Caribbeans in the borough, a reason for also twinning with historic Spanish Town in Jamaica. There were Sandinista festivals in the borough, and an activist renovated a dilapidated terrace house, donating the money after it was sold to social causes in Nicaragua. Lambeth has also acquired twins in Brooklyn, New York and Shinjuku, in Japan.

In the case of Greenwich, which became a royal borough in London in 2010, two of its twins, Maribor in Slovenia and Reinickendorf in Germany, were the product of sympathies in the Cold War; the link with Maribor was made in 1966, when Slovenia was still part of Yugoslavia, and Reinickendorf was a working class district of West Berlin, when the city was still divided. In the 1980s, when there was a major coal strike aimed at the then Conservative government, Greenwich was briefly twinned with Easington, a coal mining district in north-east England.

Although Labour has kept control in both of these London boroughs, a changing degree of political enthusiasm has meant some wavering in the significance of the twinnings. There are serious travel costs in the more distant links. There are no direct flights, for instance, from Lambeth, or even London Heathrow, to Bluefields, or even to the international airport at Managua, capital of Nicaragua. Citizens of Greenwich were not encouraged to visit Maribor in 2012, the year the Slovenian city was European Capital of Culture. Twinning for school students has become more possible with Skype, Facetime and the tools of social media, but that requires leadership, commitment and persistence from often overworked teachers.

The sheer cost of town twinning is a major obstacle. The twenty-first century has seen a number of British towns "untwinning" from European counterparts, the product of austerity and disillusion with the European project. When Peter Davies became mayor of Doncaster in 2009 he scrapped its five town twinning arrangements, as a cash-saving measure. "Only about a dozen people ever benefited from these trips. I can see that it arose out of altruistic motives after the war, but it just became about junkets," he said.

The idea that Italian towns of modest size may be able to put much effort or resources into twinning with partners in southern Brazil is at least questionable. Current politics in Italy may not be helpful. Italy, particularly in the north, is going through a rightist upsurge. The town of Predappio near Bologna, where Mussolini was born and is buried, is seeing a boom in visits from admirers of fascism, and the mayor wants to open his crypt throughout the year. Garibaldi represents a totally different tradition. Further, Brazilian towns do not share the European culture of twinning. This may be different in Central America. Interestingly, in spite of political divisions between Nicaragua and the United States, many Nicaraguan towns have links with the USA.

Following publication of his book in Italy in 2011 Gavillucci was invited to return to South America later in the year to present his findings and to follow up on the tourism connections he had promoted. His visit was timed to coincide with the Farroupilha Week in September, and included nine days in Mostardas. He was the only foreigner present in Piratini on 1 October for the ceremony of the *Chama Permanente*, the arrival of a spark from the flame that had been carried round the state, ending Farroupilha Week in Porto Alegre.

The "sacred flame" had recently been written into state law no. 13.600 "to continue to illuminate the path of those who value our traditions", the result of successful lobbying by those who were pushing the *Farroupilha* heritage. The presidents of the Movimento Tradicionalista Gaúcha and the Ordem dos Cavalarianos de Rio Grande were among the participants.

So what can one conclude? Gavillucci is unique as a contemporary Italian in undertaking an extensive pilgrimage in the steps of Garibaldi, and keeping a record. Plainly he enjoyed his road trip and opportunities to chat up random acquaintances intrigued by the notices on his car, as well as more significant Garibaldi enthusiasts. His interest in tourism, and twinning possibilities with Italian towns, shines through. His chapters of history show a careful respect for what is known of Giuseppe and Anita in South America.

His perspective was that of someone who enjoyed being a tourist himself, and was also an expert who could see the potential for increased Garibaldi-related tourism between the Plate region and Italy. His contacts in the Italian communities he visited gave him local information, but may have made him too ready to believe what he wanted to hear. In Uruguay it is plain that Garibaldi is not an undisputed national hero. My own approach and findings were more sceptical, more affected by political awareness, understanding the weak educational underpinning of knowledge in the public at large.

For Gavillucci, both Giuseppe and Anita were unquestioned heroes of the two worlds, and there is an element of hagiography in his road trip. More than once, too, he acknowledges a moment of sadness when he has to move on from a town where they lived and fought, to the next stop on his odyssey. He filmed and wrote blogs to try to fix his memories.

There is also a sub-text to his travels and writing. This is emphasised by his frequent references to "our hero". He is reminding compatriots of a heroic era, before modern Italy was created, of courage, altruism and romance in every sense of the word. The idea of Italy, dreamed of in southern Brazil and Uruguay, may have been more attractive than the messy reality, with the compromises as well as heroics that attended unification.

Garibaldi and the Risorgimento may seem like ancient history in the twenty-first century, and less heroic populists occupy the country's airtime and bandwidth. What Gavillucci seems to be saying is that there was, and maybe still could be, an idealised Italy of bravery, single-mindedness and concern for other peoples, as well as for those who live in the peninsula.

PART 4

REFLECTIONS

13

GARIBALDI, HISTORY, SOUTH AMERICA

The British historian, A.J.P. Taylor (1906–90), once described Garibaldi as "the only admirable figure in modern history". This was a twentieth-century European view, reflecting Giuseppe's austerity, courage and single-minded devotion to the unification of Italy. But with the passage of time his star has waned in Europe and he was no hero to the recent right-wing government in Italy. As I discovered in my travels in southern Brazil and Uruguay, knowledge of him there, too, has diminished. It is overlaid by issues of tourism, contemporary politics and amnesia even among those of Italian descent. When Melvyn Bragg, the British broadcaster, discussed Garibaldi in a BBC radio programme on 1 December, 2016, he was plainly surprised to learn that the standard-bearer of the Risorgimento had spent such a significant period in South America.[1]

As a "hero of two worlds" it is perhaps inevitable that so far as he is remembered at all he is recalled separately by different populations on either side of the Atlantic. Few would agree with Henry Ford, the US car manufacturer, who said history was "bunk". The inventor and entrepreneur was a disrupter in his day, creating a system of mass production which made a new means of transport affordable for ordinary families, offering new freedoms. The past, for Ford, was irrelevant.

This is not the case for most people, for history comprises their family, their identity, and their social situation. It is only partly mediated through the formal education system, which in most countries is erratic, and inevitably nationalistic. What is covered in the curriculum is partial, slow to change and vulnerable to the enthusiasms of an education minister. How it is taught depends on the teacher. I still recall with pleasure how a history teacher at my secondary school, taking our standard textbook about the Tudors and Stuarts, which was a favourite period for study in sixteenth- and seventeenth-century English history, used the same material to reach opposite conclusions to the author's.

At least as important as history in school is the historical information passed down by films, TV and the media, by politicians, tourism and the heritage industry. Inevitably there are clashes of fact and interpretation. Certain periods in a nation's history can rise or fall in contemporary awareness, depending on current needs, sensitivities and the power of propaganda. They are also hugely different between neighbouring countries, so that Pakistan and India view the break-up of the Indian Raj in 1947 from different perspectives, while Germany and the United Kingdom do not share the same approach to the Second World War.

Attitudes towards Giuseppe and Anita Garibaldi would inevitably differ between Brazil and Uruguay. In both countries there is a strongly nationalist strain in historiography, which affects both left and right among politicians and historians, in the past and the present. An external crusader, especially one who can be dismissed as a European pirate, is suspect to those who think their own nationals are solely responsible for their history. For nationalists, therefore, Giuseppe may possibly be a hero in Italy, but his status in South America is more doubtful.

A nationalist sense of history is powerful in many countries, particularly at the popular level. In the United Kingdom the myth of 1940, when "Britain fought alone" after the Dunkirk evacuation, remains potent. Yet the role of the dominions and the colonial empire was crucial in supplying personnel, food and supplies. Young airmen who flew in the Battle of Britain also included Poles and Free French pilots. More recently, many young South Africans considering the end of apartheid in the early 1990s are ignorant or disparaging of the support from the black caucus in the US Congress, the Commonwealth and the international Anti-Apartheid Movement, believing that their success was unaided.

In Brazil as a whole the *Farroupilhas* are just one episode in a country's history which includes many other revolts and struggles. One of the most famous, because it was immortalised in a classic book by Euclides da Cunha,[2] was the 1897 war against a fanatical sect in Canudos, in the backlands of Bahia. The followers of Antônio Conselheiro forced crushing defeats on the army of the young republic, creating a political crisis in Rio de Janeiro before they were overwhelmed. More recently, the twentieth century has witnessed the successful revolutions of 1930 and 1964. The fact that São Paulo and Rio are the book publishing and media centres for the country means that for the Brazilian public at large, the *Farroupilhas* in the south, let alone Garibaldi, have reduced salience.

However, modern Brazil is a huge territory and the adoption of the *Farroupilhas* by the state of Rio Grande do Sul as a mark of identity is a significant and contemporary commitment. Tall flagpoles, with a state flag incorporating that of the old Piratini republic of nearly 200 years before, stand out at intervals by roadsides. Celebrations of Farroupilha Day, 20 September, coincidentally the date of Italian unity, can be bigger than those of 7 September, Brazil's independence day.

This is, of course, extremely curious. In Scotland, for example, the Scottish National Party does not make so much of the Jacobite rebellions against the English in the eighteenth century, almost certainly because a majority of the Scottish population at that time supported a protestant king against the Catholic Jacobites. Gaelic, the Celtic language of the Highlanders who rose up for the Stuarts, was already in retreat. During the civil war in southern Brazil there was always a substantial group, particularly among the *charqueadors* and in Porto Alegre, who supported the Brazilian emperor against the *Farroupilhas*. When Júlio de Castilhos and his allies enlisted the *Farroupilhas* for their own version of state-building they were capturing a contested part of *gaúcho* history for their own purposes. They were arguing that Rio Grande do Sul, on the frontier, remained a special place.

But Garibaldi was marginal to this *Castilhista* endeavour. In spite of exciting enterprises such as taking ships overland and the capture of Laguna, his role was not so great as to secure a certain place in the forefront of official *Farroupilha* memory, as did Bento Gonçalves or General Canabarro. As has been seen in the naming of the town of

Garibaldi in 1900, more than twenty years after Italian migrants founded a mutual aid society there, it was they who pushed his cause for recognition. What recognition he now enjoys seems restricted to Rio Grande do Sul; in Santa Catarina, where his seaborne attack took Laguna and he met his valiant partner Anita, he has a walk-on status in her shadow.

Memorialisation of the *Farroupilhas* has not promoted a wider "southern" consciousness. *O Sul é o Meu País* has achieved only a tiny response in unofficial referenda in the three states of Rio Grande do Sul, Santa Catarina and Paraná. Unlike the Scots compared to the English, or the Catalans compared to the Spanish majority, the citizens of these states are not distinct in culture or language from other Brazilians. Minor differences in demography and accent do not provide a strong enough basis for separatism.

Objectively, the role of Garibaldi in the Uruguayan civil war was much more important. His small fleet harried Admiral Brown's block-ading ships off Montevideo, making it possible for some food and supplies to reach the besieged citizens. His Italian Legion was one of the forces which protected the city from attack, raising morale at a desperate time. Apart from the black troops of the freed slaves and British and French regulars during the formal Anglo-French intervention, Montevideo had few reliable Uruguayan defenders. Fructuoso Rivera, its key general whose reputation was founded at the time of independence, suffered serious defeats at Arroyo Grande in 1842 and again at India Muerta in 1845, leaving the city exposed on both occasions.

Garibaldi's diversionary expedition up the Rio Uruguay in 1845 following his earlier naval exploits in the Paraná in 1842 were more than morale-boosting efforts. They were designed to show that the reach of the Gobierno de la Defensa was not just limited to the capital, and that this government was serious in seeking to open trade up the Plate tributaries by overcoming the embargo by Rosas. For Montevideo there were customs income and trade to be secured, and a demonstration to Britain and France that it was serious about promoting free navigation. The expedition to Salto, held by Garibaldi and Anzani for over six months, was also a chance to bring in recruits who had fled to Brazil.

Giuseppe's subsequent career in Italy, and Italian migration to Uruguay, secured his reputation in the country in the nineteenth century, at the cost, however, of giving it a partisan, *Colorado* quality. By the early twenty-first century there were bigger issues at stake, in terms of the amount of attention that modern Uruguayans can pay to the independence and civil war period. Although so critical to the establishment of the nation, this period is not without its embarrassments. Both Artigas and Rivera were expelled from the country. Heroes like Lavalleja, Oribe and Rivera fell out and fought with each other.

The demand for history in any contemporary country, by the public at large and educators, is limited. All searchlights on the past switch according to present needs, brightening some periods and allowing others to fall into darkness. Events in twentieth-century Uruguay were dramatic, requiring analysis and debate, and the first half of the nineteenth century now seems far away. There is no part of the country, even the capital, that has embraced this early history with the enthusiasm with which Rio Grande do Sul recalls its *Farroupilhas*.

It is therefore not surprising that awareness of Garibaldi in Uruguay and his symbolic international role as a fighter for freedom against tyranny is limited to a handful of dedicated enthusiasts in Montevideo. As with other civil society and historical bodies the Asociación Garibaldina has been powered by a few keen experts, notably Professora Maria Sagario, widow of Carlos Novello, the founder, and Milka Rappa, its energetic secretary. As such, it will be vital to find younger, qualified successors to carry on their work and to continue their journal, *Garibaldi*. Should they fail, a precious piece of Uruguay's past, linking it to neighbours and wider intellectual currents in European history, could be lost.

The challenge they face, in trying to bring the Casa Garibaldi back to life raises the issue of history as cultural tourism. Much understanding of the past everywhere now depends on the attractiveness of houses and heritage objects. The problem faced by the National Historical Museum, which is now responsible for the Casa Garibaldi, is that without investment and marketing it is hard to justify the staff and maintenance costs of keeping it open. The items on display were not numerous, and lacked modern video and exhibition expertise.

I came across similar closures in southern Brazil, in Laguna, where Anita's museum was being refurbished, and in Piratini, where funds for the refurbishment of the building used by Garibaldi and Rossetti had run out. *Prefeitos* in Piratini and Mostardas admitted how difficult it is for local government to raise finance for cultural and heritage projects. The absence of a bridge, which would permit larger vehicles to visit Piratini in September, was an obstacle to the growth of *Farroupilha* tourism in the first capital of the breakaway republic. The waymarked walk around the town, passing *Farroupilha* places of interest, shows that Piratini is keen to make the most of its past.

Tourism can rescue history but, like some of the films and TV involving Giuseppe and Anita, this may involve blurring, sexing up or fictionalising the evidence. It is arguable that Anita, with the support of the two institutions in her name and the August celebrations in Laguna, receives more touristic support than her husband. In southern Brazil she has the status of a local girl who became a celebrity, even though some members of her family never quite forgave her as a runaway.[3] She was brave, loyal to her man, and became equally committed to the cause of Italy. Nonetheless, the battle site near Curitibanos, tucked away in woodland, where she looked for Giuseppe's body among the dead, is not yet a place of pilgrimage.

The dressing-up and *gaúcho* cavalcades associated with the *Farroupilha* celebrations today are fun events. They act as reminders. When people today can participate in something derived from the past, that past comes alive for them. But many would argue that the impact is skin-deep, not unlike the battle re-enactments which in Britain, for instance, see Cavaliers fight Roundheads in a physically exciting recall of the seventeenth-century civil war. The more complex history represented in these pageants, and the extent to which it survives in contemporary DNA, is beyond their reach or purpose.

Tourism is a favoured route into history, but it requires imagination in presenting houses and objects as attractive and worth visiting. It needs investment, and ideally historic buildings and artefacts should be brought alive by audio and visual aids and current activities of pleasure to both adults and children. My own inquiries showed that, whether in Piratini or Montevideo, history suffers where places that could attract visitors were not open to the public. Underfunding and other priorities for local authorities or cultural institutions meant that the heritage of Giuseppe and Anita was not attracting significant attention. Gavillucci's strategy of stimulating town twinning and a

Garibaldi pilgrimage route round South America has yet to bear fruit. As implied earlier, there are costs involved, and such an initiative would need support from the travel industry from outside the region. Town twinning can be vulnerable to changes in the political landscape and in the interests of the public.

He is right, of course, that more could be made of the two Garibaldis as an inspiration for tourists, particularly from Italy, Europe and North America. But this would ideally require collaboration across the Brazil-Uruguay border. Adílcio Cadorin sees an opportunity in the bicentenary of Anita's birth, in 2021. He wishes to stimulate committees in all the towns with connections to the couple. They can arrange memorial events, and plant roses in Anita's honour. If this comes about, it could assist an overdue reassessment of the Garibaldis. It would enable people today to see them as real actors in the South American dramas of the early nineteenth century, not marginal figures awaiting their moment of fame in Europe. Giuseppe devoted all his resourceful thirties, when he was physically at his strongest, to South America.

There is something remarkable and generous about the Italians who took up arms for the Rio Grande republic and the Gobierno de la Defensa. At their core was a group of revolutionaries and conspirators, often Freemasons, dedicated to the creation of Italy. In a period when communications were erratic, before radio let alone social media could be imagined, they managed to keep in touch with each other in the Americas and across Europe. Count Livio Zambeccari, scientist and patriot, was an outstanding representative of this type. Required to leave Brazil in 1839 after three years in prison, he returned to Europe and was involved in Mazzinian uprisings in the 1840s. When the Roman Republic was declared in 1849 he was put in command of the stronghold of Ancona. His friendship with Garibaldi was re-established and he fought with him at the Volturno. He dedicated his final years, for he died in 1862 when he was scarcely sixty, to the rebuilding of Freemasonry in Italy.

Communities of Italian descent in Brazil, Uruguay and Argentina are now often a century or more away from ancestors who crossed the Atlantic from the peninsula. It is unrealistic to suppose that many of them will have more interest in the Garibaldis today than other citizens. Indeed, when the financial crash occurred in 2008 young Italians left for jobs in Germany, France and the United Kingdom rather than crossing to South America. One reason was that the European crisis coincided with what had been a serious economic downturn in Uruguay and Argentina.

While adventure and reward could be factors, idealism was perhaps the strongest motivation of the nineteenth-century activist migrants to South America. They were rallying to small republics in peril. Many, like Giuseppe's friends, Eduardo Mutru and Luigi Carniglia, who died in a shipwreck after the epic overland transport of the boats, lost their lives. Their help was not always appreciated, and in Montevideo there was friction between members of the Italian Legion and Uruguayans. The idealism that was honed in the Plate region was a flame that could recruit volunteers to fight, often against the odds, and was perhaps the most precious item that crossed the Atlantic in 1848.

History can be manufactured, and anniversaries are often used as building-blocks. In Rio Grande do Sul the magic date when the republic was declared was 20 September—when the Garibaldi Association and Italian officials in Montevideo also celebrate the incorporation of Rome and the Papal States in a united Italy. From 1905 onwards both Uruguay and Argentina have associated this date with freedom of thought, and in 1917 the Uruguayan parliament confirmed this as a public holiday; two years later, when the list of holidays was published in Uruguay it was described as Italy Day.

In 1933 the dictatorship of Gabriel Terra abolished the majority of public holidays and, when they were revived after it fell, the 20 September holiday had a merely optional quality. It was thanks to the Garibaldi Association that in 2004 Uruguay reinstated it as a day off work for all, to be celebrated as the Day of Freedom of Thought. The association of this holiday with Garibaldi and freethinking may also have something to do with Freemasonry. By chance, it is often a holiday in Chile, too, as 18 September is Chile's day of independence from the Spanish empire, 19 September is Army Day, and families can extend their break if they have a third day off.[4]

There is sometimes a bogus quality to anniversaries. In 2019, for instance, the United Kingdom government made a fuss of this year as the 70th anniversary of the London Declaration of the Commonwealth, an agreement in 1949 by which the republic of India could remain in what had hitherto been a monarchical association. This was lauded, largely in London alone, as the birth of the modern multicultural Commonwealth, where the majority of member states are republics.

But 2015, the jubilee of the intergovernmental Commonwealth Secretariat, had also been celebrated to mark the birth of the modern Commonwealth. Previous anniversaries of the London Declaration had passed unnoticed at decade-long intervals, and a panel of historians at London University's Institute of Commonwealth Studies concluded that other dates had as good a claim to this birth certificate.[5] Its significance was being puffed as a side-effect of UK government policy, making more of the Commonwealth association as it struggled in the toils of Brexit.

What is interesting in the context of Garibaldi, and the modest way in which he is now remembered in South America, is that there is no specific anniversary dedicated to him, or place at which he is memorialised. Anita has Laguna, and the August dates of her birth and death. Garibaldi has no comparable recognition, and the irony of celebrating 20 September 1870 as the incorporation of Rome into Italy is that he was not there. The obvious date for him in South America is 6 February, the anniversary of the battle in 1846 at San Antonio outside Salto, where the remains of Italian legionaries are interred inside the towering monument to him.

Salto is the second largest city in Uruguay, across the river from Argentina and not far from the border with Brazil. But whether it has the will to mount annual events to remember the battle of San Antonio may seem doubtful, when even its Italian society, of which Garibaldi is styled perpetual president, does little for him now. The 2016 inscription on his bust in the Avenida Barbieri, "from the citizens of Salto", hints at possibilities, however. It lists his ideals: freedom of conscience, freedom of thought, freedom of expression, social equality and solidarity. The Garibaldi Association is based in Montevideo and would lack the capacity to promote celebrations in Salto. But it may be that Salto itself, as part of a wide-ranging tourism strategy which might utilise all its resources—the river, its farms, vineyards and even its casino—could promote attention for this remarkable man.

Given the way the world works today, the best prospects for more systematic recognition of Garibaldi in South America must lie through the routes of tourism, partnership and sponsorship. The partnership might involve local rather than national governments; the sponsorship might involve Italian companies with interests in Latin America; the tourism and celebrations could be marketed to engage public support in southern Brazil and Uruguay, rather as the beaches of Florianópolis and Punta del Este attract both national and international visitors.

In an era when identity politics offer a divisive route to power for demagogues and rascals, the story of Giuseppe and Anita stands out in contrast. They made sacrifices. They supported countries and peoples which were not their own. They were not disheartened by setbacks. They were not seeking to make money. They do not sit comfortably with excessively nationalist histories, and where progressives stress their nationalism they find it convenient to overlook them. It is shaming in the twenty-first century to compare their courage with the record of an elected president and commander-in-chief of the United States who avoided conscription.

George Macaulay Trevelyan, a British historian at the start of the twentieth century and admirer of Garibaldi, stressed his courage at the centenary of his birth. He argued that it was only because he was in the front line and the thick of the battle that he could lead a mixed bag of volunteers to capture seemingly impregnable positions, defended by superior numbers of well-armed regular troops: "Wherever the old grey cloak was seen ahead, they would follow. The moral power of his personal presence, the smouldering fire that kindled in those small, deep eyes, the melody of that low, appealing voice, were his weapons that made up for artillery, and good rifles, and military training, and steep, entrenched positions."

Trevelyan went on to signal the crucial role of Garibaldi's idealism, and his beliefs in peace and brotherhood.

> Only where there was vile tyranny, where one race ruled another by the sword, where cruelty and oppression were a system of government, and ignorance a system of education, he knew that there could be no peace but death. The story of his life was an ever-enduring protest against the acceptance by men of the intolerable as the inevitable. His life belonged not to one country or one century alone.[6]

This peroration, addressed to friends, was interrupted by frequent cheers. But how far was Garibaldi a true democrat, even in nineteenth-century terms? Did his attitude towards "uncivilised" Amerindians belie his commitment to the rule of one race over another, in a blindness during the age of empires when his liberal admirers in England, for example, could sometimes justify punitive expeditions among "savages"? The Anglo-Zulu War in 1879, just before his death, saw the prince imperial, son of Napoleon III, killed in a British war of conquest in southern Africa.

Garibaldi was clear-cut in his abhorrence of slavery, both with the *Farroupilhas* and when he was fighting for the Gobierno de la Defensa in Uruguay. The devotion of Andrés Aguiar in Uruguay and in Rome was a testimony to how he was seen by those of African descent. This was one of his viewpoints that drew admiration in the United States, where emancipation did not occur until 1863, and in Britain and France.

Yet, like most of Spanish and Portuguese origin in South America at that time, he did not see indigenous Amerindians in the same light. Driving by remnant communities in southern Brazil today, or learning of the attempts by those of Charrúa heritage to gain recognition in Uruguay, is to appreciate that the dominant societies of southern South America have been established after wars that killed many of the original inhabitants. Ironically the name "Uruguay", from the river of the same name, derives from a Guarani word; its meaning is disputed, but is probably either "painted birds", after the attractive *Tero* or *Teru-Teru*, the Southern Lapwing which is now the national bird, or "freshwater shellfish".

It was an unusual progressive in Garibaldi's era who would stand up for the rights of indigenous peoples, and his own horizons were fixed on Italy and Europe. There he envisaged both freedom and for Europe, in a sense, a coming together in a sort of federation. He was totally opposed to absolutism. More difficult is to assess the extent to which he was a democrat. He was certainly jaundiced by the politicking in Montevideo, and he carried support for a temporary dictatorship into his struggle in Italy, where he became Dictator of the Two Sicilies. He had no love for the plebiscite which confirmed the acquisition of Nice by France. Yet he himself was elected a deputy for the parliament of united Italy.

He took some of his image from the inspiration of *caudillos* like Bento Gonçalves, but became critical of the military failures of Montevideo's leading *caudillo*, Fructuoso Rivera. The South American *caudillos*, like Garibaldi in Uruguay and Italy, were usually leading untrained volunteers, *gaúcho* horsemen from the *estancias* or recruits from the patronage networks they controlled. They were not well-drilled troops, but fighters learning on the job who depended on the charisma and skill of their leaders. They could be brutal, decapitating their defeated enemies. After setbacks, or if they became too hungry or worn out, they might simply go home. Garibaldi admired the toughness of the *gaúchos*, but saw the weaknesses in the *caudillo* system.

He was no ideologist. When Garibaldi visited England, where there were huge public demonstrations in his honour in 1864, Marx dismissed it all as "deplorable buffoonery". Marx's comrade-in-arms, Friedrich Engels, wisely remarked, however, that "an ounce of action is worth a ton of theory", and Garibaldi, except when he was taking compulsory or voluntary time out, was certainly the Action Man of his day. Because he was uninterested in the finer points of ideology and was inconsistent in his positions, he can be dismissed as, for instance, anti-Catholic or, as a conservative Brazilian told me at the start of my recent inquiries, "a communist".

The issue of his relationship with Catholicism is complex and has continued to poison his status among devout Catholics. The sheer power and authority of the Catholic Church in Italy and Latin America, until it began to wane in the face of secularism and evangelical Protestantism in the late twentieth century, meant that many were hostile towards him. Now, with the Argentinian and more liberal Pope Francis, there is scope for a reassessment. He was a Freemason, and the Vatican had banned Catholics from becoming Masons, in part because of their undoctrinal theism and progressive views. Nonetheless, throughout history there have been some Masons who were also Catholics. He was violently opposed to the temporal power of the pope, whose Papal States he saw as an obstacle to Italian unity. He shed no tears when the pope escaped from the Roman Republic.

At the same time he was happy to register his marriage in Montevideo in a church. He was pleased when Ugo Bassi, a priest, joined him as a chaplain to the Italian Legion in Rome. He attended Mass in Palermo cathedral. If indeed religion is the opium of the people, as Marx has written, he was prepared to smoke it on occasion.

GARIBALDI, HISTORY, SOUTH AMERICA

Garibaldi can be an uncomfortable character in the eyes of some today. He did not respect inherited state boundaries. Those who share his ideals can applaud the *Garibaldini*, men of many nations who joined Italians to enlist with the Redshirt brand. But his approach might also be understood by the Muslims of many countries who signed up for ISIS in the Middle East, or their opponents who have volunteered for the Kurdish and anti-ISIS forces in Syria. He is the forefather of all those who think that a cause or ideal that is worth fighting for justifies a break from conventional loyalties to country, family or friends. With the Italian Legion in Montevideo, and after he came to Europe, he was often leading private armies only loosely linked to an overall command. The problems this could create were illustrated during the Rio Uruguay episode in his insubordinate relationship with his allies in the British Navy. Yet at the same time this independent, privateering approach was a crucial element in success in Sicily and southern Italy, when he cut through and set aside the devious policies of the king and Cavour. It led, however, to defeat and temporary arrest when he attempted the premature and unauthorised liberation of the Papal States in 1861.

A combination of nationalism, on behalf of a nation still to be forged, with internationalism was rare in the nineteenth century. It is possibly rarer still nearly 200 years later. His insights were strengthened by his birth in Nice, on the edge of an Italian world which was divided into many states and dialects, and by meeting his liberal supporters in France and the Anglo-Saxon countries. When in 1848 revolutions broke out in Europe, threatening the reactionary despotisms entrenched at the Congress of Vienna after the defeat of Napoleon 1, he cheered them all as he headed back to Europe.

Garibaldi is a modern figure who would deny that a nationalist must oppose the ideals of liberalism and internationalism. He would reject Vladimir Putin's assertion that liberalism is obsolete. Attempts at thought control, as in communist or totalitarian societies, would have been abhorrent to him. Uruguay's recognition of freedom of expression, on a day also linked to Italian history, is a direct tribute to his ideas.

Nelson Mandela resisted attempts to sanctify him and Garibaldi, though treated by the credulous in southern Italy as a latter-day Jesus, was not so vain as to lose touch with reality. He did, however, tell

Abraham Lincoln, who had offered him command of a corps, that he should have leadership of the whole Northern army in the civil war. He was not lacking in self-respect.

In an era of widespread machismo, he acknowledged Anita as his full partner. This was a problematic partnership, for he was handsome, with an eye for women and with the talents to attract them. But in the context of southern Brazil and Uruguay it is impossible to separate the two persons in this couple. He welcomed Anita's arrival in the Roman Republic as that of "another soldier", and she stayed with him, although pregnant and ailing, up until her death on the retreat from Rome. Her children, and the roles they went on to undertake, were a tribute to her as well as to him.

It is probably a mistake to paint Anita as a proto-feminist, though she broke away from a loveless marriage and family disapproval to join Giuseppe in Laguna. She fought bravely with the *Farroupilhas*, helping to build morale. In Montevideo, where she was looking after four children, she was also acting as a nurse for the wounded in the Italian Legion, and it was said that she cared for casualties from both sides during the civil war. When she joined her husband in Salto she carried on nursing.

Her small home in Montevideo, lacking even candles at one point and with housekeeping funds in short supply, saw a constant flow of military and Italians passing through. It must have been like 10 Downing Street during the Anglo-French intervention in Suez in 1956, when Lady Eden said the Suez Canal was flowing through her living room. She was on her own with young children for months at a time. Nonetheless she learnt other languages besides her native Portuguese, and was sufficiently expert in diplomacy to act as her husband's ambassador, when he sent her on ahead to Genoa on board the *Carolina* in December 1847. She understood the nuances of Uruguayan politics, for she was a friend of Bernardina Rivera, wife of Fructuoso, with whom her husband had an on-off relationship.

In southern Brazil she was a warrior. In Uruguay she was not a warrior, but was much more than the mother of four children. She was supporting Garibaldi's work with the Italian Legion and the fleet, and gathering intelligence for him. This was a partnership of soulmates in spite of Garibaldi's indiscretions, and it is appropriate that she has been styled "a heroine of two worlds".

GARIBALDI, HISTORY, SOUTH AMERICA

It was during Garibaldi's lifetime that he became a legend, and the relationship between legends and ongoing awareness of history is subtle and unpredictable. At the 1907 centenary of his birth, the then Italian Ambassador in the United Kingdom said:

> Legend is sometimes as truthful, at least in its spirit, and almost always more powerful and efficient than history, because it influences for centuries the mind, the feeling and the action of a nation. Garibaldi, who fought in two continents for liberty and independence, will perhaps in the distant future be considered, not as a real and living individual, but as the mythical and legendary personification of a period of history—of that period of history which was almost everywhere dominated by the great struggle for liberty.

The ambassador's reflections, preceding two world wars and a Cold War, assumed that memories of Garibaldi would live on, whether legendary or firmly rooted in the teaching of history. In the early years of the twenty-first century this is not really the case, either in South America or Europe. Even Che Guevara, a twentieth-century hero for many on the left, is an often forgotten figure outside Cuba. In the 1970s and 1980s it was common to see Che posters in the student bedrooms of Europe, his face on youngsters' T-shirts. When Gavillucci saw a bust of Che near Montevideo it was a surprise to the political scientist who was showing him round, who did not know when it was unveiled. Its inscription stated that it was sited in a plaza named for the *comandante*, but there was no such plaza.

To compare Guevara with Garibaldi is to compare one individual with a fixed ideology, which combined communism with national independence, with another whose commitments to freedom and national independence were different but equally strong. Both shared a sense of internationalism and willingness to fight in several countries. As a guerrilla leader Garibaldi, who fought on water and land, was definitely superior. Arguably, while both were charismatic, Garibaldi was more successful at welding enthusiasts into a fighting force, though possibly less good on detail. In politics he was probably more willing to compromise. Like Che and Fidel Castro, who took power in Cuba in 1959, he had had good luck in Sicily and southern Italy. When around a thousand revolutionaries overthrew Batista and his army of 40,000 in Cuba, it was a sequel to Garibaldi's outnumbered force overcoming the

207

Bourbon armies. In both cases, the governments they defeated were in reality rotten to the core.

Former heroes can be mislaid, and for some who look to wider currents of opinion or social class the very idea of a hero is misleading. The twentieth century has been described as the age of the common man and it was allergic to the mass ascription of "heroes", comparable to the large number of men denominated as "saints" in the early Christian Church. While tabloid media may scatter the "hero" epithet rather freely, to people who have undertaken a single act of courage, there is also reluctance to award the title, and some feeling that a hero has to demonstrate nobility and fixity of purpose over a long period, against tough odds, for an honourable purpose. Hero status is awarded by the public, and over more than one generation; it is not an honour granted by a government.

One of the ironies of the explosion of internet information is that here-and-now instant knowledge, whether accurate or fake, has over-whelmed collective memory. Yet memory is still called on to support the identity of communities and nations, especially when they make claims based on oppression and victimisation.

The Garibaldi story remains a reminder of the links between Europe and Latin America, links that are different from those that bind Europe and North America, for instance in NATO or use of the English lan-guage. The Garibaldis and the other Europeans who volunteered to fight for Montevideo helped preserve Uruguay as an independent state open to free trade and the ideas of the Enlightenment. At the same time, the Italians from Uruguay contributed energy and experience to the campaign for a united Italy.

Much later, when a Brazilian expeditionary force was sent to Italy to fight with the Allies during the Second World War, this gesture of libera-tion from across the Atlantic was reciprocated. Now, when China is such a dominant trade partner with Brazil, Uruguay and other South American countries, and the European Union has just negotiated a huge trade agreement with the Mercosur states of Argentina, Brazil, Chile, Paraguay and Uruguay, it is valuable to remember the Garibaldi connection as part of a historic, wide-ranging and European-oriented context.

It will be interesting to see whether Anita's bicentenary in 2021 encourages a fresh assessment of the Garibaldis alongside the media coverage of her romantic story that may be expected. If so, it will have to reach beyond the partisan capture of Giuseppe's history in Uruguay and the folkloric mixture of the real Anita Garibaldi with *gaúcho* festivals linked to the *Farroupilhas* in southern Brazil. There is scope for documentaries, intellectual seminars and a review in both Brazil and Uruguay of how the post-independence era is currently studied in schools and universities. This was an era of sometimes brutal warfare, when the map of southern South America could have been redrawn, and Britain and France were powerful external players.

One reason why the Garibaldis have suffered mainstream neglect lies in a certain lack of interest on the part of the newer leftist parties which have held power in the early years of the current century—the PT in Brazil and Frente Amplio in Uruguay. Both were new coalitions, cutting their teeth in opposition to the military dictatorships in their respective countries. Their campaigns were immediate, aiming for social reform and an end to the relics of dictatorship. While intellectuals were prominent in both the PT and the Frente Amplio, the earlier history of their countries seemed too remote to be relevant. Garibaldian connections to internationalism or women's liberation seemed very far removed from the present day.

Finally, it is worth asking the most difficult question: If Giuseppe and Anita had not played heroic roles in the Roman Republic and the struggle to unify Italy, would they ever have acquired significant status in South America? Would they be heroes of one world, if it was not possible to describe them as heroes of two?

Looking at what actually happened in South America, and forgetting what they did later, it is clear that they would always have merited a place in the history of the wider Plate region. Anita was a brave and romantic young woman. Giuseppe was a bold and courageous leader, on the water and on land. They were part of the Italian group which tried to assist the *Farroupilha* republic, and was even more crucial, along with other Europeans, in ensuring the survival of Montevideo during a long civil war.

Yet it was the struggle for and ultimate success of the Risorgimento in Italy which made Garibaldi, after Anita's death, one of the most renowned figures of the nineteenth century. Had he not been a hero of the Old World he might not have been so readily seen as a hero in the

New World, and his actions on both sides of the Atlantic then heightened his reputation. The arrival of large numbers of Italian migrants in Brazil, Uruguay and Argentina ensured that at around the time of his death an ocean could not keep his admirers apart.

NOTES

INTRODUCTION

1. Lucy Riall, *Garibaldi: Invention of a Hero* (New Haven, CT, and London: Yale University Press, 2007) p. 41.

1. A JOURNEY TO SOUTH AMERICA, FROM NICE TO RIO DE JANEIRO

1. Klemens von Metternich dismissed the idea of "Italy" in two letters of 1847, to the Austrian Ambassador to France and to Lord Palmerston, British foreign minister.
2. R. Lahlou, *Garibaldi: les révolutions d'un siècle* (Paris: Bernard Giovanangeli, 2007) p. 38.
3. D. Mack-Smith, *Mazzini* (New Haven, CT, and London: Yale University Press, 1996) p. 46.
4. There was a famous row in London in 1844 after the failure of another Italian plot which Mazzini had tried to discourage. Parliament exposed the fact that Mazzini's correspondence was being opened by the authorities under Lord Aberdeen's government, as were the letters of many ambassadors.
5. Venezuela, Colombia, Ecuador and Peru.
6. Letter to General Juan José Flores, head of state of Ecuador, 9 November 1830.
7. It is arguable that this British policy, backed up by the Royal Navy, was more significant than the Monroe Doctrine of President James Monroe, which he announced in 1823; Monroe stated that any attempt by European powers to establish or retain colonies in the Western Hemisphere would be regarded as unfriendly by the United States.

8. He had inherited the Portuguese throne in 1826 and, though he relinquished his claim, he sent his five-year-old daughter, Maria da Gloria, back on condition that she marry her uncle Miguel.

9. Slavery was abolished by the *Farroupilhas*, but reintroduced after their defeat; slaves were not finally freed in Rio Grande do Sul and the rest of Brazil until 13 May 1888, by which time there were still 60,000.

10. The word comes from *farrapo*, the fringed leather clothing commonly worn then by the cowboy *gaúchos* of the cattle lands of Rio Grande do Sul, dismissed as rags by other Brazilians; in time all people in the state came to be known as *gaúchos*.

11. *Garibaldi: An Autobiography*, ed. Alexandre Dumas, trans. William Robson (London: Routledge, Warne and Routledge, 1861), p. 49. Cited hereafter as *Garibaldi, op. cit.*

12. In 2013 the Italian Embassy in Brazil estimated that 15 per cent of Brazilians had Italian ancestry, many in São Paulo and southern states, and there was a rush to claim dual nationality during the Brazilian recession; by the twenty-first century it was estimated that half of Argentinians and some 60 per cent of Uruguayans had Italian ancestors.

13. Lindolfo Collor, *Garibaldi e a Guerra dos Farrapos* (Rio de Janeiro: José Olympio, 1938) pp. 83–4.

14. A *caramurú* is an indigenous Tupinamba name for a type of sea fish found in Bahia; it was the nickname given to a Portuguese aristocrat, Diogo Álvares Correia, who was shipwrecked there in 1509, married the daughter of a chief, and played an important role in spreading the Portuguese empire in Brazil.

15. Collor, *op. cit.*, p. 99.

2. FROM RIO DE JANEIRO TO ROMANCE

1. Collor, *op. cit.*, pp. 110–11.

2. *Garibaldi, op. cit.*, p. 69.

3. Collor, *op. cit.*, p. 158.

4. *Garibaldi, op. cit.*, p. 81.

5. The motto of the French Revolution had been "Liberty, Equality and Fraternity" but the Rio Grande Republic borrowed Mazzini's gender-neutral Humanity to replace Fraternity.

6. G.M. Trevelyan, *Garibaldi's Defence of the Roman Republic* (London: Longmans Green, 1919) p. 31.

7. Information confirmed by a descendant of the Ribeiro family, Luisa Calvete.

8. A. Cadorin, *Anita: A Guerreira das Repúblicas* (Florianópolis: IOSC, 1999) p. 43.

3. FIGHTING SIDE BY SIDE

1. Floriano Peixoto (1839–95) was one of the generals who presented an ultimatum to Emperor Pedro II in 1889 and established a republic; he ruled as a dictator from 1891 to 1894 and Desterro was renamed Florianópolis as a punishment for its support for opponents of the new republic, in a civil war in southern Brazil which had echoes of the *Farroupilha* rising.
2. *Garibaldi*, *op. cit.*, p. 100.
3. Wolfgang L. Rau, *Anita Garibaldi: o perfil de uma heroína Brasileira* (Florianópolis: Lunardelli, 1997) p. 177.
4. There is dispute among historians as to whether this was at Lages, or the more distant Vacaria. Yvonne Capuano, *De Sonhos e Utopias... Anita e Giuseppe Garibaldi* (São Paulo: Melhoramentos, 1999), p. 379, concluded that the couple must have been reunited in Lages, whereas Cadorin, *Anita*, *op. cit.*, p. 138, decided it was Vacaria, which seems more credible.
5. Capuano, *op. cit.*, p. 391; Garibaldi, in his autobiography, pp. 116–19, suggests that the empire had 4,000 infantry and some 3,000 cavalry, and that at least 500 men were killed on each side; other estimates were larger still, with 4,000 infantry and 8,000 cavalry for the empire, and only a thousand infantry and 5,000 cavalry for the republic.
6. *Garibaldi*, *op. cit.*, p. 117.
7. Capuano, *op. cit.*, p. 401, quoting a letter from F. Álvarez Machado e Vasconcelos.
8. *Garibaldi*, *op. cit.*, p. 131. Rossetti was a key ideologist for the republic, and edited 160 numbers of *O Povo*.
9. *Ibid.*, p. 133.
10. Cadorin, *Anita*, *op. cit.*, p. 165.
11. He died on 3 March 1841, and Garibaldi thought of returning to Nice to be with his widowed mother.

4. MONTEVIDEO, AND ANOTHER WAR

1. *Garibaldi*, *op. cit.*, p. 144.
2. Capuano, *op. cit.*, pp. 453–6.
3. Famously the *General Belgrano* was an Argentine warship controversially sunk by the British in 1982; like its predecessor in the 1840s it was named after General Manuel Belgrano, who had founded the School of Navigation (Escuela de Náutica) in 1799 and fought for Argentine independence.
4. Entre Rios, "Between the Rivers", is the low-lying region between the Paraná and Uruguay rivers.

5. The siege of Montevideo lasted from 1842 to 1851, and became one of the great progressive causes for European and international sympathisers in the nineteenth century. Alexandre Dumas promoted this narrative with his novel, *Montevideo ou une nouvelle Troie (The New Troy)*, published in 1850.

5. ITALIAN LEGION, AND NAVAL COMMANDER

1. See David McLean, "Trade, Politics and the Navy in Latin America: The British in the Paraná, 1845–1846", *Journal of Imperial and Commonwealth History*, September 2007, p. 354.
2. See David McLean, *War, Diplomacy and Informal Empire—Britain and the Republics of La Plata, 1836–1853* (London: British Academic Press, 1995) p. 43.
3. *Garibaldi, op. cit.*, p. 191.
4. *Ibid.*, p. 194. Garibaldi's claims seem exaggerated.
5. Capuano, *op. cit.*, p. 482, quoting Cuneo.
6. An alternative explanation is that Garibaldi captured the shirts at sea from a boat running the blockade towards Buenos Aires.
7. *Garibaldi, op. cit.*, p. 202.
8. Louis Philippe I was forced to abdicate in February 1848; later in the year Louis Napoleon Bonaparte, nephew of the Emperor Napoleon who was defeated at Waterloo, became French president; he was Emperor Napoleon III from 1851 until his defeat and capture by the Prussians in 1870.
9. For a full discussion see David McLean, "Garibaldi in Uruguay: A Reputation Reconsidered", *English Historical Review*, no. 458, 1998, pp. 351–68.
10. Director: Gerardo Caetano; Coordinadora: Ana Frega, *Uruguay: revolución, independencia y construcción del Estado* (Montevideo: Fundación MAPFRE, 2016) p. 123.
11. See McLean, "Garibaldi in Uruguay", *op. cit.*
12. McLean, *War, Diplomacy and Informal Empire*, *op. cit.*, p. 100.
13. *Garibaldi, op. cit.*, p. 205.
14. Federico Anschütz, resident of Gualeguaychú and guide during my visit, was able to clarify this confusion by consulting Professor Marcos Henchoz, a local historian, at my request.
15. Others have stated as certain that she died of diphtheria, but see Cadorin, *Anita, op. cit.*, p. 185.
16. Cadorin states that Anita left her other children in Montevideo with people she trusted (p. 185); but it is also possible, as described by B. Gerson in *Garibaldi e Anita, guerrilheiros do liberalismo* (São Paulo:

José Bushatsky, 1971), p. 91, that she brought them with her, for he describes a touching reunion in Salto.

17. *Garibaldi, op. cit.*, p. 210; Rau suggests that thirty-six were killed.
18. *Ibid.*, p. 215.
19. *Ibid.*, pp. 225–6.
20. C.M. Rama, *Garibaldi y el Uruguay* (Montevideo: Nuestro Tiempo, 1968) p. 81.
21. McLean, "Garibaldi in Uruguay", *op. cit.*, p. 360 et seq.
22. Lord Palmerston, who was also twice prime minister, was the dominant foreign secretary during Queen Victoria's reign, serving in the Foreign Office 1830–4, 1835–41 and 1846–51. A belligerent figure in promoting Britain's imperial interests, he tended to see the Plate intervention as a diversion.

6. LIFE IN MONTEVIDEO, AND THOUGHTS OF EUROPE

1. H.F. Winnington-Ingram, *Hearts of Oak* (London: W.H. Allen & Co, 1889), p. 93, brought to my attention by Professor Ana Frega.
2. *Garibaldi, op. cit.*, p. 199.
3. McLean, *War, Diplomacy and Informal Empire, op. cit.*, p. 121.
4. *The Times*, 2 June 1932.
5. Collor, *op. cit.*, p. 483.
6. *Garibaldi, op. cit.*, p. 220.
7. Ibid., p. 219.
8. M. Oliveira, *Garibaldi: herói dos dois mundos* (São Paulo: Contexto, 2013) states (p. 116) that because removal of a corpse met bureaucratic obstacles, one of his soldiers dug up the body at night; it was then reburied in Nice and subsequently transferred to Caprera.

7. SOUTH AMERICAN LEGACIES IN ITALY

1. Anti-monarchical revolutions broke out in Sicily, France, Austria and Germany, with more peaceful demonstrations in other countries. In non-revolutionary Britain there was a peak of protest by Chartists, calling for a secret universal ballot. Only in France, where the monarchy was replaced by a republic, was the movement successful, and what has been described as "a Spring of Peoples" was as largely abortive as the "Arab Spring" in the early twenty-first century.
2. Cadorin, *Anita, op. cit.*, p. 199.
3. *Ibid.*, p. 207, quoting three historians.
4. He was able to authenticate a rare portrait of his mother, painted in Montevideo, as a true likeness.

5. C. Hibbert, *Garibaldi and his Enemies* (Harmondsworth: Penguin Books, 1987) p. 361.

6. Medici had a realistic view of his chief: "Poor Garibaldi. He ruins himself in times of inaction; he talks too much, writes too much, and listens too much to those who know nothing." Letter quoted by Hibbert, *op. cit.*, p. 186.

7. Capuano, *op. cit.*, p. 509 after Rau.

8. Quoted in Hibbert, *op. cit.*, p. 240.

9. Quoted in G.M. Trevelyan, *Garibaldi and the Making of Italy* (London: Longmans Green, 1911) p. 184, based on an earwitness, W.G. Clark.

10. Hibbert, *op. cit.*, p. 82n.

11. Information courtesy of Edward Mortimer.

12. Alexandre Dumas, *Montevideo ou une nouvelle Troie* (Paris, 1850) pp. 84–91, quoted in D. Mack-Smith (ed.), *Garibaldi* (Englewood Cliffs, NJ: Prentice-Hall, 1969), pp. 88–9.

13. In spite of the dangers he had courted, Garibaldi outlived his three brothers and a sister who died in childhood.

14. Trevelyan, *Garibaldi and the Making of Italy, op. cit.*, p. 151.

15. C.S. Forbes, *The Campaign of Garibaldi in the Two Sicilies: A Personal Narrative* (Edinburgh and London: William Blackwood & Sons, 1861), pp. 92–3.

16. See Hibbert, *op. cit.*, p. 199.

17. Trevelyan, *op. cit.*, p. 198.

18. Hibbert, *op. cit.*, p. 215.

19. Hibbert, *op. cit.*, p. 83.

20. M. Gilbert, *Churchill: A Life* (New York: Henry Holt, 1991) p. 77.

21. A.J.P. Taylor, *English History, 1914–1945* (Oxford: Oxford University Press, 1965) p. 475.

8. AFTERMATH IN BRAZIL

1. Academics dispute how far this territory was ever truly Spanish, or subsequently Uruguayan, as against Portuguese, or subsequently Brazilian. Enrique Hernández, professor of international relations at the Universidad de la República in Montevideo, argues that the *cabildo* of Montevideo had had limited reach northwards and that by a treaty of 1801 between Spain and Portugal the Chuí river had already been recognised as the southern boundary of the Portuguese territory.

2. More recently the members of the Social Democratic Party of Brazil (PSDB) of Fernando Henrique Cardoso, president from 1995 to 2003, were known as *Toucanos* (toucans) because of their vivid party colours.

3. J.M. Bello, *A History of Modern Brazil, 1889–1964* (Stanford, CA: Stanford University Press, 1966) p. 118.

4. *Ibid.*, p. 115.
5. R. Bourne, *Getúlio Vargas of Brazil, 1883–1954* (London & Tonbridge: Charles Knight, 1974) p. 46.
6. Brazil had declared war on Germany and the Central Powers in 1917, after several vessels had been sunk by German submarines.
7. L. Collor, *Garibaldi e a Guerra dos Farrapos* (Rio de Janeiro: Livraria José Olympio, 1938).
8. J. Zalla and C. Menegat, "History and Memory in the Farroupilha Revolution: A Brief Genealogy of the Myth", *Revista Brasileira de História*, São Paulo, vol. 31, no. 62, 2011, pp. 49–70.

9. AFTERMATH IN URUGUAY

1. N. Duffau and R. Pollero, "Poblacíon y Sociedad", in G. Caetano (ed.), *Uruguay: Revolucíon, Independencia y construccíon del Estado, Tomo 1 1808/1880* (Montevideo: Planeta, 2016) p. 218.
2. The debates are recorded in *Compilación de leyes y decretos, 1825–1930*, Montevideo MCMXXX, kindly made available by the historian Nicolás Duffau.
3. Whereas *El País* continues to publish, *El Día* closed in 1993.
4. It seems more or less definite that Garibaldi took Rosita's coffin with him to Europe in 1848.
5. Information from Milka Rappa.
6. Information from Professor Ana Frega, Universidad de la República, Montevideo.
7. J.M. Sanguinetti and M. Canessa de Sanguinetti, *Garibaldi y el Partido Colorado* (Montevideo: Ed Fb, 2007).
8. M. Gavillucci, *Um Italiano seguindo o caminho de Garibaldi: José e sua Anita entre Brasil, Uruguai e Argentina* (São José do Norte: Atalaia do Norte Produções, 2016).
9. *Ibid.*, p. 207.

12. AN ITALIAN IN THE STEPS OF A HERO

1. Gavillucci, *op. cit.*
2. *Ibid.*, p. 84.
3. *Ibid.*, p. 108.
4. In fact, the British Empire, which included Caribbean colonies and on the mainland what are now the independent states of Guyana and Belize, passed the Slavery Abolition Act in 1833, six years earlier than the Julian Republic.

13. GARIBALDI, HISTORY, SOUTH AMERICA

1. In the BBC Radio Four series, "In Our Time".
2. *Os Sertões*, 1902, was translated as *Rebellion in the Backlands* (Chicago, IL: University of Chicago Press, 1944). Da Cunha had been a war correspondent in the campaign.
3. Information from Luisa Calvete, descendant of the Ribeiro family.
4. I am grateful to Milka Rappa for researching the history of 20 September as a public holiday in Uruguay. Intriguingly, 20 September in 2019 has been adopted as a day for international action to combat the world's climate emergency.
5. Panel chaired by Philip Murphy, Director, Institute of Commonwealth Studies, 20 May 2019.
6. *The Times*, 5 July 1907. There were celebrations of the centenary in London, Southampton and Newcastle. Trevelyan, author of a three-volume history, was the foremost British historian of Garibaldi and the unification of Italy in his day.

BIBLIOGRAPHY

Bethell, Leslie. *The Abolition of the Brazilian Slave Trade: Britain, Brazil and the Slave Trade Question*. Cambridge: Cambridge University Press, 1970.

———— *The Paraguayan War*, 1864–1870. London: Institute of Latin American Studies, 1996.

———— *Brazil: Essays on History and Politics*. London: Institute of Latin American Studies, 2018.

———— (ed.). *The Cambridge History of Latin America (12 vols)*. Cambridge: Cambridge University Press, 1984–2008.

Boiteux, Henrique. *A heroína brasileira: Annita Garibaldi*. Rio de Janeiro: Imprensa Naval, 1935.

Bourne, Richard. *Political Leaders of Latin America*. Harmondsworth: Penguin Books, 1969.

———— *Getulio Vargas of Brazil, 1883–1954*. London and Tonbridge: Charles Knight, 1974.

———— *Lula of Brazil: The Story So Far*. Berkeley and Los Angeles, CA: University of California Press, 2008.

Cadorin, Adílcio. *Anita: A Guerreira das Repúblicas*. Florianópolis: IOSC, 1999.

Cadorin, Adílcio and Cadorin, Lucas. *Laguna, Terra Mater, Cronologia Histórica*. Blumenau: Nova Letra, 2013.

Caetano, Gerardo, Director. *Uruguay, 1808–1880: Revolución, independencia y construcción del Estado*. Montevideo: Editorial Planeta, 2015.

———— *Uruguay, 1880–1930: Reforma social y democracia de partidos*. Montevideo: Editorial Planeta, 2016.

———— *Uruguay, 1930–2010: En busca del desarrollo entre el autoritarismo y la democracia*. Montevideo: Editorial Planeta, 2016.

Capuano, Yvonne. *De Sonhos e Utopias... Anita e Giuseppe Garibaldi*. São Paulo: Melhoramentos, 1999.

Collor, Lindolfo. *Garibaldi e a Guerra dos Farrapos*. Rio de Janeiro: Livraria José Olympio, 1938.

BIBLIOGRAPHY

Corbellini, Helena. *El sublevado: Garibaldi, corsario del Río de la Plata*. Montevideo: Sudamericana, 2009. (A novel.)

Docca, E.F. de Souza. *História do Rio Grande do Sul*. Rio de Janeiro: Organização Simões, 1954.

Dumas, Alexandre. *Montevideo, ou une nouvelle Troie*. Paris: 1850.

Forbes, C.S. *The Campaign of Garibaldi in the Two Sicilies: A Personal Narrative*. Edinburgh and London: William Blackwood & Sons, 1861.

Garibaldi, A. *Anita Garibaldi: a mulher do General*. São Paulo: Martins Fontes, 1989.

Garibaldi, G. ed. Alexandre Dumas, trans. William Robson. *Garibaldi: An Autobiography*. London: Routledge, Warne & Routledge, 1861.

———— *Garibaldi en el Plata: autobiografia*. Montevideo: Proyección, 1990.

Gavillucci, Mauro. *Um Italiano Seguindo o Caminho de Garibaldi: José e sua Anita entre Brasil, Uruguai e Argentina*. Portuguese-language edition. São José do Norte: Atalaia do Norte Produções, 2016.

Gerson, Brasil. *Garibaldi e Anita, guerrilheiros do liberalismo*. São Paulo: José Bushatsky, 1971.

Guerzoni, Giuseppe. *Garibaldi*. Firenze: G. Barbera, 1929.

Herrera, Luis Alberto de. *Orígenes de la Guerra Grande*. Montevideo: A. Monteverde, 1941.

Hibbert, Christopher. *Garibaldi and his Enemies*. Harmondsworth: Penguin Books, 1987.

Lima, João Francisco de. *Anita Garibaldi, heroína de dois mundos*. São Paulo: Nova Época, 1977.

Mack-Smith, Denis (ed.). *Garibaldi*. Englewood Cliffs, NJ: Prentice-Hall, 1969.

McLean, David. *War, Diplomacy and Informal Empire: Britain and the Republics of La Plata, 1836–1853*. London and New York: British Academic Press, 1995.

Markun, Paulo. *Anita Garibaldi: uma Heroína Brasileira*. Rio de Janeiro: Editora Senac, 1999.

Novello, Carlos. *Garibaldi: un exilio providencial*. Montevideo: author published, 2008.

———— *Garibaldi: luchador ideológico? filibustero? mercenario? héroe?* Montevideo: author published, 2008.

———— *Garibaldi: su primera acción en un proyecto mazziniano*. Montevideo: author published, 2008.

Oliveira, Maurício. *Garibaldi: herói dos dois mundos*. São Paulo: Contexto, 2013.

Pereda, Setembrino E. *Los Italianos en la Nueva Troya*. Montevideo: Estado mayor del ejército, Departamento de estudios históricos, División historia, 1969.

Rama, Carlos M. *Garibaldi y el Uruguay*. Montevideo: Nuestro Tiempo, 1968.

BIBLIOGRAPHY

Rau, Wolfgang Ludwig. *Vida e Morte de José e Anita Garibaldi*. Laguna, author published, 1989.

————— *Anita Garibaldi: o perfil de uma heroína Brasileira*. Florianópolis: Lunardelli, 1997.

Riall, Lucy. *Garibaldi: Invention of a Hero*. New Haven, CT and London: Yale University Press, 2007.

Ridley, Jasper. *Garibaldi*. London: Constable, 1974.

Sanguinetti, Julio María. *Garibaldi y el Partido Colorado*. Montevideo: Ed Fb, 2007.

Sanguinetti, Marta Canessa de. *Garibaldi: Cronología de una vida*. Montevideo: Ed Fb, 2007.

Sant'Ana, Elma. *Menotti, o filho gaúcho de Anita e Garibaldi*. Porto Alegre: Editora Tchê, 2003.

Sant'Ana, Elma and Girondi, Elenita. *Garibaldi: a cidade e o herói*. Caxias do Sul: Editora Maneco, 2007.

Santos, João Felício dos. *A guerrilheira: o romance da vida de Anita Garibaldi*. São Paulo: Círculo do Livro, 1987.

Scirocco, Alfonso. *Garibaldi: Battaglie, amori, ideali di un cittadino del mondo*. Rome: Laterza, 2007.

Trevelyan, George Macaulay. *Garibaldi's Defence of the Roman Republic, 1848–9*. London: Longmans Green, 1909.

————— *Garibaldi and the Thousand*. London: Longmans Green, 1909.

————— *Garibaldi and the Making of Italy*. London: Longmans Green, 1911.

Varela, Alfredo. *Historia da grande revolução: o cyclo farroupilha no Brasil*. Porto Alegre: Livraria do Globo, 1933.

INDEX

Note: Page numbers followed by "*n*" refer to notes.

INDEX

INDEX

INDEX

INDEX

INDEX

INDEX

INDEX

INDEX